SOUTH EA
HANDB

Capital Transport

CONTENTS

ISBN 185414 183 X

First published 1990
Fourth edition 1997

Published by Capital Transport Publishing
38 Long Elmes, Harrow Weald, Middlesex

Printed by Bath Midway Press Ltd
Midland Industrial Estate, Holt, Wiltshire

The front cover photo is by Geoff Rixon
The back cover photos are by Martin Smith
The title page photo is by Eric Baldock
The photo overleaf is by Richard Godfrey

INTRODUCTION

This handbook is an expanded version of South East Buses, incorporating some of the operators neighbouring Greater London formerly included in London Bus Handbook Part 2.

Since the previous edition of this handbook, a number of operators have been absorbed by others. Blue Admiral and Red Admiral have been taken over by Provincial; Berks Bucks (Bee Line) by CentreWest; Mercury Passenger Services by Maidstone & District; Sussex Bus by Stagecoach South. Much rationalisation of fleets and operations has occurred, and this process continues. Hants & Sussex have ceased trading, though some of their vehicles have passed to Southampton. Maidstone & District passed into the ownership of British Bus, all of whose concerns have in turn come under the Cowie wing, and its administration has come under integrated control with that of Kentish Bus and Londonlinks at Maidstone.

Within the larger fleets, low-floor single-deckers have started to appear in some quantity. Double-deckers continue to form a significant part of several fleets, with an upsurge in new deliveries. Stagecoach South have renewed more than one-third of the East Kent fleet, and the London & Country fleet has also seen substantial updating.

Acknowledgement is due to the operators covered in this handbook, almost all of whom have displayed generous assistance in confirming details of their fleets. Valuable assistance has also been received from Eric Baldock, Jef Johnson, Dave Jolliffe, Colin Lloyd, Dave Stewart and Don Vincent, and officers of the specialist enthusiast groups covering this area – The M&D and East Kent Bus Club, Southdown Enthusiasts' Group, the PSV Circle and London Omnibus Traction Society. The customary request that readers who are interested in more details of the fleets should not trouble the operators direct is coupled with a recommendation to contact these societies.

Finally, please remember that operator premises are private property, and should not be entered unless proper permission has first been obtained.

NICHOLAS KING   Hemel Hempstead, November 1996

AUTOPOINT

B.P. & J. Rodemark, Gardner Street, Herstmonceux, East Sussex, BN27 4LE

From small beginnings as a country minibus operator, Autopoint expanded to a fleet of nearly 30 vehicles in the years following deregulation, operating a network of local bus services and contracts. Many of these have been under contract to East Sussex County Council. However, there have been some losses in recent rounds of retendering. The present fleet includes a number of full-size coaches.

Vehicle policy has shown some enterprising trends. Many vehicles have been re-registered with private AP marks originally issued in East Sussex. Fleet colours are white, dark blue and light blue and the fleet is based at Bodle Street.

AUTOPOINT

545XFM	Leyland Leopard PSU5C/4R	Duple Dominant I	C51F	1977	Ex Maidstone & District, 1993
5501AP	Bedford YMT	Van Hool McArdle 300	C53F	1978	Ex Day & Butland, Westham, 1987
3442AP	Leyland Leopard PSU3E/4R	Van Hool Aragon	C53F	1979	Ex Horlock, Northfleet, 1987
8903AP	Volvo B10M-61	Van Hool Alizée H	C49FT	1983	Ex Smiths-Shearings, Wigan, 1989
7693AP	Leyland Royal Tiger B50	Plaxton Paramount 3500	C53F	1986	Ex Armchair, Brentford, 1994
2317AP	Mercedes-Benz L608D	PMT	B20F	1986	Ex Southdown, 1991
5536AP	Mercedes-Benz L608D	PMT	B20F	1986	Ex Southdown, 1991
9163AP	Bedford YMPS	Plaxton Paramount 3200 3	C33F	1987	
4058AP	Mercedes-Benz 709D	Advanced Vehicle Builders	DP25F	1987	
1241AP	Ford Transit	Dormobile	B20F	1987	Ex Dormobile, Folkestone (demonstrator), 1991
9415AP	Mercedes-Benz 609D	Reeve Burgess	DP19F	1988	
9925AP	Toyota HB31R	Caetano Optimo	C21F	1989	Ex Horseman, Reading, 1994
1509AP	Mercedes-Benz 609D	North West Coach Sales	DP24F	1989	
3069AP	Mercedes-Benz 811D	Wright Nim-Bus	B33F	1992	
5752AP	Mercedes-Benz 811D	UVG Citi-Star	DP33F	1996	

Previous registrations

1241AP	E863UKO	5536AP	C592SHC
1509AP	F255KDM	7693AP	C758FMC
2317AP	C590SHC	8903AP	ENF578Y, SPR124, GNF470Y
3069AP	K171YVC	9163AP	D39WDY
3442AP	CTM417T	9415AP	F361JYJ
4058AP	D759TTU	9925AP	G102APC
5501AP	BUR428T	545XFM	UKR144S

All but one of the Autopoint fleet carry locally-based AP registrations. One of the more unusual recipients is 4058AP, a Mercedes-Benz 709D with Advanced Vehicle Builders dual-purpose body, new to the operator in 1987 and found in Tunbridge Wells in July 1995.
Richard Godfrey

THE BEE LINE

The Berks Bucks Bus Co Ltd, Macmillan House, Paddington Station, London W2 1TY

The present company arose from the division of the former Thames Valley & Aldershot Omnibus Company Ltd on 1st January 1986, when it was named Alder Valley North. Becoming Berks Bucks Bus Co in January 1987, it was sold by the NBC to Q Drive, part of the Len Wright group, in December 1987. Operations in the High Wycombe area were transferred to Oxford Bus Company in November 1990. The Londonlink service went to Reading Transport in October 1991 and operations at Newbury and Reading followed in July 1992. Work in the Slough area was taken over from Luton & District in January 1993. The most recent change of ownership took place on 20th March 1996, when the operation was sold to the CentreWest group. They plan to retain its independent identity. The operational area corresponds closely with that of the former Thames Valley Traction Company.

The current livery is golden yellow with blue skirt and orange stripe.

The fleet is operated from depots at Bracknell, Maidenhead and Slough.

THE BEE LINE

112	E982DNK	MCW Metrorider MF150/81	Metro-Cammell-Weymann	B23F	1988	Ex Luton & District, 1993
113	E983DNK	MCW Metrorider MF150/81	Metro-Cammell-Weymann	B23F	1988	Ex Luton & District, 1993
131	J31KLR	Mercedes-Benz 811D	Plaxton Denver	B28F	1991	Ex London Buslines, 1996; on loan to CentreWest
132	J32KLR	Mercedes-Benz 811D	Plaxton Denver	B28F	1991	Ex London Buslines, 1996; on loan to CentreWest
133	J33KLR	Mercedes-Benz 811D	Plaxton Denver	B28F	1991	Ex London Buslines, 1996; on loan to CentreWest
134	J34KLR	Mercedes-Benz 811D	Plaxton Denver	B28F	1991	Ex London Buslines, 1996; on loan to CentreWest
135	J35KLR	Mercedes-Benz 811D	Plaxton Denver	B28F	1991	Ex London Buslines, 1996; on loan to CentreWest

162-181		Mercedes-Benz 609D	Robin Hood	B20F	1987	175 ex London Buslines, 1990

162	E458CGM	171	E467CGM	176	E472CGM	180	E476CGM
169	E465CGM	174	E470CGM	177	E473CGM	181	E477CGM
170	E466CGM	175	E471CGM	179	E475CGM		

191	K379DBL	Mercedes-Benz 709D	Plaxton Beaver	B23F	1992	

195-197		Mercedes Benz 709D	Reeve Burgess	B25F	1990	Ex London Buslines, 1995

195	G645YVS	196	G646YVS	197	G647YVS

201-208		Dennis Dart 9.8SDL3017*	Plaxton Pointer	B40F	1993-94	* 205-208 are 9.8SDL3035

201	K279XJB	203	K282XJB	205	L205GMO	207	L207GMO
202	K281XJB	204	K283XJB	206	L206GMO	208	L208GMO

211-217		Dennis Dart SLF 10m	Plaxton Pointer	B37F	1996	

211	N211WRD	213	N213WRD	215	N215WRD	217	N217WRD
212	N212WRD	214	N214WRD	216	N216WRD		

326-349		Leyland National 11351/1R		B49F	1974-75	Ex Thames Valley & Aldershot, 1986

326	TBL170M	336	GPC736N	347	KPA360P
329	TBL 174M	342	HPK501N	349	KPA370P

359	NPJ484R	Leyland National 11351A/1R		B49F	1976	Ex Alder Valley, 1990
362	TPE162S	Leyland National 11351A/1R		B49F	1978	Ex Thames Valley & Aldershot, 1986
363	TPE164S	Leyland National 11351A/1R		B49F	1978	Ex Thames Valley & Aldershot, 1986
364	TPE165S	Leyland National 11351A/1R		B49F	1978	Ex Thames Valley & Aldershot, 1986
407	YPL407T	Leyland National 10351B/1R		B41F	1978	Ex Luton & District, 1993
453	UPB303S	Leyland National 10351A/1R		B41F	1977	Ex Luton & District, 1993

501-505		Leyland Olympian ONCL10/1RZ	Northern Counties	H45/29F	1988	

501	F172LBL	502	F173LBL	503	F174LBL	504	F175LBL	505	F176LBL

533	CJH144V	Bristol VRT/SL3/6LXB	Eastern Coach Works	H43/31F	1980	Ex Thames Valley & Aldershot, 1992
539	GGM89W	Bristol VRT/SL3/6LXB	Eastern Coach Works	H43/31F	1980	Ex Thames Valley & Aldershot, 1992
540	GGM90W	Bristol VRT/SL3/6LXB	Eastern Coach Works	H43/31F	1980	Ex Thames Valley & Aldershot, 1992
560	GGM107W	Bristol VRT/SL3/6LXB	Eastern Coach Works	H43/31F	1980	Ex Thames Valley & Aldershot, 1992

740-746   Scania K113CRB   Berkhof Excellence 2000   C53F   1991

| 740 | TJI4830 | 742 | TJI4832 | 744 | TJI4834 | 746 | TJI4836 |
| 741 | TJI4831 | 743 | TJI4833 | 745 | TJI4835 | | |

752	TJI4821	Leyland Tiger TRCTL11/3R	Plaxton Paramount 3500	C50F	1983	Ex Thames Valley & Aldershot, 1986
754	TJI4824	Leyland Tiger TRCTL11/3R	Plaxton Paramount 3500	C50F	1983	Ex Alder Valley, 1992
768	TJI4838	Leyland Tiger TRCTL11/3R	Plaxton Paramount 3200 3	C53F	1988	Ex Luton & District, 1993

782-789   Volvo B10M-60   Jonckheere Jubilee P50   C53F   1989   Ex Alder Valley, 1992

| 782 | TJI4822 | 783 | TJI4823 | 786 | TJI4826 | 788 | TJI4828 | 789 | TJI4829 |

| 790 | TJI4820 | Volvo B10M-60 | Jonckheere Jubilee P50 | C53F | 1989 |

791-798   Scania K113CRB   Berkhof Excellence 1000   C53F   1995

| 791 | M791TCF | 793 | M793TCF | 795 | N795WAN | 797 | N797WAN |
| 792 | M792TCF | 794 | M794TCF | 796 | N796WAN | 798 | N798WAN |

| 801 | K801CAN | Leyland Lynx LX2R11C15Z4S | Leyland | B47F | 1992 | Ex Alder Valley, 1992 |
| 802 | K802CAN | Leyland Lynx LX2R11C15Z4S | Leyland | B47F | 1992 | Ex Alder Valley, 1992 |

803-808   Leyland Lynx LX112TL11ZR1RS   Leyland   B49F   1987   Ex London Buslines, 1995

| 803 | D751DLO | 804 | D752DLO | 805 | D753DLO | 806 | D754DLO | 808 | D755DLO |

810-819   Scania L113CRL*   Northern Counties Countybus Paladin   B51F   1995   *810 is L113CLL

| 810 | M810PGM | 812 | M812PGM | 814 | M814PGM | 816 | M816PGM | 818 | M818PGM |
| 811 | M811PGM | 813 | M813PGM | 815 | M815PGM | 817 | M817PGM | 819 | M819PGM |

RW1-30   Renault-Dodge 875   Wright   B28F   1990   Ex CentreWest, 1996

RW1	HDZ5401	RW7	HDZ5407	RW14	HDZ5414	RW20	HDZ5420	RW26	HDZ5426
RW2	HDZ5402	RW8	HDZ5408	RW15	HDZ5415	RW21	HDZ5421	RW27	HDZ5427
RW3	HDZ5403	RW9	HDZ5409	RW16	HDZ5416	RW22	HDZ5422	RW29	HDZ5429
RW4	HDZ5404	RW10	HDZ5410	RW17	HDZ5417	RW23	HDZ5423	RW30	HDZ5430
RW5	HDZ5405	RW11	HDZ5411	RW18	HDZ5418	RW24	HDZ5424		
RW6	HDZ5406	RW13	HDZ5413	RW19	HDZ5419	RW25	HDZ5425		

Previous registrations

TJI4820 F760OJH
TJI4821 YPJ203Y
TJI4822 F772OJH
TJI4823 F773OJH
TJI4824 YPJ206Y
TJI4826 F756OJH
TJI4828 F758OJH
TJI4829 F759OJH
TJI4830 J740TDP
TJI4831 J741TDP
TJI4832 J742TDP
TJI4833 J743TDP
TJI4834 J744TDP
TJI4835 J745TDP
TJI4836 J746TDP
TJI4838 E322OMG

Special liveries

Green Line: 740-6/52/4/68/82/3/6/8/9/90
Great Western Trains/Railair Link: 791-8
Overall advertisement: 169/81, 203, 326, 407, 503-5/40
Legoland Shuttle: 212
Airportlink: 204-8

Bristol VRTs with standard Eastern Coach Works bodies are down to a handful. No.539 was caught at Heathrow in September 1995, showing the brighter effect of the new livery with blue skirt and orange stripes thereon. Ivor Norman

1995 saw the arrival of ten Scania L113 vehicles with Northern Counties Countybus Paladin bodywork. No. 816 is seen in this view at Bracknell. Richard Godfrey

Following purchase of Bee Line by the CentreWest group, 28 Renault-Dodge S75 midibuses with Wright bodywork were transferred from London to replace older machines. Mike Harris

In advertising livery for Heathrow Airport, Bee Line No. 605 (since renumbered 505 to avoid duplication) is a Leyland Olympian with Northern Counties bodywork, used mainly on the Reading to Heathrow service. This view was caught mid-route in Windsor during February 1995. Richard Godfrey

The most recent new buses are seven low-floor Dennis Darts with Plaxton bodywork. No. 212 was new in the spring of 1996 and is seen at Legoland in June 1996 in dedicated livery for the shuttle service to and from that site. Ivor Norman

In 1995 the Rail Air link was updated with eight Scania K112 vehicles bodied in Holland by Berkhof. No.791, the first of the batch, shows the dignified livery used for this service at Hatton Cross in July 1995. Colin Lloyd

BLUE LAKE

Tramcourt Ltd, 44 Clayton Road, Selsey, West Sussex, PO19 2PR

Under the ownership of J.A. Redford, Blue Lake operated a city service in Chichester for some years. From 30th October 1995 this was replaced by local route 67 between Bognor Regis and Glenwood Estate. Operations had been taken over by Tramcourt Ltd in September 1993, using the same operating centre at Quarry Lane, Chichester.

BLUE LAKE

BPH106H	AEC Swift 4MP2R	Park Royal	B38D	1970	Ex Dinner, Launceston, 1989
TCD490J	Bristol RESL6L	Marshall Camagna	B45F	1970	Ex Sussex Bus, Pagham, 1993
MYD599L	AEC Reliance 6U3ZR	Plaxton Panorama Elite III	C51F	1972	Ex Berry & Hemming, Taunton, 1995
LNM511V	Bedford YMT	Duple Dominant II	C53F	1980	Ex Carlone, Godalming, 1994
DLB789Y	Bova EL26/581	Bova Europa	C53F	1983	Ex Athelstan, Malmesbury, 1989
UUY60Y	Bova EL26/581	Bova Europa	C49FT	1983	Ex Associated, Worcester, 1993
E459ANC	Mercedes-Benz 609D	Made-to-Measure	DP24F	1988	

Previous registrations
UUY60Y   FUA403Y, TXI3752

BRIGHTON BLUE BUS

Brighton Transport Ltd, 43-45 Coombe Terrace, Lewes Road, Brighton, BN2 4AQ

Brighton Borough Transport derives from the former Brighton Corporation operation which opened on 25th November 1901 with a network of 25 trams. Motor-buses were introduced on 31st March 1939, trolleybuses following on the next day (although not officially inaugurated until 1st June 1939). Trams were withdrawn on 1st September 1939 and trolleybuses last ran on 30th June 1961. For many years pooling arrangements were conducted with Brighton, Hove & District and also latterly with Southdown.

Deregulation in October 1986 was anticipated by the adoption in March 1986 of subsidiaries covering Brighton Buses, Brighton Coaches and, for non-operational activities, Brighton Transport. The 11-vehicle fleet of Chapman, Lewes was purchased in May 1988 and the fleetname of Lewes Coaches retained for operations. On 30th June 1989 the Campings Luxury Coaches business was purchased and continued as a separate division until eventually absorbed into the main operation. The present fleetname was introduced in May 1994.

The fleet carries a livery of mainly blue, with dark blue skirt and lining and black window surrounds. Atlanteans also have white relief, whilst the most recent deliveries carry route-specific branding logos. Vehicles in the Lewes Coaches fleet carry that name on standard livery. Vehicles are kept at the garage in Lewes Road, Brighton, with outstations at Meadow Road, Worthing, and at Cliffe Industrial Estate, Lewes.

BRIGHTON BLUE BUS

1-15		Leyland Atlantean AN68A/1R	East Lancs		H43/31F		1978			
1	TYJ1S	4	TYJ4S	7	TYJ7S	10	TYJ10S	13	TYJ13S
2u	TYJ2S	5	TYJ5S	8	TYJ8S	11	TYJ11S	14u	TYJ14S
3	TYJ3S	6u	TYJ6S	9	TYJ9S	12	TYJ12S	15u	TYJ15S

24	SPN669X	Leyland Leopard PSU3E/4R	Duple Dominant IV	C53F	1982	Ex Southend, 1988

25-31 Leyland National 2 NL116HLXB/1R B49F* 1983 *28-30 are B47F

25	XFG25Y	27	XFG27Y	29	XFG29Y	**31**	XFG31Y
26	XFG26Y	28	XFG28Y	30	XFG30Y		

38	F538LUF	Leyland Lynx LX112L10ZR1R	Leyland	B47F	1989
44	F544LUF	Leyland Lynx LX112L10ZR1R	Leyland	B47F	1989
45	F545LUF	Leyland Lynx LX112L10ZR1R	Leyland	B47F	1989
46	F546LUF	Leyland Lynx LX112L10ZR1R	Leyland	B47F	1989
47	E447FWV	Leyland Lynx LX1126LXCTZR1S	Leyland	B47F	1988
48	E448FWV	Leyland Lynx LX1126LXCTZR1S	Leyland	B47F	1988
49	E449FWV	Leyland Lynx LX1126LXCTZR1S	Leyland	B47F	1988
50	E450OAP	Renault S56	Alexander AM	B23F	1988
51	E451OAP	Renault S56	Alexander AM	B23F	1988
52	E452OAP	Renault S56	Alexander AM	B23F	1988
60	E460WJK	Dodge S56	Alexander AM	DP25F	1987
61	E461CWV	Renault S56	Alexander AM	B23F	1987
62	E462CWV	Renault S56	Alexander AM	B23F	1987
63	E463CWV	Renault S56	Alexander AM	B23F	1987
64	E464CWV	Renault S56	Alexander AM	B23F	1987
65	M65CYJ	Dennis Dart 9.8SDL3054	Plaxton Pointer	B40F	1995
67	OYJ67R	Leyland Atlantean AN68/1R	East Lancs	H45/32F	1977
68	M68CYJ	Dennis Dart 9.8SDL3054	Plaxton Pointer	B40F	1995
69	M69CYJ	Dennis Dart 9.8SDL3054	Plaxton Pointer	B40F	1995
71	M71CYJ	Dennis Dart 9.8SDL3054	Plaxton Pointer	B40F	1995
73	M73CYJ	Dennis Dart 9.8SDL3054	Plaxton Pointer	B40F	1995
75	OJI8786	Dennis Javelin 11SDL1905	Duple 320	C53F	1988
76	M76CYJ	Dennis Dart 9.8SDL3054	Plaxton Pointer	B40F	1995
78	M78CYJ	Dennis Dart 9.8SDL3054	Plaxton Pointer	B40F	1995
79	M79CYJ	Dennis Dart 9.8SDL3054	Plaxton Pointer	B40F	1995
80	J980JNJ	Dennis Dart 9.8SDL3017	Plaxton Pointer	B40F	1992
81	PIB5144	Leyland Leopard PSU3E/4RT	Willowbrook Warrior(1991)	B48F	1980	Ex Southend, 1988
82	TDZ4705	Volvo B10M-61	Plaxton Paramount 3500 2	C49FT	1985	Ex Clarke, Lower Sydenham, 1995
83	J983JNJ	Dennis Dart 9.8SDL3017	Plaxton Pointer	B40F	1992
84	J984JNJ	Dennis Dart 9.8SDL3017	Plaxton Pointer	B40F	1992
85	PIB5145	Leyland Leopard PSU3E/4RT	Willowbrook Warrior(1991)	B48F	1980	Ex Southend, 1988
86	J986JNJ	Dennis Dart 9.8SDL3017	Plaxton Pointer	B40F	1992
87	J987JNJ	Dennis Dart 9.8SDL3017	Plaxton Pointer	B40F	1992
88	J988JNJ	Dennis Dart 9.8SDL3017	Plaxton Pointer	B40F	1992
89	J989JNJ	Dennis Dart 9.8SDL3017	Plaxton Pointer	B40F	1992

92-96 Leyland Lynx LX112L10ZR1R Leyland B47F 1990

92	G992VWV	**93**	G993VWV	**94**	G994VWV	**95**	G995VWV	**96**	G996VWV

97	H909SKW	Renault S75	Whittaker-Europa Enterprise	B29F	1990
99	MNK424V	Leyland Leopard PSU5C/4R	Duple Dominant II	C57F	1980	Ex Thamesdown, 1996
188	TDZ4706	Volvo B10M-61	Plaxton Paramount 3500 2	C53F	1986	Ex Clarke, Lower Sydenham, 1995
189	PJI2845	Volvo B10MT-53	Plaxton Paramount 4000RS	CH55/9FT	1985	Ex HAD Coaches, Shotts, 1996

201-215 Dennis Dart SLF 10.6m Plaxton Pointer B39F 1996

201	N201NNJ	204	N204NNJ	207	N207NNJ	210	N210NNJ	213	N213NNJ
202	N202NNJ	205	N205NNJ	208	N208NNJ	211	N211NNJ	214	N214NNJ
203	N203NNJ	206	N206NNJ	209	N209NNJ	212	N212NNJ	215	N215NNJ

216	N216NPN	Dennis Dart 9.8SDL3054	Plaxton Pointer	B40F	1996	
217	N217NPN	Dennis Dart 9.8SDL3054	Plaxton Pointer	B40F	1996	
218	N218NPN	Dennis Dart 9.8SDL3054	Plaxton Pointer	B40F	1996	
	E639MTP	Renault S56	Wadham Stringer	B25F	1988	On extended loan from E Sussex County Council
	M112EUF	Dennis Dart 9SDL3034	Leicester Carriage Builders	DP28FL	1995	On extended loan from E Sussex County Council
	M814EWV	Dennis Dart 9SDL3034	Leicester Carriage Builders	DP28FL	1995	On extended loan from E Sussex County Council

Previous registrations

OJI8786	E475FWV	PIB5145	UTD204T		TDZ4705	C482HAK
PIB5144	UTD203T	PJI2845	B925BGA, WLT447, B931EGG		TDZ4706	C488HAK

Special liveries
Overall advertisements: 5, 13/4, 26-9. 38, 44/6-8, 60/5, 81/5, 94
Lewes Coaches: 30, 73/5/8, 189
Holmbush Express: 86/8

Above **Brighton Blue Bus have received fifteen Dennis Dart low-floor buses with Plaxton Pointer bodywork, replacing older double-deckers. No.206 shows off the new livery introduced for these vehicles.**
Terry Blackman

Left **The livery of the immediate privatisation period is shown by Leyland Lynx No.44, new in 1989 as part of a second generation of single-deckers to be introduced into the fleet within the decade.**
Malc McDonald

Below **The first modern single-deckers in the Brighton fleet had been seven Leyland National 2 vehicles received in 1983, of which the first was No.25.**
Gerald Mead

The ubiquitous Dennis Dart with Plaxton Pointer bodywork forms a significant part of the present-day Brighton fleet. No.65, new in 1995, was found at Denton Corner roundabout displaying Lewes Coaches fleetnames. *Calvin Churchill*.

Double-deckers, in the form of Leyland Atlanteans, are rapidly declining in the Brighton fleet. No.67, bodied by East Lancs in 1977, is now the oldest survivor, and was located in North Street in May 1996. *Mark Lyons*

BRIGHTON & HOVE

Brighton & Hove Bus & Coach Co. Ltd, Conway Street, Hove, East Sussex, BN3 3LT

The present fleetname was adopted from 21st April 1986 following the transfer of the Brighton and Hove activities of Southdown into a separate division on 1st March 1985. The former Brighton, Hove & District Ltd company had been reactivated from 1st January 1986 for the purpose. The firm was sold by the National Bus Company to a management-led team in May 1987, and absorbed within the Go-Ahead Group on 17th November 1993.

From the autumn of 1985 the fleet was gradually repainted into a distinctive new livery of cream with black skirt and dark red bands on the lower panels flying to the roof at the rear axle. The fleet was also renumbered from the former Southdown system into a three-digit scheme. An elderly Bristol KSW6G was retrieved from private ownership in 1986 and carries traditional livery. Since autumn 1995, new route-branded liveries have been introduced. New Scanias have jade relief for use on route 25, Lances have burgundy relief for use on route 1, and ex-Bournemouth minibuses are receiving plum relief for use on route 7.

The fleet is housed in garages at Hove and Whitehawk and at outstations in Newhaven, Shoreham and Steyning.

BRIGHTON & HOVE

1-20   Dennis Dart 9.8SDL3054   Marshall C37   B40F   1995

1	N501KCD	5	N505KCD	9	N509KCD	13	N513KCD	17	N517KCD
2	N502KCD	6	N506KCD	10	N510KCD	14	N514KCD	18	N518KCD
3	N503KCD	7	N507KCD	11	N511KCD	15	N515KCD	19	N519KCD
4	N504KCD	8	N508KCD	12	N512KCD	16	N516KCD	20	N520KCD

101-120   Dennis Lance 11SDA3113   Optare Sigma   B47F*   1996   *119/20 are DP47F

101	N401MPN	105	N405MPN	109	N409MPN	113	N413MPN	117	N417MPN
102	N402MPN	106	N406MPN	110	N410MPN	114	N414MPN	118	N418MPN
103	N403MPN	107	N407MPN	111	N411MPN	115	N415MPN	119	N419MPN
104	N404MPN	108	N408MPN	112	N412MPN	116	N416MPN	120	N420MPN

150-157   Leyland National 2 NL116HLXCT/1R   B49F   1985   Ex Southdown, 1986

150	C450OAP	152	C452OAP	154	C454OAP	156	C456OAP
151	C451OAP	153	C453OAP	155	C455OAP	157	C457OAP

206	C206PCD	Mercedes-Benz L608D	Alexander AM	B20F	1985	Ex Wycombe Bus, 1995
210	C210PCD	Mercedes-Benz L608D	Alexander AM	B20F	1985	Ex Wycombe Bus, 1995
211	C211PTY	Mercedes-Benz L608D	Alexander AM	DP19F	1986	Ex Wycombe Bus, 1995

250-265   Bristol VRT/SL3/6LXB   Eastern Coach Works   H43/31F   1980-81 Ex Southdown, 1986

250	JWV250W	259	JWV259W	261	JWV261W	264	JWV264W
257	JWV257W	260	JWV260W	262	JWV262W	265	JWV265W

270	JWV270W	Bristol VRT/SL3/680	Eastern Coach Works	H43/31F	1981	Ex Southdown, 1986 Modified to Gardner 6LXB
272	JWV272W	Bristol VRT/SL3/680	Eastern Coach Works	H43/31F	1981	Ex Southdown, 1986 Modified to Gardner 6LXB
273	JWV273W	Bristol VRT/SL3/680	Eastern Coach Works	H43/31F	1981	Ex Southdown, 1986 Modified to Gardner 6LXB
277	VVV964W	Bristol VRT/SL3/6LXB	Eastern Coach Works	H43/31F	1981	Ex Milton Keynes City Bus, 1986
278	VVV958W	Bristol VRT/SL3/6LXB	Eastern Coach Works	H43/31F	1981	Ex Milton Keynes City Bus, 1986
279	VVV959W	Bristol VRT/SL3/6LXB	Eastern Coach Works	H43/31F	1981	Ex Milton Keynes City Bus, 1986

340-359   Mercedes-Benz 811D   Wadham Stringer Wessex B31F*   1989   Ex Bournemouth, 1990   * 359 is DP31F

340	F40XPR	344	F44XPR	348	F48XPR	352	G52BEL	356	G56BEL
341	F41XPR	345	F45XPR	349	F49XPR	353	G53BEL	357	G57BEL
342	F42XPR	346	F46XPR	350	G50BEL	354	G54BEL	359	G59BEL
343	F43XPR	347	F47XPR	351	G51BEL	355	G55BEL		

419	H717DKM	Renault S75	Wadham Stringer Wessex	B26FL	1991	On extended loan from East Sussex C.C.
420	H714FWD	Talbot Freeway	Talbot	B16FL	1991	On extended loan from East Sussex C.C.
421	K927LPO	Mercedes-Benz 709D	Wadham Stringer Wessex	B23FL	1993	On extended loan from East Sussex C.C.
504	F504LAP	Dennis Javelin 12SDA1913	Plaxton Paramount 3200 3	C53FT	1989	
505	F505LAP	Dennis Javelin 12SDA1913	Plaxton Paramount 3200 3	C53FT	1989	
506	F506LAP	Dennis Javelin 12SDA1913	Plaxton Paramount 3200 3	C53FT	1989	
507	G507SAP	Dennis Javelin 12SDA1928	Duple 320	C53FT	1990	
508	G508SAP	Dennis Javelin 12SDA1928	Duple 320	C53FT	1990	
509	G509SAP	Dennis Javelin 12SDA1928	Duple 320	C53FT	1990	
510	F679OVK	Leyland Tiger TRCL10/3ARZM	Plaxton Paramount 3500 3	C49FT	1989	Ex Northern National, 1995
511	F790OVK	Leyland Tiger TRCL10/3ARZM	Plaxton Paramount 3500 3	C49FT	1989	Ex Northern National, 1995
512	N512MPN	Volvo B10M-62	Plaxton Première 350	C51FT	1995	
513	N513MPN	Volvo B10M-62	Plaxton Première 350	C51FT	1995	
606	UWV606S	Bristol VRT/SL3/6LXB	Eastern Coach Works	CO43/31F	1977	Ex Southdown, 1986
615	UWV615S	Bristol VRT/SL3/6LXB	Eastern Coach Works	CO43/31F	1978	Ex Southdown, 1986
619	UWV619S	Bristol VRT/SL3/6LXB	Eastern Coach Works	CO43/31F	1978	Ex Southdown, 1986
631	UFG631S	Bristol VRT/SL3/6LXB	Eastern Coach Works	H43/27D	1977	Ex Southdown, 1986

635-650 Bristol VRT/SL3/6LXB Eastern Coach Works H43/31F 1978 Ex Southdown, 1986

635	XAP635S	639	XAP639S	642	XAP642S	646	AAP646T
638	XAP638S	641	XAP641S	645	XAP645S	650	AAP650T

674	EAP974V	Bristol VRT/SL3/6LXB	Eastern Coach Works	H43/31F	1979	Ex Southdown, 1986
675	EAP975V	Bristol VRT/SL3/6LXB	Eastern Coach Works	H43/31F	1979	Ex Southdown, 1986
679	EAP979V	Bristol VRT/SL3/6LXB	Eastern Coach Works	H43/31F	1979	Ex Southdown, 1986
683	EAP983V	Bristol VRT/SL3/6LXB	Eastern Coach Works	H43/31F	1980	Ex Southdown, 1986

701-710 Scania N112DRB East Lancs H47/33F 1988

701	E701EFG	703	E703EFG	705	E705EFG	707	E707EFG	709	E709EFG
702	E702EFG	704	E704EFG	706	E706EFG	708	E708EFG	710	E710EFG

711-730 Scania N113DRB East Lancs H47/33F 1989-90

711	F711LFG	715	F715LFG	719	F719LFG	723	G723RYJ	727	G727RYJ
712	F712LFG	716	F716LFG	720	F720LFG	724	G724RYJ	728	G728RYJ
713	F713LFG	717	F717LFG	721	G721RYJ	725	G725RYJ	729	G729RYJ
714	F714LFG	718	F718LFG	722	G722RYJ	726	G726RYJ	730	G730RYJ

740	C110UBC	Scania N112DR	East Lancs	H46/33F	1986	Ex Leicester, 1989
741	C111UBC	Scania N112DR	East Lancs	H46/33F	1986	Ex Leicester, 1989
742	C112UBC	Scania N112DR	East Lancs	H46/33F	1986	Ex Leicester, 1989
743	C113UBC	Scania N112DR	East Lancs	H46/33F	1986	Ex Leicester, 1989

751-760 Scania N113DRBAA East Lancs Cityzen H47/31F 1996

751	N751OAP	753	N753OAP	755	N755OAP	757	N757OAP	759	N759OAP
752	N752OAP	754	N754OAP	756	N756OAP	758	N758OAP	760	N760OAP

6447	HAP985	Bristol KSW5G	Eastern Coach Works	H32/28R	1953	Ex preservation, 1986

Previous registrations
F679OVK F579BTG, JSK328
F790OVK F596BTG, FCU190

Special liveries
Traditional BH&D livery: 6447

Privatisation in 1986 brought three Bristol VRTs with Eastern Coach Works bodies from the Milton Keynes City Bus fleet. No.278 is one of a type which is becoming increasingly rare in the town. Gerald Mead

From 1988 to 1990 ten Scanias with East Lancs bodywork were added to the fleet each year. No.712, seen in Eastbourne in February 1995, demonstrates the 1989 batch of such vehicles. Richard Godfrey

Brighton & Hove added to their collection of Scania/East Lancs double-deckers in 1989 when four such vehicles became available from Leicester. No.741, with electronic destination display, typifies these vehicles. Gerald Mead

It is not long since single-deckers were the exception rather than the norm in the fleet. No.153, a Leyland National 2 of 1985, formed part of the opening fleet when transferred from Southdown, and was amongst the last of the type to be built. Colin Lloyd

Brighton & Hove is following the example of Brighton Blue Bus in converting some operations to single-deck. No.19 is one of twenty Dennis Darts with Marshall C37 bodywork purchased in 1995, and shows the new livery application in North Street in May 1996. Malc McDonald

Further updating of the fleet has been provided by twenty Dennis Lances with Optare Sigma bodywork, such as No.109, delivered in 1996. As in the Blue Bus fleet, double-deckers have been the chief casualties. No.109 loads in North Street in May 1996. Gerald Mead

In 1990 Brighton & Hove snapped up nineteen Mercedes-Benz minibuses with Wadham Stringer bodywork which had quickly become surplus to the requirements of Bournemouth. No.343 is seen in Old Steine in April 1996. Ivor Norman

1996 has seen the arrival of ten Scania N113s with East Lancs Cityzen bodywork. No.751, the first of the batch, shows the jade green relief used for branding of route 25, seen in Old Steine in June 1996. Malc McDonald

Amongst several distinguished veterans retained in immaculate condition by their owners within the area is Brighton & Hove No.6447, a Bristol KSW5G of 1953 with Eastern Coach Works body, restored in original livery. Alan Simpkins

CHALKWELL COACH HIRE

Chalkwell Garage & Coach Hire Ltd (Chalkwell Coaches), 195 Chalkwell Road, Sittingbourne, Kent, ME10 1BJ

Chalkwell Coach Hire had operated excursions and private hire in the Sittingbourne area for many years before starting local bus operations in April 1990, when Kent County Council contracts were obtained in the Swale area. The fleet has expanded considerably since then, both in terms of coach and bus operation, and the operations of Donsway Coaches, Faversham were acquired in October 1993, together with a number of vehicles. 1993 also saw Chalkwell take over local excursion work formerly operated by Maidstone & District from the Medway Towns, and the introduction of commuter services to and from London. In April 1996 commuter services of Smith, Sittingbourne were absorbed into an expanded network. The local network was, however, cut back on 30th September 1996.

The fleet is operated from Sittingbourne, with an outstation at Dunkirk, in a livery of white and red with black stripes.

New in 1995, M870SKP, the newest vehicle in the ever-expanding Chalkwell fleet, is an Optare MetroRider. This view at Chatham in May 1995 shows it in use for private hire, though it is also frequently found on contracted services for Kent County Council. Richard Godfrey

CHALKWELL COACH HIRE

Reg	Chassis	Body	Type	Year	History
RHS861W	Leyland Leopard PSU3/4R	Plaxton Supreme IV	C53F	1967	Ex Hearson, Chesterton, 1995; rebodied 1980
VIB5228	Bedford YMT	Duple Dominant II	C53F	1978	Ex Harris, Dunkirk, 1993
VIB5230	Leyland National 10351A/2R		B44F	1978	Ex Harris, Dunkirk, 1993
VIB9308	Bedford YMT	Plaxton Supreme	C49F	1978	Ex Harris, Dunkirk, 1993
VIB5229	Bedford YMT	Plaxton Supreme	C53F	1978	Ex Harris, Dunkirk, 1993
VIB8319	Leyland National 10351A/2R		B44F	1978	Ex Wellhouse NHS Trust, Edgware, 1995
BBW24V	Leyland Leopard PSU3E/4R	Duple Dominant IIExp	C49F	1979	Ex City of Oxford, 1994
VIB8682	Leyland National 10351B/1R		B44F	1979	Ex Sovereign, 1995
LJU836V	Ford R1014	Plaxton Supreme IV	C45F	1980	Ex Fisher, New Ollerton, 1996
PPV199W	Bedford YMT	Plaxton Supreme IVExp	C53F	1980	Ex Craker, Maidstone, 1996
MUD26W	Leyland Leopard PSU3F/4R	Duple Dominant IVExp	C49F	1981	Ex City of Oxford, 1994
VIB5231	Leyland Tiger TRCTL11/3R	Plaxton Supreme V	C57F	1982	Ex Cottrell, Mitcheldean, 1992
VIB5232	Leyland Tiger TRCTL11/3R	Plaxton Supreme V	C57F	1982	Ex Cottrell, Mitcheldean, 1993
KIW5235	Leyland Tiger TRCTL11/2R	Plaxton Paramount 3200Exp	C53F	1983	Ex Davies, Pencader, 1992
A438NKL	Talbot Express	Rootes	B14FL	1983	Ex Leybourne Grange Hospital, 1990
KIW6419	Leyland Tiger TRCTL11/2R	Plaxton Paramount 3200Exp	C53F	1983	Ex Mainwaring, Gilfach Goch, 1990
KIW7360	Leyland Tiger TRCTL11/2R	Plaxton Paramount 3200	C53F	1984	Ex Mainwaring, Gilfach Goch, 1990
KIW8923	Leyland Tiger TRCTL11/3R	Plaxton Paramount 3200	C53F	1984	Ex Brown, South Kirkby, 1989
KIW8924	Leyland Tiger TRCTL11/3R	Plaxton Paramount 3500	C53F	1984	Ex Elgar & Fox, Inkpen, 1989
KIW4965	Leyland Tiger TRCTL11/3R	Plaxton Paramount 3200	C53F	1984	Ex Hague, Platts Common, 1993
VIB9378	Leyland Tiger TRCTL11/3R	Plaxton Paramount 3200	C57F	1984	Ex Premier, Cambridge, 1994
VIB9379	Leyland Tiger TRCTL11/3R	Plaxton Paramount 3200	C57F	1984	Ex Premier, Cambridge, 1994
XOI5903	Leyland Tiger TRCTL11/3R	Plaxton Paramount 3500	C53F	1984	Ex Stringer, Pontefract, 1996
VIB5240	Leyland Tiger TRCTL11/3RH	Alexander TC	C53F	1985	Ex Docherty, Auchterader, 1994
VIB5241	Leyland Tiger TRCTL11/3RZ	Plaxton Paramount 3500 2	C53F	1985	Ex Filer, Stanton Wick, 1993
EAZ8421	Leyland Tiger TRCTL11/3R	Plaxton Paramount 3500	C53F	1985	Ex Smith, Sittingbourne, 1996
B748KCU	Volvo B10M-61	Plaxton Paramount 3500 2	C53F	1985	Ex Nesbit, Somerby, 1996
C148GGP	Mercedes-Benz L508D	Devon Conversions	C16FL	1985	Ex Kent County Council, 1990
C147CKL	Mercedes-Benz L307D	Robin Hood	C12F	1985	
C552DKE	Ford Transit 190	Chassis Developments	C16F	1985	
C480TAY	Ford Transit	Dormobile	B16F	1985	Ex Midland Fox, 1994
C487TAY	Ford Transit	Dormobile	B16F	1985	Ex Midland Fox, 1994
C490TBC	Ford Transit	Dormobile	B16F	1985	Ex Midland Fox, 1994
NIW4406	Leyland Tiger TRCTL11/3RZ	Plaxton Paramount 3500 3	C57F	1986	Ex Hulley, Baslow, 1996
VIB9375	Leyland Tiger TRCTL11/3R	Plaxton Paramount 3200 2	C57F	1986	Ex Premier, Cambridge, 1984
OIW1608	Leyland Tiger TRCTL11/3RH	Duple 320	C57F	1986	Ex Findlands, Rusholme, 1996
SIB1361	Leyland Tiger TRCTL11/3RH	Duple 320	C57F	1986	Ex Findlands, Rusholme, 1996
D991WDY	Mercedes-Benz 609D	Pilcher-Greene	B16FL	1987	Ex Sochulbus, Ashford, 1990
D575PKW	Ford Transit 130	Coachcraft	C12F	1987	
D271XRG	Volvo B10M-61	Plaxton Paramount 3200 3	C57F	1987	Ex Moor Dale, Newcastle, 1996
D881FYL	Volvo B10M-61	Plaxton Paramount 3200 2	C53F	1987	Ex London Coaches (Kent), 1996
E451BFT	Ford Transit	Jubilee	11	1987	Ex private owner, 1993
VIB5237	Volvo B10M-61	Plaxton Paramount 3500 3	C53F	1987	Ex Premier, Cambridge, 1994
VIB9485	MCW Metrorider MF150/72	Metro-Cammell-Weymann	B25F	1988	Ex Welwyn-Hatfield Line, 1995
E26XKP	Mercedes-Benz L307D	Devon Conversions	C12F	1988	
E360KPO	Iveco Daily 49.10	Robin Hood	C25F	1988	Ex Farnham Coaches, 1988
VIB5072	MCW Metrorider MF150/59	Metro-Cammell-Weymann	B25F	1988	Ex Hydes, Thurcroft, 1995
CSU960	Volvo B10M-61	Plaxton Paramount 3500 3	C53F	1988	Ex Mott, Stoke Mandeville, 1996
F939KKX	Talbot Express	Chassis Developments	C14F	1988	
F749EKM	Mercedes-Benz L307D	Devon Conversions	C12F	1988	
F486NYJ	Iveco Daily 49.10	Dormobile	B21F	1989	Ex Kenning, Waterlooville, 1995
H847DKL	Mercedes-Benz 814D	Phoenix	C33F	1990	
VIB9460	Iveco Daily 49.10	Dormobile	C25F	1991	Ex demonstrator, 1993
H651ENK	DAF 400	Jubilee	C16FL	1991	Ex private owner, 1993
L775CKM	Iveco Daily 59.12	Dormobile	B29F	1993	Ex demonstrator, 1994
M457OVM	LDV 400	Compact	B16FL	1994	
M870SKP	Optare MetroRider MR15	Optare	B31F	1995	

Previous registrations

B748KCU	B367HNL,SVJ529	RHS861W	JUA301E	VIB8682	EPD533V
CSU960	E486BFM	VIB5072	E95WKY	VIB9308	SJK938S
EAZ8421	B46XKJ	VIB5229	YMJ546S	VIB9375	C328PEW, HSV195,
KIW4965	A240ADT	VIB5230	THX235S		C795UEW
KIW5235	8124DD, PDW275Y	VIB5231	XPP285X	VIB9378	A832PPP, HSV196,
KIW 6419	A379ROU	VIB5232	XPP286X		A541WAV
KIW7360	A234GNR	VIB5237	E558UHS	VIB9379	A833PPP, HSV194,
KIW8923	A719OWT	VIB5240	B531LSG, GSU378,		A534WAV
KIW8924	A152RMJ		B734XES	VIB9460	H46FNK
LJU836V	LHS183V, AFJ199A	VIB5241	B501UNB	VIB9485	E482CNM
NIW4406	D104ERU	VIB8319	THX130S	XOI5903	B252AMG

CHILTERN QUEENS

Chiltern Queens Ltd, Greenmore, Woodcote, Oxfordshire, RG8 0RP

Chiltern Queens was formed in July 1955 as the successor to Kemp's Motor Services Ltd, also of Woodcote. Leyland Leopards and Volvos are now the staple fare with the recent decline of AEC availability. Three main services are operated from Reading together with town services in Didcot and Henley-on-Thames and a number of occasional rural services

CHILTERN QUEENS

EUD256K	AEC Reliance 6MU4R	Plaxton Derwent	B47F	1972	
OJO835M	Leyland Leopard PSU3B/4R	Plaxton Derwent	B55F	1974	
VBW581	Leyland Leopard PSU5A/4R	Plaxton Supreme III	C57F	1976	
RFC10T	Leyland Leopard PSU3E/4R	Duple Dominant I Express	C49F	1978	Ex City of Oxford, 1989
RFC12T	Leyland Leopard PSU3E/4R	Duple Dominant I Express	C49F	1978	Ex City of Oxford, 1989
WUD815T	Leyland Leopard PSU3E/4R	Duple Dominant I Express	C49F	1978	Ex City of Oxford, 1989
591STT	Leyland Leopard PSU3E/4R	Plaxton Supreme IV Exp	C53F	1979	
YFC18V	Leyland Leopard PSU3E/4R	Duple Dominant II Exp	C49F	1979	Ex City of Oxford, 1991
BBW20V	Leyland Leopard PSU3E/4R	Duple Dominant II Exp	C49F	1979	Ex City of Oxford, 1993
BBW22V	Leyland Leopard PSU3E/4R	Duple Dominant II Exp	C49F	1979	Ex City of Oxford, 1992
MUD25W	Leyland Leopard PSU3F/4R	Duple Dominant II Exp	C53F	1981	Ex City of Oxford, 1993
PPJ65W	Leyland Leopard PSU5C/4R	Wadham Stringer Vanguard	B54F	1981	Ex Ministry of Defence (RAF), 1993
PJH582X	Leyland Leopard PSU3E/4R	Plaxton Supreme IV	C53F	1982	
EBW106Y	Leyland Tiger TRCTL11/3R	Duple Dominant IV Exp	C51F	1983	Ex City of Oxford, 1995
B911SPR	Volvo B10M-61	Plaxton Paramount 3200 2	C53F	1985	Ex Excelsior, Bournemouth, 1987
C644SJM	Volvo B10M-61	Plaxton Paramount 3200 2	C53F	1986	
C114PUJ	Volvo B10M-61	Caetano Algarve	C49FT	1986	Ex Hughes, Llanfair Caerelnon, 1993
D262HFX	Volvo B10M-61	Plaxton Paramount 3200 3	C53F	1987	Ex Excelsior, Bournemouth, 1988
E533PRU	Volvo B10M-61	Plaxton Paramount 3200 3	C48FT	1987	
F986TTF	Mercedes-Benz 811D	Optare StarRider	B33F	1987	Ex Lee & Back, Caversham, 1991
F344TSC	Mercedes-Benz 811D	Alexander AM	DP29F	1988	Ex Bowen, Bridgenorth, 1992
H788RWJ	Scania K93CRB	Plaxton Paramount 3200 3	C55F	1990	
TSV804	Volvo B10M-61	Jonckheere Jubilee P599	C49FT	1986	Ex Gunton, Ongar, 1994
D504NWG	Mercedes-Benz L608D	Alexander AM	B20F	1986	Ex Lincolnshire, 1995
D506NWG	Mercedes-Benz L608D	Alexander AM	B20F	1986	Ex Lincolnshire, 1995
D34ENH	Volvo B10M-61	Duple 340	C55F	1987	Ex Country Lion, Northampton, 1994

Previous registrations

PPJ65W	50 AC 08	VBW581	SFC32P	591STT	UUD623T
TSV804	C28GNK	C114PUJ	C690KDS, SEL4X		

Following the demise of the AEC Reliance, of which Chiltern Queens had been a long-time supporter, allegiance switched to the Leyland Leopard. OJO835M, with Plaxton Derwent bodywork, was the first such vehicle, delivered in 1974 and still in use with its original owner in June 1996. Terry Blackman

Like many other operators, Chiltern Queens has purchased mini-buses which are surplus to the requirements of larger operators. D504NWG is one of two Mercedes-Benz L608D vehicles of 1986 with Alexander bodywork acquired from Lincolnshire in 1995, and was caught at the depot in June 1996. John Grubb

COASTAL COACHES

P.H. Jenkins, 18 West Point, Newick, East Sussex, BN8 4RU

Coastal Coaches gained an East Sussex County Council contract for service 346 between Silverhill (Hastings) and Pett in October 1990. After a period of operation by others, this was regained in January 1996. Coastal also operate route 355 between Heathfield and Hollington via Battle, and route 96, a Bexhill town service. A livery of green, white and blue is used.

COASTAL COACHES

103	M103CYJ	Iveco Daily 59.12	Marshall C31	B29F	1994	
104	XS2210	Iveco Daily 49.10	Robin Hood City Nippy	B21F	1989	Ex R&I Tours, London NW10, 1995
105	VY2150	Iveco Daily 49.10	Robin Hood City Nippy	B25F	1988	Ex Evans, Prenton, 1995
106	E633KDG	MCW Metrorider MF150/60	Metro-Cammell-Weymann	B25F	1988	Ex Swindon & District, 1995

Previous registrations
VY2150   E221XJA
XS2210   G209LGK, RIB4315, G121CLD

Changes in East Sussex contracts brought this Iveco Daily with Marshall C31F into the Coastal fleet as No.103 in 1994. In January 1996 it was photographed at Pett Church shortly after the acquisition of route 346 from Bexhill Buses after a short period of cover by South Coast Buses. Richard Godfrey

COUNTY RIDER

East Sussex County Council, Sackville House, Brooks Close, Lewes, East Sussex, BN7 1UE.

In addition to contracted Local Rider services, for which operators provide their own vehicles, East Sussex County Council owns a small number of vehicles which are loaned on a long-term basis to operators for County Rider services. These are painted in ESCC colours of dark green with yellow relief. They include the three vehicles listed under Brighton Blue Bus, which are operated by Lewes Coaches on routes in the Crowborough area; vehicles listed under RDH Services, used in the Uckfield area; and 419-421 under Brighton & Hove.

The following two vehicles owned by ESCC are operated by Renown of Bexhill:

C602PUF	Mercedes-Benz L608D	Reeve Burgess	B16FL	1985	Ex Community Transport, Hove, 1991
H538CTR	Leyland Cub ST2R44C97A4	Wadham Stringer Vanguard B34FL		1990	

Empress Coaches of Hastings, Warrens Coaches of Ticehurst and Autopoint of Herstmonceux also contribute vehicles from their own fleets to County Rider services.

Amongst services for which East Sussex County Council provide the vehicle is a network of County Rider routes to and from the Conquest Hospital at St Leonards, Hastings. H538CTR is a Leyland Swift with Wadham Stringer bodywork, and was found working for Renown Coaches on the Bexhill area route. Terry Blackman

Brighton & Hove also hold vehicles for ESCC County Rider use, including No.418, a Renault S75 with Wadham Stringer bodywork. It was encountered in Marine Parade in November 1995. Richard Godfrey

EASTBOURNE BUSES

Eastbourne Buses Ltd, Birch Road, Eastbourne, East Sussex, BN23 6PD

Municipal bus operation started in Eastbourne in 1903, being a world first. As a result of deregulation legislation, services are now marketed as Eastbourne Buses. From May 1987 Eastbourne collaborated with Southdown in the Hastings Top Line venture until selling out their share in September 1989.

The once-substantial presence of Leyland Atlanteans in the fleet has almost been eliminated, though some secondhand examples of this type remain. Leyland Olympians form the backbone of the double-deck fleet. An increasing number of Dennis single-deckers has been supplemented by Ikarus Citibuses, and Volvos provide a small coaching element. A notable event was the re-acquisition for the 90th anniversary of a vintage AEC Regal.

Fleet colours are biscuit and aircraft blue for buses, while coaches bear silver and blue. All vehicles are accommodated at the Birch Road site.

EASTBOURNE BUSES

1	N601PFG	DAF DE33WSSB3000	Ikarus Blue Danube	C53F	1996	
2	H388CFT	Toyota Coaster HDB30R	Caetano Optimo II	C18F	1991	Ex Ramage, Ferryhill, 1992
3	C580KNO	Volvo B10M-61	Plaxton Paramount 3500 2	C53F	1986	Ex Adams, Chelmsford, 1991
4	E804DPN	Volvo B10M-61	Plaxton Paramount 3500 3	C53F	1988	
5	E805DPN	Volvo B10M-61	Plaxton Paramount 3500 3	C53F	1988	
6	C347GSD	Volvo B10M-61	Caetano Algarve	C53F	1986	Ex Park, Hamilton, 1989
7	H908DTP	Dennis Dart 9SDL3002	Wadham Stringer Portsdown	B35F	1991	Ex Wadham Stringer demonstrator, 1991
8	H840GDY	Dennis Dart 9SDL3002	Wadham Stringer Portsdown	B35F	1990	
9	H841GDY	Dennis Dart 9SDL3002	Wadham Stringer Portsdown	B35F	1990	
10	G114FJK	Dennis Javelin 11SDL1914	Duple 300	B55F	1990	
11	AHC411	AEC Regal III	East Lancs	DP30R	1950	Ex preservation, 1992
12	G911RPN	Dennis Javelin 11SDL1914	Duple 300	B55F	1989	
13	K90EBL	Dennis Lance 11SDA3101	Wadham Stringer VanguardII	B52F	1992	
14	K90DRH	Dennis Lance 11SDA3101	Wadham Stringer VanguardII	B52F	1992	
15	K315MWV	Dennis Lance 11SDA3101	Wadham Stringer VanguardII	B52F	1993	
16	L416UNJ	DAF SB220LC550	Ikarus Citibus	B48F	1994	
17	L417UUF	DAF SB220LC550	Ikarus Citibus	B48F	1994	
18	N518LUF	DAF DE02LTSB220	Ikarus Citibus	B48F	1995	
21	J221FUF	Dennis Dart 9.8SDL3012	Wadham Stringer Portsdown	B43F	1992	
22	J122FUF	Dennis Dart 9.8SDL3004	Wadham Stringer Portsdown	B43F	1992	
23	J223FUF	Dennis Javelin 11SDL1924	Wadham Stringer VanguardII	B55F	1992	
24	J124FUF	Dennis Javelin 11SDL1914	Wadham Stringer VanguardII	B55F	1991	
25	G25HDW	Dennis Javelin 11SDL1914	Duple 300	B55F	1990	Ex Bebb, Llantwit Fardre, 1991
26	G28HDW	Dennis Javelin 11SDL1914	Duple 300	B55F	1990	Ex Bebb, Llantwit Fardre, 1991
27	J127LHC	Dennis Javelin 11SDL1924	Plaxton Derwent II	DP53F	1991	
28	M528DPN	DAF SB220LT550	Ikarus Citibus	B49F	1995	
29	M529DPN	DAF SB220LT550	Ikarus Citibus	B49F	1995	
30	M530DPN	DAF SB220LT550	Ikarus Citibus	B49F	1995	
31	N631CDY	DAF DEO2LTSB220	Ikarus Citibus	B49F	1996	
33	H533YCX	DAF SB220LC550	Ikarus Citibus	B55F	1991	Ex Merseyside, 1995
41	M441CCD	DAF DB250RS	Northern Counties Countybus Palatine 2	H47/30F	1994	

47-58			Leyland Olympian ONCL10/2RZ	Northern Counties		H47/30F	1988
47	E847DPN	50	E850DPN	53	E853DPN	56	E856DPN
48	E848DPN	51	E851DPN	54	E854DPN	57	E857DPN
49	E849DPN	52	E852DPN	55	E855DPN	58	E858DPN

62	NNO62P	Leyland Atlantean AN68A/1R	Eastern Coach Works	H43/31F	1976	Ex Colchester, 1991
63	WAG368X	Leyland Atlantean AN68C/1R	Roe	H43/31F	1982	Ex Kingston-upon-Hull, 1994
64	NNO64P	Leyland Atlantean AN68A/1R	Eastern Coach Works	H43/31F	1976	Ex Colchester, 1991
66	LDX76G	Leyland Atlantean PDR1/1	Eastern Coach Works	O43/31F	1968	Ex Ipswich, 1980
67	JWF47W	Leyland Atlantean AN68/1R	Roe	H43/29F	1980	Ex London Cityrama, London SW8, 1994
68	JFV315S	Leyland Atlantean AN68A/2R	East Lancs	H50/36F	1978	Ex Blackpool, 1994
69	JFV316S	Leyland Atlantean AN68A/2R	East Lancs	H50/36F	1978	Ex Blackpool, 1994
82	DHC782E	Leyland Titan PD2A/30	East Lancs	H32/28R	1967	

Special liveries
Overall advertisements: 21/9, 58
Traditional livery: 11

Eastbourne is another south coast fleet in which single-deckers have gradually replaced double-deckers. No.14, a Dennis Lance of 1992 with Wadham Stringer bodywork, was registered to reflect the 90th anniversary of operations, using the initials of the Managing Director.
Richard Godfrey

Most Eastbourne vehicles continue the long-standing tradition that the first number of the registration relates to the year of delivery. No.18 is an Ikarus Citibus on DAF chassis delivered in 1995, photographed in April 1996. Local customers would understand that the bus will serve the District General Hospital.
Terry Blackman

Eastbourne's support for Dennis vehicles included a number of Javelins. No.27 was delivered in 1991 with dual-purpose Plaxton Derwent II bodywork, and was seen in April 1996 on the route from Brighton to Battle, recently cut back from an even more distant destination at Rye.
Terry Blackman

The bulk of double-deck work in Eastbourne is now carried by twelve Leyland Olympians with Northern Counties bodywork delivered in 1988. No.55 is seen at the station in April 1996. Terry Blackman

A rare type so far, with a unique example in the Eastbourne fleet, No.41 is a DAF DB250RS with Northern Counties bodywork new in 1994. Calvin Churchill

Eastbourne also took the Dennis Javelin with unusual Duple 300 bodywork. No.12 was new in 1989, and carried the fleet number 11 until that was appropriated for the return of a vintage AEC Regal into the fleet, hence its registration. Terry Blackman

EASTONWAYS

E.L. & Y.M. Easton (Eastonways), Manston Road, Ramsgate, Kent, CT12 5BH

From a fleet of three coaches for contract and private hire work, Eastonways has developed extensively in recent years. A group of local bus services has been built up within the Isle of Thanet from 1991, and Eastonways have gained work to and from the developing Port Ramsgate complex, for which a large number of second-hand vehicles have been acquired. The dockside identity numbers used for Port Ramsgate operations have been developed into an orthodox fleet numbering scheme.

The main fleet livery is white and blue.

EASTONWAYS

2	OJD903R	Leyland National 10351A/2R		B24+27D	1977	Ex Port Ramsgate (npsv), 1994
3	THX146S	Leyland National 10351A/2R		B36D	1978	Ex Warren, Ticehurst, 1994
4	UFG62S	Leyland National 11351A/2R		B34+40D	1977	Ex Manchester Airport (npsv), 1994
5	YYE293T	Leyland National 10351A/2R		B21+42DL	1979	Ex London Central, 1994
6	THX246S	Leyland National 10351A/2R		B24+48D	1978	Ex Vanguard, Bedworth, 1994
7	WYJ164S	Leyland National 11351A/2R		B34+40D	1978	Ex Manchester Airport (npsv), 1994
8	BYW372V	Leyland National 10351A/2R		B24+48D	1979	Ex Evag Cannon, Bolton, 1994
9	YCD78T	Leyland National 11351A/2R		B34+40D	1978	Ex Manchester Airport (npsv), 1994
10	YCD88T	Leyland National 11351A/2R		B34+40D	1978	Ex Manchester Airport (npsv), 1994
11	BYW376V	Leyland National 10351A/2R		B24+48D	1979	Ex Port Ramsgate (npsv), 1994
12	RUF44R	Leyland National 11351A/2R		B34+40D	1977	Ex Manchester Airport (npsv), 1994
14	VKE569S	Leyland National 11351A/1R		B49F	1977	Ex Roffey, Flimwell, 1994
15	OJD895R	Leyland National 10351A/2R		B36D	1977	Ex Port Ramsgate (npsv), 1994
16	OJD396R	Leyland Fleetline FE30ALRSp	Park Royal	H44/27D	1977	Ex Camm, Nottingham, 1994
17	OJD211R	Leyland Fleetline FE30AGR	Metro-Cammell-Weymann	H45/28D	1977	Ex Wealden PSV, Five Oak Green, 1994
18	OJV118S	Leyland Fleetline FE30AGR	Roe	H45/29D	1977	Ex Wealden PSV, Five Oak Green, 1994
19	THM614M	Daimler Fleetline CRL6	Metro-Cammell-Weymann	H44/28D	1974	Ex New Enterprise, Chatham, 1993
20	OJD235R	Leyland Fleetline FE30AGR	Metro-Cammell-Weymann	H44/28D	1977	Ex Wealden PSV, Five Oak Green, 1994
21	OJD389R	Leyland Fleetline FE30ALRSp	Park Royal	H44/27D	1977	Ex Camm, Nottingham, 1994
22	LIL2515	Leyland Titan TNLXB2RRSp	Park Royal	H44/26D	1979	Ex London Buses, 1994
51	D611BCK	Iveco Daily 49.10	Robin Hood City Nippy	B21F	1987	Ex Ribble, 1993
52	D39DNH	Iveco Daily 49.10	Robin Hood City Nippy	B21F	1987	Ex United Counties, 1993
53	E306FYJ	Iveco Daily 49.10	Robin Hood City Nippy	B25F	1988	Ex Sussex Bus, Pagham, 1994
54	G744DSG	Iveco Daily 49.10	Carlyle Dailybus	B25F	1989	Ex Moffat & Williamson, Gauldry, 1995
55	F586OOU	Iveco Daily 49.10	Dormobile	B25F	1988	Ex Bristol, 1996
56	D624BCK	Iveco Daily 49.10	Robin Hood City Nippy	B23F	1987	Ex Sussex Bus, Pagham, 1995
57	F220AKG	Iveco Daily 49.10	Carlyle Dailybus	B21F	1988	Ex Collinson, Longridge, 1995
58	G402DPD	Iveco Daily 49.10	Carlyle Dailybus	B25F	1989	Ex Tillingbourne, Cranleigh, 1996
59	J431PPF	Iveco Daily 49.10	Carlyle Dailybus	B25F	1991	Ex Tillingbourne, Cranleigh, 1996
61	K165VEJ	Ford Transit	Ford	14	1992	Ex private owner, 1996
62	F726EKR	Ford Transit VE6	Dormobile	C16F	1988	
63	L830MJN	Ford Transit	Ford	14	1993	Ex private owner, 1995
64	E474JYT	Ford Transit	Dormobile	11L	1987	Ex private owner, 1995
65	E998SWT	Volkswagen LT55	Optare CityPacer	B12FL	1987	Ex Leeds City Council (npsv), 1996
66	EUI1586	Leyland Leopard PSU3B/4R	Plaxton Panorame Elite III	C51F	1973	Ex Kemp, Chillenden, 1989
68	GBZ7128	Leyland Leopard PSU3E/4R	Duple Dominant II	C53F	1978	Ex Kemp, Chillenden, 1991
69	GBZ7129	Leyland Leopard PSU3B/4R	Duple Dominant	C53F	1974	Ex Fylde, 1991
70	C806TLF	Bedford YMP	Plaxton Paramount 3200 2	C35F	1986	Ex Lewis, Dunstable, 1996
71	VOR813N	Bedford YRQ	Plaxton Elite Express III	C45F	1974	Ex Kemp, Chillenden, 1993
72	PJI3533	Leyland Royal Tiger	Leyland Doyen	C49FT	1987	Ex Reliance, Gravesend, 1995
73	HIL5681	FAP Famos S315.21	FAP Famos Charisma	C49F	1989	Ex Thompson, Uxbridge, 1995
74	BAZ7296	Leyland Tiger TRCTL11/3RH	Berkhof Everest 370	C49FT	1985	Ex Airport Coaches, Stansted, 1996
75	EUI1587	MCW Metroliner DR130/4	Metro-Cammell-Weymann	CH53/16DT	1984	Ex Mancunian, Bradford, 1994
76	976NE	MCW Metroliner DR130/15	Metro-Cammell-Weymann	CH55/16DT	1986	Ex Ensign, Rainham, 1995
77	C811JGR	MCW Metroliner DR130/28	Metro-Cammell-Weymann	CH53/16DT	1986	Ex Ensign, Rainham, 1996

Previous registrations

BAZ7296	C128PPE		EUI1587	A161TGE	LIL2515	WYV64T
C811JGR	C155LJR, KSU465		GBZ7128	VYK201S	PJI3533	D164HML
C806TLF	C806TLF, 261HTF		GBZ7129	YNA398M	976NE	C755CWX
EUI1586	KBU895L		HIL5681	F751SPU		

Named vehicles
EUI1586 Duchess of Kent, GBZ7128 Princess of Kent, OJD396R Herbert, OJD211R Pee-Wee, THM614M Buster,
OJV118S Sampson, OJD235R Thomas the Tank, OJD389R Boo-Boo.
Special liveries
Sally Ferries: RUF44R, UFG62S, OJD903R.

EAST SURREY

East Surrey Bus Services Ltd, Lambs Business Park, Tilburtstow Hill, South Godstone, RH9 8JZ

East Surrey Buses have gained a higher profile in local bus work since deregulation, and in recent times have gained some significant contracts from both Kent and Surrey County Councils, in addition to expanding commercial initiatives. On 9th October 1995 the business of Oates, South Godstone (Minicruisers) was acquired. Most recently the network of routes between Edenbridge and Tunbridge Wells has been won, so that the firm now has a significant presence in West Kent.

The present fleet contains a variety of Dennis, Optare and Mercedes-Benz buses, supported by older Bedfords and Fords and a smattering of other machines. Some coaches are held for private hire work. Fleet livery is orange and cream, and the vehicles are based at South Godstone.

EAST SURREY

1	A994THJ	Leyland Cub CU435	Wadham Stringer Vanguard	B32F	1984	Ex Oates, South Godstone, 1995
4	F649PLW	Mercedes-Benz 609D	Reeve Burgess	B23F	1989	Ex Oates, South Godstone, 1995
5	G584ESW	Mercedes-Benz 508D	Coachcraft	C15F	1990	Ex Oates, South Godstone, 1995
6	G482PNF	Mercedes-Benz 709D	Made-to-Measure	DP20F	1989	Ex Oates, South Godstone, 1995
9	H5TGO	Mercedes-Benz		C24F	1991	Ex Harrison, Sprotborough, 1995
18	E318SYG	Mercedes-Benz 811D	Optare StarRider	B33F	1988	
19	MPE248P	Bedford YRQ	Plaxton Derwent	B47F	1976	Ex Farnham Coaches, 1988
20	VDL264K	Bedford YRQ	Plaxton Derwent	B49F	1972	Ex Gale, Haslemere, 1988
24	F70RPL	Mercedes-Benz 811D	Optare StarRider	DP33F	1989	
25	G301CPL	Mercedes-Benz 811D	Optare StarRider	B33F	1989	
26	G972WPA	Optare MetroRider	Optare	B33F	1990	
27u	UGB14R	AEC Reliance 6U3ZR	Duple Dominant	B53F	1977	Ex Moss, Sandown, 1990
32	OHV208Y	Ford R1114	Wadham Stringer Vanguard	B33F	1983	Ex London Borough of Lewisham, 1991
33	YLN636S	Ford R1014	Duple Dominant	B47F	1978	Ex London Borough of Hillingdon, 1991
34	J326PPD	Optare MetroRider	Optare	B33F	1991	
35	VNU533Y	Ford R1014	Duple Dominant	B47F	1982	Ex Lamcote, Radcliffe, 1991
36	J752PPM	Dennis Dart 9SDL3002	Wadham Stringer Portsdown	B37F	1991	
37	D602RGJ	Bedford YMT	Plaxton Derwent	B53F	1987	Ex Epsom Buses, 1991
38	D167TAU	Bedford YMT	Duple Dominant	B55F	1986	Ex National Plant, South Normanton, 1992
40	B88BVW	Ford R1015	Wadham Stringer Vanguard	B33F	1985	Ex Wealden PSV, Five Oak Green, 1992
41	C915BYP	Bedford YMP	Wadham Stringer Vanguard	B45F	1985	Ex Civil Service College, Sunningdale, 1992
42	D380BNR	Bedford YMT	Plaxton Paramount 3500 3	C53F	1987	Ex Owen, Yateley, 1992
45	K488XPG	Dennis Dart 9.8SDL3017	Plaxton Pointer	B40F	1993	
46	E132PLJ	Dennis Javelin 12SDA1907	Plaxton Paramount 3200 3	C53F	1988	Ex Taylor, Sutton Scotney, 1993
47	L726DPG	Dennis Dart 9.8SDL3035	Plaxton Pointer	B40F	1993	
48	L735MWW	Optare MetroRider	Optare	B29F	1993	
49	L354FPF	Dennis Dart 9.8SDL3035	Plaxton Pointer	B40F	1994	
50	M150HPL	Dennis Dart 9.8SDL3035	Plaxton Pointer	B40F	1994	
51	M151HPL	Dennis Dart 9.8SDL3040	Plaxton Pointer	B40F	1994	
52	M152HPL	Mercedes-Benz 709D	Plaxton Beaver	B25F	1995	
53	M153HPL	Iveco Daily 59.12	WSC	B24FL	1995	
54	E407EPE	Dodge S46	Northern Counties	B22F	1987	Ex Guildford & West Surrey, 1995
	G105DPB	Renault S56	Northern Counties	B25F	1989	Ex London & Country, 1996

Special liveries
Minicruisers: 1, 4, 5, 6, 9

The registration of Eastonways No. 22 only fleetingly disguises its pedigree as a former London Buses Leyland Titan, in this instance one of the earlier examples with Park Royal bodywork, as it awaits customers at Port Ramsgate. Martin Smith

A good proportion of the fleet comprises Leyland Nationals adapted for courtesy work to and from Port Ramsgate. More recently, some have started to appear in dedicated livery for Sally Ferries, such as No.2, also a refugee from London. Martin Smith

Eastonways have also developed a network of local routes across the Isle of Thanet. Iveco Daily No.55, photographed at King Street, Ramsgate, shows the smart condition in which this growing fleet is presented. Martin Smith

East Surrey No.52 is a Mercedes-Benz 709D with Plaxton bodywork new in 1995, and was photographed in August 1995 on a tendered Sunday operation at Sevenoaks. For a Sunday, the load appears healthy.
Terry Blackman

Dennis Darts with Plaxton Pointer bodywork have joined the East Surrey fleet. No.50, new in 1994, was found at Pembury on KCC contracted work in July 1995. Richard Godfrey

Amongst the older denizens of the fleet is No.19, a Bedford YRQ with Plaxton Derwent bodywork new in 1976, caught at East Croydon in April 1996 on the Wallington service.
Colin Lloyd

EMSWORTH & DISTRICT

P R J & M J Lea, 29 Record Road, Emsworth, Hampshire, PO10 7NS

The origins of Emsworth & District's local bus operations were in four former routes of the now-defunct Hants & Sussex company. These are now represented by route 11 from Chichester via Emsworth to Thorney Island, and route 36 from Southbourne via Emsworth and Havant to Cowplain.

Vehicles carry a bright green livery, and are garaged at Clovelly Road, Southbourne.

EMSWORTH & DISTRICT

AML30H	AEC Swift 4MP2R	Marshall	B46F	1970	Ex Solent Blue Line, 1988
EGN637J	AEC Swift 4MP2R4	Metro-Cammell-Weymann	B33D	1971	Ex ICI, Stevenston (npsv), 1990
JGV332N	Bedford YRT	Plaxton Derwent	B64F	1975	Ex Rallybeam, Debach, 1991
OPC35R	Bedford YMT	Plaxton Supreme	C53F	1977	Ex East Surrey, Waddon, 1989
OJD213R	Leyland Fleetline FE30AGR	Metro-Cammell-Weymann	H44/24F	1977	Ex Thamesdown, 1994
FTO558V	Bedford YMT	Plaxton Supreme IV	C53F	1979	Ex Booth, Eccles, 1995
OLJ192W	Bedford YNT	Plaxton Supreme IV	C53F	1981	Ex Banstead Coaches, 1993
ODL525X	Bedford YNT	Plaxton Supreme IV	C53F	1981	Ex Moss, Sandown, 1994
KTY23X	Bedford YMT	Duple Dominant	B53F	1981	Ex Jolly, South Hylton, 1995
KTY24X	Bedford YMT	Duple Dominant	B53F	1981	Ex Jolly, South Hylton, 1995
B29BMC	Ford Transit	Chassis Developments	12	1985	Ex Castle, Clanfield, 1990
B735YUD	Ford Transit	Carlyle	B20F	1985	Ex City of Oxford, 1991
C724JJO	Ford Transit	Carlyle	DP20F	1985	Ex City of Oxford, 1991
D269YDL	Ford Transit	Carlyle	DP18F	1986	Ex Solent Blue Line, 1995
E523TOV	Iveco Daily 49.10	Carlyle Dailybus	B25F	1988	Ex Tillingbourne, Cranleigh, 1996
G532VND	Iveco Daily 49.10	Carlyle Dailybus	B23F	1990	Ex Dunstan, Middleton, 1996

Named vehicles
OPC35R *Pride of the Ems*, KTY24X *Katy of the Ems*

One of the minibuses used regularly on service by Emsworth & District, D269YDL is a Carlyle-bodied Ford Transit which started life with Southern Vectis. This view was taken at Brooklands during the Cobham Open Day in April 1996. Colin Lloyd

EPSOM BUSES / EPSOM COACHES

H R Richmond Ltd, Blenheim Road, Longmead Estate, Epsom, Surrey, KT19 9AF

Epsom Buses is the trading name for local bus work undertaken by Epsom Coaches, founded in 1920 by Mr H R Richmond. The main thrust of operations comprises quality coaching work, Continental work and commuter services. Bus work started on 3rd April 1986 when the Mole Valley route between Hampton Court and Richmond was taken over, and seven routes were gained on contract from Surrey County Council at deregulation in October 1986. Subsequently there have been several adjustments to the network.

Fleet livery is maroon and cream for coaches, cream with maroon relief for buses.

The standard bus fleet has been upgraded to Dennis Darts during the past four years. K892CSX, the first to arrive in 1992, remains an individual specimen with Alexander bodywork; subsequent Darts have Plaxton or Marshall bodywork. Gerald Mead

F670NPG, a Mercedes-Benz 811D of 1988 with Optare StarRider bodywork, was acquired from East Surrey in 1991, and is seen in Kingston. Geoff Rixon

EPSOM BUSES / EPSOM COACHES

	Reg	Chassis	Body	Seating	Year	Notes
	D600RGJ	Bedford YMT	Plaxton Derwent II	B53F	1987	
	E204YGC	Mercedes-Benz 709D	Reeve Burgess Beaver	DP25F	1988	
	E205YGC	Mercedes-Benz 709D	Reeve Burgess Beaver	DP25F	1988	
	E206BLN	Mercedes-Benz 709D	Reeve Burgess Beaver	DP25F	1988	
	F207DGT	Mercedes-Benz 709D	Reeve Burgess Beaver	DP25F	1988	
	F208GGH	Mercedes-Benz 709D	Robin Hood	B26F	1988	
	F209GGH	Mercedes-Benz 709D	Robin Hood	B26F	1988	
	F670NPG	Mercedes-Benz 811D	Optare StarRider	B33F	1988	Ex East Surrey, South Godstone, 1991
	H210UGO	Mercedes-Benz 709D	Phoenix	B26F	1990	
	K892CSX	Dennis Dart 9.8SDL3017	Alexander Dash	B40F	1992	
	K593BEG	Mercedes-Benz 709D	Marshall C19	B27F	1992	
	K112NGK	Dennis Dart 9.8SDL3012	Plaxton Pointer	B40F	1993	
	K113NGK	Dennis Dart 9.8SDL3012	Plaxton Pointer	B40F	1993	
	K321GEW	Dennis Dart 9.8SDL3017	Marshall C27	B40F	1993	
	L894NAV	Mercedes-Benz 709D	Marshall C19	B27F	1993	
	M960CGF	Dennis Dart 9.8SDL3040	Plaxton Pointer	B40F	1994	
	N401SPA	Dennis Dart 9.8SDL3054	Plaxton Pointer	B40F	1995	
	N402SPA	Dennis Dart 9.8SDL3054	Plaxton Pointer	B40F	1995	
	N479VPA	Dennis Javelin	Plaxton Première 320	C53F	1996	
18.1	K460PNR	Toyota Coaster HDB30R	Caetano Optimo II	C18F	1992	
18.2	K465PNR	Toyota HDB30R	Caetano Optimo II	C18F	1993	
48.1	E512YGC	Volvo B10M-61	Van Hool Alizée H	C48FT	1988	
48.2	E513YGC	Volvo B10M-61	Van Hool Alizée H	C48FT	1988	
48.3	E514YGC	Volvo B10M-61	Van Hool Alizée H	C48FT	1988	
48.4	K288GDT	Volvo B10M-60	Van Hool Alizée H	C48FT	1993	
48.5	K289GDT	Volvo B10M-60	Van Hool Alizée H	C48FT	1993	
48.6	M791LPH	Dennis Javelin 12SDA2131	Plaxton Première 320	C48FT	1995	
48.7	M792LPH	Dennis Javelin 12SDA2131	Plaxton Première 320	C48FT	1995	
48.8	N405SPC	Dennis Javelin 12SDA2155	Plaxton Première 320	C48FT	1996	
53.1	H531WGH	Volvo B10M-60	Van Hool Alizée H	C53F	1991	
53.2	H532WGH	Volvo B10M-60	Van Hool Alizée H	C53F	1991	
53.3	H533WGH	Volvo B10M-60	Van Hool Alizée H	C53F	1991	
53.4	C331DND	Volvo B10M-61	Van Hool Alizée H	C53F	1986	Ex Shearings, Wigan, 1992
53.5	C529DND	Volvo B10M-61	Van Hool Alizée H	C53F	1986	Ex Shearings, Wigan, 1992
53.6	F516GGJ	Volvo B10M-60	Van Hool Alizée H	C53F	1989	
53.7	F517GGJ	Volvo B10M-60	Van Hool Alizée H	C53F	1989	
53.8	G518OGP	Volvo B10M-60	Van Hool Alizée H	C53F	1990	
53.9	G519OGP	Volvo B10M-60	Van Hool Alizée H	C53F	1990	
53.10	L231BUT	Dennis Javelin 12SDA2138	Plaxton Première 320	C53F	1994	
53.11	L232BUT	Dennis Javelin 12SDA2138	Plaxton Première 320	C53F	1994	
53.12	L233BUT	Dennis Javelin 12SDA2138	Plaxton Première 320	C53F	1994	
53.13	L234BUT	Dennis Javelin 12SDA2138	Plaxton Première 320	C53F	1994	
53.14	M790LPH	Dennis Javelin 12SDA2131	Plaxton Première 320	C53F	1995	
53.15	M793LPH	Dennis Javelin 12SDA2131	Plaxton Première 320	C53F	1995	
53.16	M332MPG	Dennis Javelin 12SDA2155	Plaxton Première 320	C53F	1995	
53.17	N406SPC	Dennis Javelin	Plaxton Première 320	C53F	1996	
53.18	N407SPC	Dennis Javelin	Plaxton Première 320	C53F	1996	
53.19	N408SPC	Dennis Javelin	Plaxton Première 320	C53F	1996	
53.20	N409SPC	Dennis Javelin	Plaxton Première 320	C53F	1996	

Previous registration
D447FSP   D614FSL

FARLEIGH COACHES

J.M. Smith, St Peter's Works, Hall Road, Wouldham, Kent, ME1 3XL

Farleigh Coaches commenced local coaching operations in August 1982, though not using this trading name until later. Bus operations were introduced at deregulation and although a weekday evening contract between Maidstone and Borough Green has since passed elsewhere, the main service 58 between Maidstone and Trottiscliffe remains. This is notable in having been introduced commercially to replace a Maidstone & District facility, although it is now provided as a Kent County Council contract. Several other school services are provided in the area north-west of Maidstone.

Fleet livery is white with orange relief and lettering.

FARLEIGH COACHES

WFS228K	Leyland Atlantean PDR1A/1	Alexander J	H45/30D	1972	Ex Ulsterbus, 1990
JGF410K	Daimler Fleetline CRL6	Park Royal	H44/29F	1972	Ex Tellyn, Little Baddow, 1983
VPB123M	Leyland Atlantean AN68/1R	Park Royal	H43/28D	1974	Ex Turner, West Farleigh, 1993
NOE591R	Leyland National 11351A/1R		B49F	1977	Ex Muffitt, Morley, 1992
OJD223R	Leyland Fleetline FE30AGR	Metro-Cammell-Weymann	H44/24D	1977	Acquired 1993
THX140S	Leyland National 10351A/2R		B36D	1977	Ex London Buses, 1991
XEK134S	Bedford YMT	Plaxton Supreme	C53F	1978	Ex Turner, West Farleigh, 1994
GDT442V	Ford R1114	Plaxton Supreme IV	C53F	1980	Ex Barnard, Kirton-in-Lindsey, 1994
PVV314	DAF MB200DKTL600	Caetano Alpha GT	C53F	1983	Ex Street, Bickington, 1993
SIB3059	DAF SB2300DHTD585	Plaxton Paramount 3200	C53F	1984	Ex Hallum, Southend, 1993
SIB3058	DAF SB2300DHS585	Jonckheere Jubilee P599	C51FT	1985	Ex Gillespie, Kelty, 1992
SIB3057	DAF SB2305DHS585	Caetano Algarve	C53F	1989	
WOI4006	Ward Dalesman TV8-640	Van Hool Alizée	C49FT	1983	Ex Prentice & McQuillan, Swanley, 1994

Previous registrations

PVV314	CAY215Y	SIB3059	A332PNW
SIB3057	F438RRY	WOI4006	GCP789Y
SIB3058	B496GBD		

Farleigh Coaches continue to prevail on Kent County Council route 58 between Maidstone and Trottiscliffe, using one of their acquired Leyland Nationals. NOE591R, a 49-seat 11.3metre model, has been owned since 1992, and had originated with Midland Red. Richard Godfrey

FUGGLES

Fuggles of Benenden Ltd, Bramley Orchard, Cranbrook Road, Benenden, Kent, TN17 4EU

Fuggles traces its origins back to the late 1920s and the establishment of a garage in the country village in 1927. The firm passed into new management during the summer of 1989 and the original trading name was reinstated after a period during which the limited company name of Penjon had been used for official purposes.

Stage services started in June 1980 and the company subsequently built up a network of services in the rural area bordered by Maidstone, Tunbridge Wells and Tenterden. Many of these were operated on a commercial basis. The recession has meant that most of them have since come under Kent County Council auspices, and some have been lost to other operators. Operations are now based on commercial and tendered routes across the Weald of Kent to Tonbridge and Tunbridge Wells.

Fleet livery is deep red and cream with pale red relief, and the fleet is housed in a new depot at Apple Pie Farm, Benenden.

FUGGLES

8	M8FUG	DAF SB220LT550	N Counties Countybus Paladin	B49F	1994	
9	M9FUG	Dennis Dart 9.8SDL3032	WSC Portsdown	B43F	1994	
10	L10FUG	Dennis Dart 9.8SDL3032	WSC Portsdown	B43F	1994	
11	A11FUG	Leyland Tiger TRCTL11/3RH	Plaxton Paramount 3200 Exp	C53F	1984	Ex Harrison & Brunt, Derby, 1994
12	M12FUG	Mercedes-Benz 711D	WSC Wessex	DP25F	1995	
14	N14FUG	Mercedes-Benz 711D	WSC Wessex	B24FL	1995	
	STD119L	Leyland Leopard PSU4B/2R	Seddon Pennine	B47F	1972	Ex Maidstone Borough Council, 1982
	LUG523P	Leyland Leopard PSU4C/4R	Plaxton Derwent	D52F	1976	Ex Wealden PSV, Five Oak Green, 1992
	PBO674R	Leyland Leopard PSU4D/2R	Plaxton Derwent	B53F	1977	Ex Red & White, 1993
	SKN904R	Leyland National 11351A/1R		DP48F	1977	Ex Morgan, Staplehurst, 1996
	UFT911T	Bedford YLQ	Plaxton Supreme III	C45F	1978	Ex Rowland & Goodwin, St Leonards, 1983
	APH529T	Bedford YMT	Plaxton Supreme IV	C53F	1979	Ex Lock, London SE8, 1993
	HVC10V	Bedford YMT	Plaxton Supreme IV	C53F	1979	Ex Rowland & Goodwin, St Leonards, 1984
	BUT47Y	Bedford YNT	Plaxton Paramount 3200 Exp	C53F	1983	Ex Wainfleet, Nuneaton, 1987
	B420CMC	Mercedes-Benz L608D	Reeve Burgess	C21F	1985	Ex Garcia, London W2, 1989
	E689WNE	Talbot Express	Made-to-Measure	C12F	1988	Ex Hirst, Meltham, 1994
	G904MCX	DAF SB2305DHTD585	Duple 320	C57F	1990	Ex North Kent, 1995
	L822PEG	Ford Transit	Dormobile	DP18FL	1994	Ex Kent County Council, 1994

Previous registrations
A11FUG   A76JFA

Recent new arrivals in the Fuggles fleet have carried dedicated registrations. No.8 is a Northern Counties-bodied DAF new in 1994, and was snapped in Tunbridge Wells in April 1996.
Terry Blackman

Like most of the recent purchases by Fuggles, Dennis Dart No.10 has a registration number with the first three letters of its owner's name. Terry Blackman

Not carrying its twenty years too convincingly, LUG523P is a Leyland Leopard with Plaxton Derwent bodywork new in 1976 and operated by Fuggles since 1992. Even the destination display has a suggestion of reluctance about it in its abbreviation. Martin Smith

KENTISH BUS

Kentish Bus Ltd, Invicta House, Armstrong Road, Maidstone, Kent, ME15 6TY

Kentish Bus & Coach was re-named from London Country South East on 27th April 1987, and purchased by the Proudmutual Group, later part of British Bus. In June 1996 British Bus was itself purchased by the Cowie group. There has been considerable success in obtaining London Transport contracts in recent years. From 1st January 1995 some of the London operations have been covered by the newly-formed London*links* company. This listing shows vehicles allocated to Dartford, Dunton Green and Northfleet, primarily for work within Kent, although some of those at Dartford and Dunton Green may be used on LT routes. Vehicles allocated to Battersea and Cambridge Heath for LT routes are shown in the London Bus Handbook.

The main livery is primrose yellow with maroon relief, though more recently vehicles for Kentish work have started to appear in a livery of green and yellow.

Kentish Bus had been successful in securing London Transport contracts, though changing circumstances have led to some of the vehicles being transferred to work in Kent. No.154 is a Dennis Dart of 1994 with Northern Counties body, seen in Dartford in July 1995 on local service.
Laurie Rufus

Kentish Bus was one of the stronger supporters of the Talbot Pullman at the end of the 1980s, though the type is now being withdrawn rapidly. No.873 was caught in Gravesend in April 1996.
Laurie Rufus

KENTISH BUS

FOR VEHICLES USED EXCLUSIVELY ON LONDON TRANSPORT SERVICES, SEE THE LONDON BUS HANDBOOK

AN186	XPG186T	Leyland Atlantean AN68A/1R	Roe	H43/30F	1979	Ex Londonlinks, 1996
AN196	XPG196T	Leyland Atlantean AN68A/1R	Roe	H43/30F	1979	Ex Londonlinks, 1996

AN203-232   Leyland Atlantean AN68A/1R Roe   H43/30F 1979/80

AN203 EPH203V	AN211 EPH211V	AN220 EPH220V	AN225 EPH225V
AN208 EPH208V	AN212 EPH212V	AN221 EPH221V	AN231 EPH231V
AN210 EPH210V	AN215 EPH215V	AN224 EPH224V	AN232 EPH232V

AN265-282   Leyland Atlantean AN68B/1R Roe   H43/30F 1980/81

AN265 KPJ265W	AN271 KPJ271W	AN276 KPJ276W	AN279 KPJ279W
AN269 KPJ269W	AN273 KPJ273W	AN277 KPJ277W	AN282 KPJ282W
AN270 KPJ270W	AN274 KPJ274W	AN278 KPJ278W	

9	TIB5905	Leyland Tiger TRCTL11/3RH	Duple 320	C53F	1986	
10	TIB5906	Leyland Tiger TRCTL11/3RH	Duple 320	C51F	1986	
11	XSV689	Leyland Tiger TRCTL11/3RH	Duple 320	C53F	1986	Ex London & Country, 1994
14	TSU644	Leyland Tiger TRCTL11/3R	Plaxton Paramount 3200Exp	C53F	1983	Ex Maidstone & District, 1996
15	YSU895	Leyland Tiger TRCTL11/2R	Plaxton Paramount 3200Exp	C53F	1983	Ex Maidstone & District, 1996
16	YLK281	Leyland Tiger TRCTL11/3RH	Duple Laser Express	C50F	1983	On extended loan from Maidstone & Dist, 1996
21	KBC193	Leyland Tiger TRCTL11/3RH	Berkhof Everest 370	C49FT	1984	
27	OSK776	Leyland Tiger TRCRL11/3RH	Berkhof Everest 370	C49FT	1986	
28	YYB122	Leyland Tiger TRCTL11/3RH	Berkhof Everest 370	C49FT	1986	
29	JSK994	Leyland Tiger TRCTL11/3RH	Berkhof Everest 370	C49FT	1986	
30	TIB5903	Volvo B10M-61	Van Hool Alizée	C53F	1988	Ex Jason, St Mary Cray, 1993
31	TIB5904	Volvo B10M-61	Van Hool Alizée	C53F	1988	Ex Jason, St Mary Cray, 1993
32	HIL2279	Volvo B10M-61	Plaxton Paramount 3500 3	C50F	1988	Ex Wallace Arnold, 1993
35	A11GTA	Volvo B10M-60	Plaxton Paramount 3500 3	C53F	1991	Ex Park, Hamilton, 1994
36	XSV691	Leyland Tiger TRCTL11/3RZ	Plaxton Paramount 3200 3	C53F	1988	Ex London & Country, 1994
38	IIL9168	Leyland Tiger TRCTL10/3ARZM	Plaxton Paramount 3200 3	C53F	1989	Ex Moor Dale, Newcastle, 1995
39	IIL9169	Leyland Tiger TRCTL10/3ARZM	Plaxton Paramount 3200 3	C53F	1989	Ex Moor Dale, Newcastle, 1995
40	J16AMB	DAF SB3000DKVF601	Van Hool Alizée	C52F	1992	Ex Express Travel, Speke, 1995
41	J17AMB	DAF SB3000DKVF601	Van Hool Alizée	C48FT	1992	Ex Express Travel, Speke, 1995
42	K22AMB	DAF SB3000DKVF601	Van Hool Alizée	C52F	1992	Ex Express Travel, Speke, 1995

87-98   Dennis Dart 9SDL3002   Duple/Carlyle Dartline   B36F   1990   Ex R&I Tours, London NW10, 1995

87	G217LGK	95	G125RGT	97	G127RGT
93	G123RGT	96	G126RGT	98	G128RGT

112-159   Dennis Dart 9SDL3034 N Counties Countybus Paladin   B35F   1994

112	L112YVK	131	L131YVK	138	L138YVK	145	L145YVK	154	L154YVK
113	L113YVK	132	L132YVK	139	L139YVK	146	L146YVK	155	L155YVK
114	L114YVK	133	L133YVK	140	L140YVK	148	L148YVK	156	L156YVK
127	L127YVK	134	L134YVK	141	L141YVK	149	L149YVK	157	L157YVK
128	L128YVK	135	L135YVK	142	L142YVK	150	L150YVK	158	L158BFT
129	L129YVK	136	L136YVK	143	L143YVK	152	L152YVK	159	L159BFT
130	L130YVK	137	L137YVK	144	L144YVK	153	L153YVK		

250-259   Scania L113CRL   Wright Pathfinder   B43F   1995

250	N250BKK	252	N252BKK	254	N254BKK	256	N256BKK	258	N258BKK
251	N251BKK	253	N253BKK	255	N255BKK	257	N257BKK	259	N259BKK

336	SIB6706	Leyland National 2 NL106AL11/1R	East Lancs (1992)	B41F	1981	Ex Londonlinks, 1996
345	SIB6715	Leyland National 1051/1R/0402	East Lancs (1993)	B41F	1973	Ex Londonlinks, 1996
346	SIB6716	Leyland National 1051/1R/0402	East Lancs (1993)	B41F	1974	Ex Londonlinks, 1996

348-357   Leyland National 10351B/1R   East Lancs (1992)   B41F   1978/79

348	SIB1279	350	SIB1281	352	SIB1283	354	SIB1285	356	SIB1287
349	SIB1280	351	SIB1282	353	SIB1284	355	SIB1286	357	SIB1288

361	PDZ6261	Leyland National 10351/1R	East Lancs (1994)	B41F	1977	Ex Londonlinks, 1996
362	PDZ6262	Leyland National 10351/1R	East Lancs (1994)	B41F	1977	Ex Londonlinks, 1996

403-411   Leyland Lynx LX2R11C15Z4S   Leyland   B49F   1989   Ex Boro'line Maidstone, 1992

403	G36VME	405	G38VME	407	G40VME	409	G42VME	411	G44VME
404	G37VME	406	G39VME	408	G41VME	410	G43VME		

In 1995, Kentish Bus purchased a number of Dennis Darts from R&I Tours with Duple bodywork finished by Carlyle, chiefly to support routes acquired from Maidstone & District in north-west Kent. No.95 represents both this operation, as seen at Gravesend, and the new livery which was introduced concurrently. Laurie Rufus

The new livery provides a strikingly fresh dimension to older vehicles in the fleet, such as AN276, a Leyland Atlantean with Roe bodywork found at Bromley South. This was one of the last substantial batches of Atlanteans delivered to the old London Country company before its fragmentation. Colin Brown

The most recent midibus arrivals in the fleet are eight Optare MetroRiders new in 1996. These are used in the Dartford area, as exemplified by No.803 in June 1996. The new livery provides clean lines which complement the design of the vehicle well. Laurie Rufus

With support from Kent County Council, ten low-floor Scanias were introduced on route 480 in December 1995. Bodied by Wright, these vehicles, represented by No.250, carry dedicated route branding and provide a welcome upgrade from the mixed operations previously found on this busy service. Dave Stewart

Although carrying LT insignia in the windscreen, Leyland National No.357, an East Lancs Greenway rebuild of 1992, was working the Gravesend service when captured at Sevenoaks in March 1996. Note the addition of a green stripe to the old-style livery. Eric Baldock

Green Line services to and from the Gravesend area have been subject to remarketing during the past year, including the adoption of a fresher livery. No.36 is a Leyland Tiger of 1988. Colin Lloyd

413	H813EKJ Leyland Lynx LX2R11G15Z4S	Leyland	B49F	1991	Ex Boro'line Maidstone, 1992
414	H814EKJ Leyland Lynx LX2R11G15Z4S	Leyland	B49F	1991	Ex Boro'line Maidstone, 1992
415	H815EKJ Leyland Lynx LX2R11G15Z4S	Leyland	B49F	1991	Ex Boro'line Maidstone, 1992
416	H816EKJ Leyland Lynx LX2R11G15Z4S	Leyland	B49F	1991	Ex Boro'line Maidstone, 1992
417	D155HML Leyland Lynx LX112TL11ZR1	Leyland	B49F	1987	Ex Boro'line Maidstone, 1992
419	D157HML Leyland Lynx LX112TL11ZR1	Leyland	B49F	1987	Ex Boro'line Maidstone, 1992
445	M445HPF Optare MetroRider MR17	Optare	B29F	1994	Ex Londonlinks, 1996
446	M446HPF Optare MetroRider MR17	Optare	B29F	1994	Ex Londonlinks, 1996
555	G555VBB Leyland Olympian ON2R50C13Z4	Northern Counties	H47/27D	1990	
556	G556VBB Leyland Olympian ONCL10/1RZ	Northern Counties	H47/27D	1990	

557-565   Volvo Olympian YN2RC16Z4 Northern Counties Countybus Palatine II   H47/30F   1994

557	L557YCU	559	L559YCU	562	L562YCU	564	L564YCU
558	L558YVU	561	L561YCU	563	L563YCU	565	L565YCU

601-620   Leyland Olympian ONLXB/1R   Eastern Coach Works   H45/32F* 1983-85   Ex Northumbria, 1990/91
* 601 is H44/32F

601	WDC219Y	611	A241GHN	614	A244GHN	617	B247NVN	620	C257UAJ
608	CEF231Y	612	A242GHN	615	B245NVN	618	B248NVN		
610	A240GHN	613	A243GHN	616	B246NVN	619	B256RAJ		

631-638   Volvo Citybus B10M-50   Northern Counties   H45/31F   1989   Ex Londonlinks, 1996

631	G631BPH	633	G633BPH	635	G635BPH	637	G637BPH
632	G632BPH	634	G634BPH	636	G636BPH	638	G638BPH

721-734   Volvo Citybus B10M-50   Alexander RV   H47/29D   1989   Ex Boro'line Maidstone, 1992

721	F101TML	726	F106TML	730	F110TML	733	F113TML
723	F103TML	728	F108TML	731	F111TML	734	F114TML

751-762   Leyland Olympian ONLXB/1RH Optare   H47/29F   1988/89 Ex Boro'line Maidstone, 1992

751	E151OMD	754	E154OMD	757	E157OMD	760	E160OMD
752	E152OMD	755	E155OMD	758	E158OMD	761	E161OMD
753	E153OMD	756	E156OMD	759	E159OMD	762	F991UME

764	E164OMD Volvo Citybus B10M-61	Alexander RV	H47/37F	1988	Ex Boro'line Maidstone, 1992

765-770   Leyland Olympian ON2R50C13Z4 Northern Counties   H47/30F   1991   Ex Boro'line Maidstone, 1992

765	H765EKJ	767	H767EKJ	769	H769EKJ
766	H766EKJ	768	H768EKJ	770	H770EKJ

801-808   Optare MetroRider MR15   Optare   B29F   1996

801	N801BKN	803	N803BKN	805	N805BKN	807	N807BKN
802	N802BKN	804	N804BKN	806	N806BKN	808	N808BKN

836	F393DOA Talbot Pullman	Talbot	B17FL	1989	Ex Pathfinder, Newark, 1993
841	E31NEF MCW Metrorider MF154/9	Metro-Cammell-Weymann	DP31F	1988	Ex Londonlinks, 1995
842	E32NEF MCW Metrorider MF154/9	Metro-Cammell-Weymann	DP31F	1988	Ex Londonlinks, 1995
843	E33NEF MCW Metrorider MF154/9	Metro-Cammell-Weymann	DP31F	1988	Ex Londonlinks, 1995
844	E34NEF MCW Metrorider MF154/9	Metro-Cammell-Weymann	DP31F	1988	Ex Londonlinks, 1995
852	N852YKE Optare MetroRider MR13	Optare	B25F	1995	Ex Londonlinks, 1996
858	F847EKP MCW Metrorider MF159/2	Metro-Cammell-Weymann	B25F	1988	Ex Boro'line Maidstone, 1992
859	F997EKM MCW Metrorider MF159/2	Metro-Cammell-Weymann	B25F	1988	Ex Boro'line Maidstone, 1992
860	F860LCU MCW Metrorider MF158/15	Metro-Cammell-Weymann	B31F	1988	Ex Londonlinks, 1995
861	F861LCU MCW Metrorider MF158/15	Metro-Cammell-Weymann	B31F	1988	Ex Londonlinks, 1996
864	F864LCU MCW Metrorider MF158/15	Metro-Cammell-Weymann	B31F	1988	Ex Londonlinks, 1995
866	G866TCU Optare MetroRider MR01	Optare	B31F	1989	Ex Londonlinks, 1995
867	E673DCU MCW Metrorider MF150/62	Metro-Cammell-Weymann	B21F	1987	Ex Rochester & Marshall, 1990
869	F932LKE MCW Metrorider MF154/13	Metro-Cammell-Weymann	B33F	1988	Ex Boro'line Maidstone, 1992

871-884   Talbot Pullman   Talbot   B22F*   1989/90   * 871 is B17FL

871	G871SKE	875	G875SKE	878	G878SKE	882	G882SKE	884	G884SKE
873	G873SKE	876	G876SKE	879	G879SKE	883	G883SKE		

886	H886CCU Optare MetroRider	Optare	B25F	1991	
887	H887CCU Optare MetroRider	Optare	B25F	1991	
889	H889CCU Optare MetroRider	Optare	B25F	1991	
890	H890CCU Optare MetroRider	Optare	B25F	1991	
891	K981KGY Mercedes-Benz 709D	Dormobile Routemaker	B29F	1993	Ex Transcity, Sidcup, 1993

892	K982KGY	Mercedes-Benz 709D	Dormobile Routemaker	B29F	1993	Ex Transcity, Sidcup, 1993
893	K983KGY	Mercedes-Benz 709D	Dormobile Routemaker	B29F	1993	Ex Transcity, Sidcup, 1993
894	H149NOJ	Mercedes-Benz 709D	Carlyle	B29F	1991	Ex Transcity, Sidcup, 1993
910	D910VCN	Freight Rover Sherpa	Rootes	B8F	1986	Ex Northumbria, 1993; crewbus

961-975 Optare MetroRider Optare B25F 1991

961	J961JNL	970	J970JNL	974	J974JNL
962	J962JNL	973	J973JNL	975	J975JNL

977	L837MWT	Optare MetroRider MR01	Optare	B31F	1993	Ex Darlington, 1995
978	L838MWT	Optare MetroRider MR01	Optare	B31F	1993	Ex Londonlinks, 1995
980	D340WPE	Ford Transit	Carlyle	B16F	1986	Ex Boro'line Maidstone, 1992
981	D341WPE	Ford Transit	Carlyle	B16F	1986	Ex Boro'line Maidstone, 1992
983	D318WPE	Ford Transit	Carlyle	B16F	1986	Ex Boro'line Maidstone, 1992
984	C524DKO	Ford Transit	Ford	12	1986	Ex Boro'line Maidstone, 1992; crewbus
996	D179CRE	Freight Rover Sherpa	PMT	B16F	1986	Ex Transcity, Sidcup, 1993
997	D417FEH	Freight Rover Sherpa	PMT	B16F	1987	Ex Transcity, Sidcup, 1993

Previous registrations

A11GTA	H832AHS	PDZ6261	UPB310S	SIB6715	TPD176M
F106TML	F107TML	PDZ6262	UPB313S	SIB6716	UPE196M
F107TML	F111TML	SIB1279	BPL484T	TIB5903	E316OPR
F109TML	F106TML	SIB1280	EPD541V	TIB5904	E319OPR
F110TML	F109TML	SIB1281	BPL489T	TIB5905	C261SPC
F111TML	F110TML	SIB1282	YPL439T	TIB5906	C264SPC
F932LKE	F241JWV, 217UKL	SIB1283	BPL479T	TSU644	FKL174Y
HIL2279	E300UUB	SIB1284	YPL445T	XSV689	C256SPC
IIL9168	F714ENE	SIB1285	BPL480T	XSV691	E91OJT
IIL9169	F710ENE	SIB1286	BPL482T	YLK281	A176MKE
JSK994	C153SPB	SIB1287	BPL483T	YYB122	C152SPB
KBC193	B118KPF	SIB1288	EPD522V	YSU895	A114EPA
OSK776	C150SPB	SIB6706	LFR855X		

Named vehicles
21 *Silver Belle*, 27 *Silver Bullet*, 30 *Silver Fox*, 31 *Silver Link*

Special liveries
Overall advertisements: AN211/5/7/74/8, 884
Green Line: 9-11/4, 32/6/8, 40-2

Kentish Express: 21/7, 30/1
White: 35/9

In addition to Green Line work, Kentish Bus have until recently provided vehicles on contract to Gulliver Travel Agency. No.35 is a Volvo B10 of 1991 vintage with Plaxton coachwork, originally a touring coach in the fleet of Park, Hamilton. Dave Stewart

KENT COACH TOURS

A.M., A.O., B.M. and O.L.Farmer, The Coach Station, Malcolm Sargent Road, Ashford, TN23 2NF

From October 1986 Kent Coach Tours secured a Kent County Council contract between Ashford and Faversham, with some journeys extended to Oare and Luddenham. In March 1988 a local Ashford service was added, followed by a service from Folkestone to Dover through the Alkham Valley in April 1990. A further local service in the Ashford area was introduced commercially in November 1990.

In March 1992 the Ashford local service was enhanced, and although the Faversham route was lost under retendering at this point, it was regained in October 1993. A number of other routes have since been introduced in the Ashford area, both commercial and contracted.

The fleet operates in a two-tone blue livery.

KENT COACH TOURS

Reg	Chassis	Body	Seating	Year	History
KDW333P	Leyland National 11351/1R		B49F	1975	Ex Westbus, Ashford, 1993
MOU743R	Bristol VRT/SL3/6LXB	Eastern Coach Works	H43/27D	1976	Ex Hickmott, Kingsnorth, 1995
NFN85R	Leyland National 11351A/1R		DP48F	1977	Ex Warren, Ticehurst, 1993
OJD890R	Leyland National 10351A/2R		B36D	1977	Ex Bailey, Folkestone, 1994
MFA719V	Bristol VRT/SL3/6LXB	Eastern Coach Works	CH39/28F	1980	Ex PMT, 1994
KCT353	Leyland Leopard PSU5C/4R	Plaxton Supreme IV	C57F	1981	Ex Chambers, Stevenage, 1991
KCT986	Bova FHD12-280	Bova Futura	C49FT	1985	Ex D Truelove, Liversedge, 1988
KCT638	Volvo B10M-60	Plaxton Paramount 3500 3	C53F	1989	Ex Wallace Arnold, 1994
F771GNA	Leyland Tiger TRCTL11/3ARZ	Plaxton Paramount 3200 3	C53F	1989	Ex Thamesway, 1996
G791VYJ	Volvo B10M-60	Plaxton Paramount 3500 3	C51FT	1990	Ex Rowland & Goodwin, St Leonards, 1995
K13KCT	Mercedes-Benz 814D	Plaxton Beaver	DP33F	1993	
M13KCT	Mercedes-Benz 609D	Autobus Classique	DP24F	1994	
KCT415	Mercedes-Benz 814D	Plaxton Beaver	C33F	1995	
N614DKR	Mercedes-Benz 811D	Plaxton Beaver	B31F	1996	

Previous registrations

KCT353	UUR349W	KCT986	B556KRY
KCT638	F415DUG	G791VYJ	G135UWV, TDY388

Kent Coach Tours hold two Bristol VRTs which are normally confined to schools services. MFA719V, with standard Eastern Coach Works body, was an unusual sight on local service when found at Faversham on the cross-country route from Ashford in July 1996. Martin Smith

LEISURELINK

Abacus Carriage Services Ltd, North Quay Road, Newhaven, East Sussex, BN9 0AB

Leisurelink operates two commercial services in Brighton and Newhaven and a small fleet of open-top vehicles for private hire and leisure services in Surrey and Sussex. The standard fleet livery is dark green with cream relief and this is reversed for open-top vehicles. There is also an associated operation at Cardiff.

53	JPL153K	Leyland Atlantean PDR1A/1Sp	Park Royal	H43/29D	1972	Ex Herts Railtours, 1996
117	DLJ117L	Daimler Fleetline CRL6	Alexander AL	H43/31F	1973	Ex Vintage Yellow Buses, 1996
125	OEL125M	Daimler Fleetline CRL6	Alexander AL	H43/31F	1974	Ex Vintage Yellow Buses, 1996
146	AJT146T	Leyland Fleetline FE30ALR	Alexander	H43/31F	1978	Ex Vintage Yellow Buses, 1996
422	AOR157B	Leyland Titan PD3/4	Northern Counties	FO39/30F	1964	Ex Southdown, 1992
515	SDA515S	Leyland Fleetline FE30AGR	MCW	H43/33F	1977	Ex West Midlands, 1996
537	SDA537S	Leyland Fleetline FE30AGR	MCW	H43/33F	1977	Ex West Midlands, 1996
710	SDA710S	Leyland Fleetline FE30AGR	MCW	H43/33F	1978	Ex West Midlands, 1996
714	SDA714S	Leyland Fleetline FE30AGR	MCW	H43/33F	1978	Ex West Midlands, 1996
718	SDA718S	Leyland Fleetline FE30AGR	MCW	H43/33F	1978	Ex West Midlands, 1996
800	SDA800S	Leyland Fleetline FE30AGR	MCW	H43/33F	1978	Ex West Midlands, 1996
872	TVP872S	Leyland Fleetline FE30AGR	MCW	H43/33F	1978	Ex West Midlands, 1996
891	TVP891S	Leyland Fleetline FE30AGR	MCW	H43/33F	1978	Ex West Midlands, 1996
925	ADV299A	Leyland Atlantean PDR1/1	Metro-Cammell	CO44/31F	1961	Ex preservation, 1993
928	928GTA	Leyland Atlantean PDR1/1	Metro-Cammell	CO44/31F	1961	Ex preservation, 1995
951	WDA951T	Leyland Fleetline FE30AGR	MCW	H43/33F	1978	Ex West Midlands, 1996

Previous registrations
ADV299A 925GTA
AOR157B 422DCD
928GTA 928GTA, AFE387A

Purchased from Bournemouth in 1996 after 22 years' service, OEL125M is a Daimler Fleetline with Alexander bodywork. In May 1996 it was found in North Street, Brighton. Malc McDonald

LONDON & COUNTRY GROUP

London & Country Ltd, Lesbourne Road, Reigate, Surrey, RH2 7LE
Gem Fairtax (1991) Ltd, Lesbourne Road, Reigate, Surrey, RH2 7LE
Guildford and West Surrey Buses Ltd, Lesbourne Road, Reigate, Surrey, RH7 2LE
Horsham Buses Ltd, Lesbourne Road, Reigate, Surrey, RH2 7LE

London & Country was renamed from London Country Bus South West early in 1993, having been privatised to the Drawlane group in February 1988. Drawlane became British Bus in December 1992. In June 1996 British Bus was itself purchased by the Cowie group. Gem Fairtax, Guildford & West Surrey and Horsham Buses are operating subsidiaries, but there is considerable interchange between these and the parent fleets, and the group is therefore given as one here. The former operations at Croydon, Walworth and Dunton Green, chiefly for London Transport contracts, were transferred to the newly-formed Londonlinks company on 1st January 1995; details of this fleet will be found in the London Bus Handbook.
   The livery is light green with dark green, white and red relief, and the fleet operates from bases at Addlestone, Cranleigh, Crawley, Guildford, Horsham, Hounslow, Leatherhead, Merstham, Slyfield, Warnham and Woking.

There are still several original Leyland Nationals of 1970s vintage in the fleet, although replacement must be due soon. SNB357 carries its years well in this view at Sutton Station. Mike Harris

The conventional form of the Dennis Lance, with East Lancs bodywork, provides the basis for fifteen vehicles delivered in the spring of 1996. LS21 passes through Leatherhead in June 1996. Colin Lloyd

LONDON & COUNTRY GROUP

AD1-10   Dennis Arrow   East Lancs   H45/35F*   1996
* AD9/10 are DPH45/31F

AD1	N801TPK	**AD3**	N803TPK	**AD5**	N805TPK	**AD7**	N807TPK	**AD9**	N809TPK
AD2	N802TPK	**AD4**	N804TPK	**AD6**	N806TPK	**AD8**	N808TPK	**AD10**	N810TPK

AN120 OCO120S Leyland Atlantean AN68A/1R   Roe   H43/30F 1978   Ex AML Coaches, Hounslow, 1994

AN128-182   Leyland Atlantean AN68A/1R   Park Royal   H43/30F 1978/79

AN128 UPK128S		**AN146** UPK146S		**AN149** VPA149S		**AN153** VPA153S	
AN129 UPK129S		**AN147** UPK147S		**AN151** VPA151S		**AN175** XPG175T	
AN135 UPK135S		**AN148** VPA148S		**AN152** VPA152S		**AN182** XPG182T	

AN184-229   Leyland Atlantean AN68A/1R   Roe   H43/30F 1979/80

AN184 XPG184T	**AN197** XPG197T	**AN223** EPH223V	**AN228** EPH228V
AN187 XPG187T	**AN201** XPG201T	**AN226** EPH226V	**AN229** EPH229V

AN258-288   Leyland Atlantean AN68B/1R   Roe   H43/30F 1980/81

AN258 KPJ258W	**AN267** KPJ267W	**AN283** KPJ283W	**AN285** KPJ285W	**AN287** KPJ287W
AN259 KPJ259W	**AN281** KPJ281W	**AN284** KPJ284W	**AN286** KPJ286W	**AN288** KPJ288W

BS406t	YPH406T	Bedford YMT	Plaxton Supreme IV	C53F	1978	Ex Blue Saloon, Guildford, 1996
BS407t	YPH407T	Bedford YMT	Plaxton Supreme IV	C53F	1978	Ex Blue Saloon, Guildford, 1996
BS820t	YPB820T	Bedford YMT	Plaxton Supreme IV	C53F	1978	Ex Blue Saloon, Guildford, 1996
BTL42	C142SPB	Leyland Tiger TRCTL11/3RH	Berkhof Everest 370	C53F	1986	
BTL43	C143SPB	Leyland Tiger TRCTL11/3RH	Berkhof Everest 370	C53F	1986	
BTL44	C144SPB	Leyland Tiger TRCTL11/3RH	Berkhof Everest 370	C53F	1986	
BTL45	C145SPB	Leyland Tiger TRCTL11/3RH	Berkhof Everest 370	C53F	1986	
DC693	OYD693	Hestair Duple 425	Duple 425	C57F	1989	Ex Blue Saloon, Guildford, 1996
DD1	F201OPD	Dennis Dominator DDA1020	East Lancs	H51/33F 1988	

DD2-8   Dennis Dominator DDA1026   East Lancs   H45/31F 1989

DD2	F602RPG	**DD4**	F604RPG	**DD6**	F606RPG	**DD8**	F608RPG
DD3	F603RPG	**DD5**	F605RPG	**DD7**	F607RPG		

DD9	F609RPG	Dennis Dominator DDA1017	East Lancs	H49/35F 1989	
DD10	K36XNE	Dennis Dominator DDA2005	East Lancs	H45/31F 1993	Ex Mayne, Clayton, 1995
DD11	K37XNE	Dennis Dominator DDA2005	East Lancs	H45/31F 1993	Ex Mayne, Clayton, 1995
DD12	K38YVM	Dennis Dominator DDA2005	East Lancs	H45/31F 1993	Ex Mayne, Clayton, 1995
DD13	N713TPK	Dennis Dominator DDA2006	East Lancs	H45/31F 1996	
DD14	N714TPK	Dennis Dominator DDA2006	East Lancs	H45/31F 1996	
DD15	N715TPK	Dennis Dominator DDA2006	East Lancs	H45/31F 1996	
DD16	N716TPK	Dennis Dominator DDA2006	East Lancs	H45/31F 1996	
DJ169	J169TVU	Dennis Javelin 12SDA1919	Duple 320	C57F	1991	Ex Bullock, Cheadle, 1995
DJ422	G422SNF	Dennis Javelin 12SDA1919	Duple 320	C57F	1990	Acquired by 1996

DMB4-7   Dodge S56   Northern Counties   B25F   1988

DMB4 E104JPL		**DMB5** E105JPL		**DMB6** E106JPL		**DMB7** E107JPL

DS1-9   Dennis Dart 9.8SDL3035   East Lancs EL2000   B40F   1993/94

DS1	L503CPB	**DS3**	L505CPJ	**DS5**	L507CPJ	**DS7**	L509CPJ	**DS9**	L511CPJ
DS2	L504CPB	**DS4**	L506CPJ	**DS6**	L508CPJ	**DS8**	L510CPJ		

DS10	M521HPF	Dennis Dart 9SDL3053	East Lancs EL2000	B30FL	1995
DS11	M522HPF	Dennis Dart 9SDL3053	East Lancs EL2000	B30FL	1995
DS12	M523HPF	Dennis Dart 9SDL3053	East Lancs EL2000	B30FL	1995
DS13	M524HPF	Dennis Dart 9SDL3053	East Lancs EL2000	B30FL	1995
DS14	M525MPM	Dennis Dart 9.8SDL3054	East Lancs EL2000	B40F	1995
DS15	M526MPM	Dennis Dart 9.8SDL3054	East Lancs EL2000	B40F	1995
DS16	N528SPA	Dennis Dart 9SDL3053	East Lancs EL2000	B30FL	1995
DS17	N529SPA	Dennis Dart 9SDL3053	East Lancs EL2000	B30FL	1995
DS18	N530SPA	Dennis Dart 9SDL3053	East Lancs EL2000	B30FL	1995

One of the older Leyland Atlanteans still in service, AN182 has Park Royal bodywork and formed part of the substantial London Country order delivered in the late 1970s. Gerald Mead

In the early 1980s, the London Country group received large numbers of Leyland Olympians with Roe bodywork to assist with fleet updating. LR8 formed part of the first such contingent in 1982. Gerald Mead

London & Country has become one of the first major customers for the Dennis Arrow. AD8, with East Lancs bodywork, stands at North Street, Brighton on the coastal route from Kingston in May 1996, during its first few days in service. M.E.Lyons

During the summer of 1966, London & Country received nineteen low-floor Dennis Darts with East Lancs bodywork to Spryte design. DSL45, with Guildford & West Surrey fleetname, was photographed near Knaphill in August 1996.
Geoff Rixon

Five low-floor Dennis Lances with Wright bodywork were delivered for route 408 in 1995. The first of the batch, technically numbered LSL5 but carrying fleet number 517, was tracked down at West Croydon bus station in March 1995 shortly after entering service.
Mike Harris

The current order for Dennis Darts with East Lancs bodywork includes six 9metre vehicles delivered over the turn of 1995/6. DS24 is seen at Hampton Court in May 1996 on the rump of what was once a cross-London Green Line service.
Geoff Rixon

49

DS19-24 Dennis Dart 9.8SDL3054 East Lancs EL2000 B40F 1995/96

DS19 N539TPF	**DS21** N541TPF	**DS23** N543TPK		
DS20 N540TPF	**DS22** N542TPK	**DS24** N544TPK		

DSL25-36 Dennis Dart SLF (10m) Plaxton Pointer B35F 1996

DSL25 N225TPK	**DSL28** N228TPK	**DSL31** N231TPK	**DSL34** N234TPK
DSL26 N226TPK	**DSL29** N229TPK	**DSL32** N232TPK	**DSL35** N235TPK
DSL27 N227TPK	**DSL30** N230TPK	**DSL33** N233TPK	**DSL36** N236TPK

DSL37-55 Dennis Dart SLF (9.2m) East Lancs Spryte B31F 1996

DSL37 N237VPH	**DSL41** N241VPH	**DSL45** N245VPH	**DSL49** N249VPH	**DSL53** P253APM
DSL38 N238VPH	**DSL42** N242VPH	**DSL46** N246VPH	**DSL50** P250APM	**DSL54** P254APM
DSL39 N239VPH	**DSL43** N243VPH	**DSL47** N247VPH	**DSL51** P251APM	**DSL55** P255APM
DSL40 N240VPH	**DSL44** N244VPH	**DSL48** N248VPH	**DSL52** P252APM	

GF58	UFG58S	Leyland National 11351A/2R		B49F	1977	Ex Panther, Crawley, 1991
GF60	UFG60S	Leyland National 11351A/2R		B49F	1977	Ex Panther, Crawley, 1991
GF180	THX180S	Leyland National 10351A/2R		B41F	1978	Ex Panther, Crawley, 1991
GF313	AYR313T	Leyland National 10351A/2R		B41F	1979	Ex Panther, Crawley, 1991
GS13	MXX313	Guy Special NLLVP	Eastern Coach Works	B26F	1953	Ex Sussex Bus, Ford, 1992
LA48	TSJ48S	Leyland Leopard PSU3E/4R	Alexander AY	B53F	1978	Ex Clydeside, 1995
LA49	TSJ49S	Leyland Leopard PSU3E/4R	Alexander AY	B53F	1978	Ex Clydeside, 1995
LNB19	JOX519P	Leyland National 11351A/1R		B49F	1976	Ex Shamrock & Rambler, 1988
LNB21	JOX521P	Leyland National 11351A/1R		B49F	1976	Ex Shamrock & Rambler, 1988
LNB28	JOX528P	Leyland National 11351A/1R		B25FL	1976	Ex Shamrock & Rambler, 1989
LNB36	NOE536R	Leyland National 11351A/1R		B49F	1976	Ex Midland Red (North), 1990
LNB40	CFM340S	Leyland National 11351A/1R		B52F	1978	Ex C-Line, 1992
LNB63	NOE563R	Leyland National 11351A/1R		B49F	1976	Ex Shamrock & Rambler, 1988
LNB546	PKP546R	Leyland National 11351A/1R		B49F	1976	Ex Maidstone & District, 1995
LNB553	MEL553P	Leyland National 11351/1R		B49F	1976	Ex Hampshire Bus, 1993
LNB600	NOE600R	Leyland National 11351A/1R (Urban bus)		B49F	1977	Ex Midland Red (North), 1994
LNC362	KDW362P	Leyland National 11351/1R/SC		DP48F	1975	Ex Rhondda, 1992
LNC911	SKG911S	Leyland National 11351A/1R		DP48F	1978	Ex Rhondda, 1992

LR8-50 Leyland Olympian ONTL11/1R Roe H43/29F 1982/84

LR8 TPD108X	**LR14** TPD114X	**LR27** TPD127X	**LR29** TPD129X	**LR48** A148FPG
LR13 TPD113X	**LR18** TPD118X	**LR28** TPD128X	**LR46** A146FPG	**LR50** A150FPG

LR74	B274LPH	Leyland Olympian ONTL11/1R	Eastern Coach Works	H43/29F 1985	
LR75	B275LPH	Leyland Olympian ONTL11/1R	Eastern Coach Works	H43/29F 1985	
LR501	G501SFT	Leyland Olympian ONCL10/1RZ	Northern Counties	H47/30F 1989	Ex Kentish Bus, 1992
LR502	G502SFT	Leyland Olympian ONCL10/1RZ	Northern Counties	H47/30F 1989	Ex Kentish Bus, 1992
LR503	G503SFT	Leyland Olympian ONCL10/1RZ	Northern Counties	H47/30F 1989	Ex Kentish Bus, 1992
LR504	G504SFT	Leyland Olympian ONCL10/1RZ	Northern Counties	H47/30F 1989	Ex Kentish Bus, 1992

LS10-24 Dennis Lance 11SDA3113 East Lancs EL2000 B49F 1996

LS10 N210TPK	**LS13** N213TPK	**LS16** N216TPK	**LS19** N219TPK	**LS22** N322TPK
LS11 N211TPK	**LS14** N214TPK	**LS17** N217TPK	**LS20** N220TPK	**LS23** N223TPK
LS12 N212TPK	**LS15** N215TPK	**LS18** N218TPK	**LS21** N221TPK	**LS24** N224TPK

LSL5-9 Dennis Lance SLF 11SDA3201 Wright Pathfinder B40F 1995

LSL5 M517KPA	**LSL6** M518KPA	**LSL7** M519KPA	**LSL8** M520KPA	**LSL9** N527SPA

MBM5	C305SPL	Mercedes-Benz L608D	Reeve Burgess	B20F	1986	
MBM468	N468SPA	Mercedes-Benz 709D	Alexander(Belfast) AM	B22FL	1995	
MBM469	N469SPA	Mercedes-Benz 709D	Alexander(Belfast) AM	B22FL	1995	
MBM470	N470SPA	Mercedes-Benz 709D	Alexander(Belfast) AM	B22FL	1995	
MC123	H123WFM	Mercedes-Benz 814D	North Western Coach Sales	C24F	1991	Ex Clay Lake, 1995 On ext loan to Colchester
MM471	N671TPF	Mercedes-Benz 709D	Plaxton Beaver	B23F	1995	
MR472	P472APJ	Optare MetroRider	Optare	B29F	1996	
RF315	MLL952	AEC Regal IV 9821LT	Metro-Cammell	B39F	1952	Ex Time Transport, Thornton Heath, 1995
RMA16	KGJ614D	AEC Routemaster 9RM	Park Royal	H31/24F	1966	Acquired 1996
RMC4	SLT59	AEC Routemaster 4RM	Eastern Coach Works	H32/25RD	1972	Ex London Buses, 1970; Leyland units
RP21	JPA121K	AEC Reliance 6U2R	Park Royal	DP45F	1972	Ex AML, Hounslow, 1994
RT3775	NLE882	AEC Regent III 0961	Park Royal	H30/26R	1953	Ex preservation, 1994

SNB340-366 Leyland National 10351A/1R B41F 1976-78

SNB340 UPB340S	**SNB349** UPB349S	**SNB357** XPC17S	
SNB348 UPB348S	**SNB354** XPC14S	**SNB366** YPF766T	

SNB/SNC376-540 Leyland National 10351B/1R   B41F   1978/79
SNB394 ex Northumbria, 1994; SNC420 is an Urban Bus conversion

SNB376 YPL376T	**SNB394** YPL394T	**SNB435** YPL435T	**SNB502** DPH502T	**SNB531** EPD531V
SNB377 YPL377T	**SNB395** YPL395T	**SNB440** YPL440T	**SNB507** EPD507V	**SNB535** EPD535V
SNB378 YPL378T	**SNB403** YPL403T	**SNB448** YPL448T	**SNB508** EPD508V	**SNB536** EPD536V
SNB380 YPL380T	**SNB419** YPL419T	**SNB450** YPL450T	**SNB509** EPD509V	**SNB537** EPD537V
SNB382 YPL382T	**SNC420** YPL420T	**SNB459** BPL459T	**SNB510** EPD510V	**SNB538** EPD538V
SNB385 YPL385T	**SNB423** YPL423T	**SNB475** BPL475T	**SNB511** EPD511V	**SNB540** EPD540V.
SNB390 YPL390T	**SNB425** YPL425T	**SNB478** BPL478T	**SNB518** EPD518V	**SNB543** EPD543V
SNB391 YPL391T	**SNB427** YPL427T	**SNB491** BPL491T	**SNB519** EPD519V	
SNB392 YPL392T	**SNB431** YPL431T	**SNB494** BPL494T	**SNB529** EPD529V	
SNB393 YPL393T	**SNB433** YPL433T	**SNB498** BPL498T	**SNB530** EPD530V	

SR88	E88OJT	Leyland Tiger TRCTL11/3ARZA	Plaxton Paramount 3200 2	C53F	1988	Ex Shamrock & Rambler, 1989
SR89	E89OJT	Leyland Tiger TRCTL11/3ARZA	Plaxton Paramount 3200 2	C53F	1988	Ex Shamrock & Rambler, 1989
SR90	E90OJT	Leyland Tiger TRCTL11/3ARZA	Plaxton Paramount 3200 2	C53F	1988	Ex Shamrock & Rambler, 1989
TC426	HBH426Y	Leyland Tiger TRCTL11/3R	Plaxton Paramount 3200	C53F	1983	Ex Blue Saloon, Guildford, 1996
TC776	776WME	Leyland Royal Tiger B54	Roe Doyen	C46FT	1984	Ex Blue Saloon, Guildford, 1996
TDL46	C246SPC	Leyland Tiger TRCTL11/3RH	Duple 320	C53F	1986	
TP74	B274KPF	Leyland Tiger TRCTL11/2RH	Plaxton Paramount 3200 2 Exp	C49F	1985	
TP91	AEF990Y	Leyland Tiger TRCTL11/2R	Plaxton Paramount 3200 Exp	C53F	1983	
TPL44	A144EPA	Leyland Tiger TRCTL11/3R	Plaxton Paramount 3200 Exp	C51F	1984	Ex Southend, 1995
TPL54	A154EPA	Leyland Tiger TRCTL11/3R	Plaxton Paramount 3200 Exp	C57F	1984	
TPL58	A158EPA	Leyland Tiger TRCTL11/3R	Plaxton Paramount 3200 Exp	C57F	1984	
TPL85	B285KPF	Leyland Tiger TRCTL11/3RH	Plaxton Paramount 3200 2 Exp	C53F	1985	
TPL88	B288KPF	Leyland Tiger TRCTL11/3RH	Plaxton Paramount 3200 2 Exp	C53F	1985	
TPL89	B289KPF	Leyland Tiger TRCTL11/3RH	Plaxton Paramount 3200 2 Exp	C53F	1985	
TPL90	B290KPF	Leyland Tiger TRCTL11/3RH	Plaxton Paramount 3200 2 Exp	C53F	1985	
VCB89	C89NNV	Volvo B10M-61	Caetano Stagecoach	B57F	1986	Ex Tellings-Golden Miller, Byfleet, 1995

101	F101SPM	Renault S56	Northern Counties	B25F	1989	
113	G113TND	Mercedes-Benz 811D	Carlyle	B33FL	1990	Ex Bee Line Buzz, 1992
120	G120TJA	Mercedes-Benz 811D	Carlyle	B31F	1990	Ex C-Line, 1991
132	K132XRE	Mercedes-Benz 709D	Dormobile Routemaker	B29F	1992	Ex Stevensons, Uttoxeter, 1994
133	J480XHL	Mercedes-Benz 709D	Alexander AM	DP25F	1991	Ex Stevensons, Uttoxeter, 1994
154	K154BRF	Mercedes-Benz 709D	Dormobile Routemaker	B29F	1993	Ex Stevensons, Uttoxeter, 1994
155	K155CRE	Mercedes-Benz 709D	Dormobile Routemaker	B27F	1993	Ex Stevensons, Uttoxeter, 1994
156	K156BRF	Mercedes-Benz 709D	Dormobile Routemaker	B27F	1993	Ex Stevensons, Uttoxeter, 1994
157	K157BRF	Mercedes-Benz 709D	Dormobile Routemaker	B27F	1993	Ex Stevensons, Uttoxeter, 1994
161	APM113T	AEC Reliance 6U2R	Plaxton Supreme IV Express	C53F	1979	Ex Eagle, Bristol, 1994
168	E168OMD	Volvo B10M-61	Plaxton Paramount 3200 3	C57F	1988	Ex Moon, Warnham, 1994
189	G689OHE	Mercedes-Benz 811D	Reeve Burgess Beaver	B31FL	1990	Ex Danks & Gaymer, Coseley, 1992
190	G690OHE	Mercedes-Benz 811D	Reeve Burgess Beaver	B31FL	1990	Ex Danks & Gaymer, Coseley, 1992
200	HPK502N	Leyland National 11351/1R		B49F	1975	Ex Alder Valley South, 1990
201	G101TND	Mercedes-Benz 811D	Carlyle	B31F	1989	Ex Bee Line Buzz, 1992
202	HPK504N	Leyland National 11351/1R (Urban bus)		B49F	1975	Ex Alder Valley South, 1990
205	KPA356P	Leyland National 11351/1R		B49F	1975	Ex Alder Valley South, 1990
208	D208SKD	Mercedes-Benz L608D	Reeve Burgess Beaver	B20F	1986	Ex North Western, 1992
210	D210SKD	Mercedes-Benz L608D	Reeve Burgess Beaver	B20F	1986	Ex North Western, 1991
212	KPA363P	Leyland National 11351/1R		B49F	1975	Ex Alder Valley South, 1990
213	KPA364P	Leyland National 11351/1R		B49F	1975	Ex Alder Valley South, 1990
221	KPA372P	Leyland National 11351/1R		B49F	1975	Ex Alder Valley South, 1990
222	KPA373P	Leyland National 11351/1R		B49F	1975	Ex Alder Valley South, 1990
235	KPA386P	Leyland National 11351A/1R		B49F	1976	Ex Alder Valley South, 1990
236	M236KNR	Mercedes-Benz 709D	Alexander AM	B29F	1995	
242	LPF600P	Leyland National 11351/1R/SC		DP21FL	1976	Ex Alder Valley South, 1990
246	KPA367P	Leyland National 11351/1R		DP21FL	1975	Ex Alder Valley South, 1990
251	NPJ472R	Leyland National 11351A/1R		B49F	1976	Ex Alder Valley South, 1990
252	JCK852W	Leyland National 2 NL106AL11/1R	East Lancs (1991)	B40F	1981	Ex North Western, 1991
257	NPJ478R	Leyland National 11351A/1R		B49F	1976	Ex Alder Valley South, 1990
258	NPJ479R	Leyland National 11351A/1R		B49F	1976	Ex Alder Valley South, 1990
265	PPM 892R	Leyland National 11351A/1R (Urban bus)		B49F	1977	Ex Alder Valley South, 1990
270	GFR799W	Leyland National 2 NL116690/1R		B49F	1978	Ex North Western, 1992
274	TPE151S	Leyland National 11351A/1R		B49F	1977	Ex Alder Valley South, 1990
275	TPE168S	Leyland National 11351A/1R		DP45F	1978	Ex Alder Valley South, 1990
277	BVP813V	Leyland National 2 NL116L11/1R		B49F	1980	Ex North Western, 1992
286	LFR876X	Leyland National 2 NL106AL11/1R		B44F	1981	Ex North Western, 1991
302	G302DPA	Dennis Falcon SDA421	East Lancs	B48F	1990	Ex Londonlinks, 1996
303	G303DPA	Dennis Falcon SDA421	East Lancs	B48F	1990	
304	G304DPA	Dennis Falcon SDA421	East Lancs	B48F	1990	
305	G305DPA	Dennis Falcon SDA421	East Lancs	B48F	1990	

Acquired from Tellings-Golden Miller in 1995, VCB89 is a Volvo B10 with Caetano bus bodywork new in 1986. This most unusual vehicle was photographed in Cranleigh in March 1996. Richard Godfrey

Substantial numbers of Leyland Nationals, native and acquired, have been sent for rebuilding in the past few years. LNB600, originally a Midland Red machine, is more unusual in being an Urban Bus conversion for the Guildford & West Surrey fleet, and was caught at Bramley in March 1996. Richard Godfrey

Operating from Leatherhead and maintaining use of the traditional garage code, Dennis Dominator DD5 is seen at Surbiton on a long-established route partly funded by London Transport. Geoff Rixon

Within the group, a small batch of vehicles operates in Gem Fairtax livery, following the takeover of this fleet in 1991. GF313 is an ex-London Buses Leyland National and was photographed in Crawley in April 1996. Colin Brown

Amongst the older minibuses in the fleet, No.414 is a Dodge S56 of 1987 with Northern Counties body, acquired from Hants & Surrey in 1993. This view in Horsham shows the localised fleetname, beneath which is carried the legend "A London & Country franchise". Alan Simpkins

An unusual vehicle in this fleet is MC123, a Mercedes-Benz 814D with coach-seated body by North Western Coach Sales. It was photographed in Victoria in April 1996, whilst on extended loan to Colchester. Colin Lloyd

353	JIL2193	Leyland National 11351/1R	East Lancs (1994)	B49F	1974	Ex South Coast Buses, 1994
356	JIL2196	Leyland National 11351/1R	East Lancs (1994)	B49F	1975	Ex Westbus, Ashford, 1994
357	JIL2197	Leyland National 1151/1R/0102	East Lancs (1994)	B49F	1973	Ex Midland Fox, 1994
358	JIL2198	Leyland National 11351A/1R	East Lancs (1994)	B49F	1976	Ex Midland Fox, 1994
359	JIL2199	Leyland National 11351A/1R	East Lancs (1994)	B49F	1976	Ex Midland Fox, 1994
360	JIL2190	Leyland National 11351/1R	East Lancs (1994)	B49F	1976	Ex Midland Red (North), 1994
363	PDZ6263	Leyland National 11351A/1R	East Lancs (1994)	B49F	1977	Ex Tellings-Golden Miller, Byfleet, 1992
364	PDZ6264	Leyland National 11351A/1R	East Lancs (1994)	B49F	1979	Ex Tellings-Golden Miller, Byfleet, 1992
365	PDZ6265	Leyland National 11351/1R	East Lancs (1994)	B49F	1975	Ex Alder Valley South, 1990
366	SJI5066	Leyland National 11351A/1R	East Lancs (1994)	B49F	1977	Ex Tellings-Golden Miller, Byfleet, 1992
367	JIL5367	Leyland National 11351A/1R	East Lancs (1994)	B49F	1977	Ex Tellings-Golden Miller, Byfleet, 1992
368	IIL2168	Leyland National 11351A/1R	East Lancs (1994)	B49F	1977	Ex Tellings-Golden Miller, Byfleet, 1992
369	SJI5569	Leyland National 11351A/1R	East Lancs (1994)	B49F	1977	Ex The Bee Line, 1994
370	SJI5570	Leyland National 11351A/1R	East Lancs (1994)	B49F	1976	Ex Midland Fox, 1994
371	SJI5571	Leyland National 11351A/1R	East Lancs (1994)	B49F	1976	Ex Midland Fox, 1994
372	SJI5572	Leyland National 11351/1R/SC	East Lancs (1994)	B49F	1976	Ex The Bee Line, 1994
373	PDZ6273	Leyland National 11351A/1R	East Lancs (1994)	DP49F	1976	Ex Midland Fox, 1994
374	PDZ6274	Leyland National 11351A/1R	East Lancs (1994)	DP49F	1976	Ex Midland Fox, 1994
375	PDZ6275	Leyland National 11351A/2R	East Lancs (1994)	DP49F	1977	Ex Panther, Crawley, 1991
376	PDZ6276	Leyland National 11351A/1R	East Lancs (1994)	DP49F	1975	Ex Northumbria, 1994
377	PDZ6277	Leyland National 11351A/1R	East Lancs (1994)	DP49F	1978	Ex Alder Valley South, 1990
378	RDZ4278	Leyland National 11351/1R	East Lancs (1995)	B49F	1975	Ex Shamrock & Rambler, 1988
379	RDZ4279	Leyland National 11351/1R	East Lancs (1995)	B49F	1975	Ex Alder Valley South, 1990
380	LIL2180	Leyland National 11351/1R	East Lancs (1995)	B49F	1975	Ex Alder Valley South, 1990
402	K402VPK	Mercedes-Benz 709D	Dormobile	B25FL	1992	
403	K403VPK	Mercedes-Benz 709D	Dormobile	B25FL	1992	
404	K404VPK	Mercedes-Benz 709D	Dormobile	B25FL	1992	
405	K405VPK	Mercedes-Benz 709D	Dormobile	B25FL	1992	
411	E411DPE	Dodge S56	Northern Counties	B27F	1987	Ex Hants & Surrey, 1993
414	E414DPE	Dodge S56	Northern Counties	B27F	1987	Ex Hants & Surrey, 1993
418	E418EPE	Renault S56	Northern Counties	B27F	1988	Ex Hants & Surrey, 1993
420	E420EPE	Renault S56	Northern Counties	B27F	1988	Ex Hants & Surrey, 1993

421-427   Mercedes-Benz 709D   Dormobile   B25F*   1993   *425/6 are B27F

421	L421CPB	423	L423CPB	425	L425CPB	427	L427CPB
422	L422CPB	424	L424CPB	426	L426CPB		

428	L428CPC	Mercedes-Benz 709D	Danescroft	B27F	1993
429	L429CPC	Mercedes-Benz 709D	Danescroft	B27F	1993
438	L438FPA	Mercedes-Benz 709D	Plaxton Beaver	B23F	1994
439	L439FPA	Mercedes-Benz 709D	Plaxton Beaver	B23F	1994

454-460   Mercedes-Benz 709D ·   Alexander AM   B23F   1994

454	M454HPG	456	M456HPG	458	M458JPA	460	M460JPA
455	M455HPG	457	M457HPG	459	M459JPA		

461	M461JPA	Mercedes-Benz 709D	Plaxton Beaver	B31F	1995
462	M462JPA	Mercedes-Benz 709D	Plaxton Beaver	B31F	1995
463	M463JPA	Mercedes-Benz 709D	Plaxton Beaver	B23F	1995
464	M464JPA	Mercedes-Benz 709D	Plaxton Beaver	B23F	1995
465	M465LPG	Mercedes-Benz 709D	Alexander (Belfast)	B29F	1995
466	M466MPM	Mercedes-Benz 709D	Plaxton Beaver	B21F	1995
467	M467MPM	Mercedes-Benz 709D	Plaxton Beaver	B21F	1995

512-516   Volvo B6-50   Plaxton Pointer   B41F   1994

512	L512CPJ	513	L513CPJ	514	L514CPJ	515	L515CPJ	516	L516CPJ

543	MOR581	AEC Reliance MU3RV	Metro-Cammell-Weymann(1966)	B40F	1954	Ex preservation, 1994

610-622   Volvo B10M-50   East Lancs   H49/39F 1989

610	G610BPH	613	G613BPH	616	G616BPH	619	G619BPH	622	G622BPH
611	G611BPH	614	G614BPH	617	G617BPH	620	G620BPH		
612	G612BPH	615	G615BPH	618	G618BPH	621	G621BPH		

701	M701HPF	Volvo Olympian YN2RC16Z4	East Lancs	H44/30F	1994
702	M702HPF	Volvo Olympian YN2RC16Z4	East Lancs	H44/30F	1994
703	M703HPF	Volvo Olympian YN2RC16Z4	East Lancs	H44/30F	1994
704	M704HPF	Volvo Olympian YN2RC16Z4	East Lancs	H44/30F	1994

901-910 Leyland Olympian ONLXB/1RZ Alexander RL   H47/32F 1988 Ex Alder Valley South, 1990

| 901 | F571SMG | 903 | F573SMG | 907 | F577SMG | 908 | F578SMG | 910 | F580SMG |

3641	PUK641R Leyland National 11351A/1R	B49F	1977	Ex Tellings-Golden Miller, Byfleet, 1992
3663	SOA663S Leyland National 11351A/1R	B49F	1978	Ex Tellings-Golden Miller, Byfleet, 1992
3713	TOF713S Leyland National 11351A/1R	B49F	1978	Ex Tellings-Golden Miller, Byfleet, 1992
3715	TOF715S Leyland National 11351A/1R	B49F	1978	Ex Tellings-Golden Miller, Byfleet, 1992
3799	LUP899T Leyland National 11351A/1R	B49F	1979	Ex Tellings-Golden Miller, Byfleet, 1992
3831	EON831V Leyland National 2 NL116L11/1R	B49F	1980	Ex Midland Fox, 1994
4712	JTU593T Leyland National 10351B/1R	B41F	1979	Ex Southend, 1993
4721	GGE165T Leyland National 10351A/1R	B41F	1979	Ex Southend, 1993
5107	H107JAR Volvo B10M-60 Ikarus	C49FT	1990	Ex Colchester, 1993

Vehicles on order
26 Dennis Dart SLF (10.6m) - B—F.

Previous registrations

IIL2168	SGR134R	OYD693	G602LKU	RDZ4278	JOX481P
JIL2190	JOX499P	PDZ6263	NOE562R	RDZ4279	KPA380P
JIL2193	RKE520M	PDZ6264	ERP551T	SJI5066	NEN961R
JIL2194	CBV779S	PDZ6265	GPJ891N	SJI5569	NPJ471R
JIL2197	BCD808L	PDZ6273	JOX490P	SJI5570	JOX491P
JIL2198	SCK703P	PDZ6274	UHG744R	SJI5571	SCK709P
JIL2199	UHG736R	PDZ6275	UFG54S	SJI5572	LPF601P
JIL5367	NOE598R	PDZ6276	GOL403N		
LIL2180	KPA375P	PDZ6277	TPE161S		

Special liveries
Overall advertisements: AN184, AN201/29/87, DD2, LNB19/31, LR14, IR504, SNB310/3, SNB419/27,
SNB509/10/8/29/35/40, 200/5/51/9/86
Gem Fairtax: GF58, GF180, GF313, 3713
Guildford Link: 236, 402-5/21
Route 441: 525/6
Countryliner: BS820, BTL42/3/5, DJ169, DJ422, TC426, TC776, TDL46, SR89/90, 168
Green Line: BTL44, TP91, TPL54
Kent Karrier: 468/70/1
Blue Saloon: BS406/7, DC693
Traditional liveries: GS13, RF315, RMA16, RMC4, RP21, RT3775, 543
Green Line 373-7

Amongst the last major second-generation orders for the revitalised Green Line network before the fragmen-tation of the London Country group in the 1980s were ninety-five Leyland Tigers delivered with Plaxton coachwork. These are typified by TPL88, now carrying local bus livery although used on the remnant of a former Green Line route when found in Kingston in June 1996.
Colin Lloyd

Dating from 1953, RT3775 is one of a number of vintage vehicles used by London & Country on heritage services. It carries Park Royal bodywork on its AEC Regent III chassis, and was photographed at Kingscote Station, Bluebell Railway on special route 473. Richard Godfrey

London & Country RF315 is chiefly used on summer Sunday services in Surrey. Apart from the fleetnames, only the trafficators and the lower-case lettering on the blind provide immediate betrayal that this vehicle is in its 44th year, as seen at Westerham in May 1996. Richard Godfrey

The former Aldershot & District name is perpetuated in No.543, purchased from private preservation in 1994 and returned to service on heritage services. An early AEC Reliance chassis of 1954 is surmounted by 1966 Metro-Cammell bodywork in this view at Walton-on-Thames on the Cobham Bus Museum special services in April 1995. Keith Grimes

LUCKETTS

Lucketts Garage (Watford) Ltd, Unit 2, Olds Approach, Tolpits Lane, Watford, WD1 8TD

Lucketts purchased a Volkswagen minibus in October 1988 for services in the Watford area. A major step forward was the acquisition of two contract routes for Hertfordshire County Council in October 1989. The network has expanded since, both with commercial and contract services, using the "Luckybus" fleetname. Vehicles operate in a livery of grey with dark blue and red relief. A notable feature is the recent use of L-BUS private registrations, even for newer vehicles.

LUCKETTS

XBR657R	Ford R1114	Plaxton Supreme	C53F	1977	Ex Ward, Watford, 1990
VGV443S	Bedford VAS5	Plaxton Supreme III	C29F	1977	Ex Ward, Watford, 1990
HIL2358	Bedford YNT	Plaxton Paramount 3200	C49DTL	1982	Ex Classical Hire, Beeston, 1990
C525EWR	Volkswagen LT55	Optare City Pacer	B25F	1986	Ex Ward, Watford, 1990
D989JYG	Volkswagen LT55	Optare City Pacer	DP20FL	1986	Ex Ward, Watford, 1990
D203RGH	Volkswagen LT55	Optare City Pacer	B25F	1987	Ex Ward, Watford, 1990
DIL7916	Bedford YNV	Duple	C57F	1987	Ex Swanbrook, Cheltenham, 1993
L100BUS	Dennis Dart 9.8SDL3035	Plaxton Pointer	B39F	1994	
L200BUS	Dennis Dart 9.8SDL3035	Plaxton Pointer	B39F	1994	
L300BUS	Dennis Dart 9SDL3031	Marshall C36	B34F	1994	
L400BUS	Dennis Dart 9SDL3031	Marshall C36	B34F	1994	
L600BUS	Optare MetroRider MR11	Optare	B31F	1995	
L500BUS	Iveco Daily 480.10.21	Wadham Stringer	B47F	1995	Ex demonstrator, 1995
L700BUS	Optare MetroRider	Optare	B32F	1996	
L800BUS	Optare MetroRider	Optare	B31F	1996	

Previous registrations

DIL7916 D121EFH	HIL2358 AEG121Y	L500BUS M289OUR

Lucketts re-registered this former Iveco Daily demonstrator, bodied by Wadham Stringer, with an older mark when they acquired it in 1995. Here it represents Lucketts' contract on a Watford town service from Hertfordshire County Council.
Capital Transport

By contrast, L300BUS is pictured on a commercial operation in Watford. This vehicle is a ubiquitous Dennis Dart, of the 9.8-metre variety, with Plaxton bodywork.
Capital Transport

MAIDSTONE & DISTRICT

The Maidstone & District Motor Services Ltd, Armstrong Road, Maidstone, Kent, ME15 6TY

Maidstone & District was formed in 1911 and at one time held sway throughout the western half of Kent and into East Sussex. Today its operations are rather more compact, taking in the Medway Towns, Maidstone, Tonbridge, Tunbridge Wells and the Swale area, together with a presence in the Weald of Kent. There is a London commuter service from the Medway Towns and Maidstone, now marketed under the 'Green Line' banner, and from May 1996 operation has been shared with Speedlink of a direct service between the Medway Towns and Gatwick Airport.

Maidstone & District was one of the first National Bus Company subsidiaries to be privatised when it was sold to a management team on 6th November 1986. In June 1988 the competing New Enterprise Coaches of Tonbridge was bought out, providing a base for school, excursion and private hire work. The residual vehicles of Boro'line Maidstone were purchased on 12th June 1992 (though all were quickly sold), together with their Maidstone depot, and from 29th May 1994 M&D took over the bus operations of Bygone Buses in the Maidstone area after three-and-a-half years of at times difficult competition. On 14th April 1995 control of M&D and New Enterprise passed to British Bus, who from October 1995 brought the management of both companies together at Maidstone with that of Kentish Bus and Londonlinks, though each company continues to operate independently. In June 1996 British Bus was itself purchased by the Cowie group.

Fleet livery is grass green with cream relief, except for the Green Line fleet. The fleet operates from garages at Gillingham, Hawkhurst, Maidstone and Tunbridge Wells, together with open outstations at Sheerness, Sittingbourne and Tenterden. The New Enterprise fleet has its own site in Tonbridge, and a livery of off-white, red and blue for coaching operations, or cream, blue and black for contract and stage carriage work. On 27th September 1996. M&D absorbed the buses and operations of Mercury, Hoo. This will continue as a separate unit within the fleet, using the existing maroon livery.

Still the backbone of the fleet, M&D's collection of Bristol VRTs with standard Eastern Coach Works bodies is nearing the point of major replacement. No.5848 climbs out of Gravesend on its way to cross the Medway Towns in October 1995. Laurie Rufus

MAIDSTONE & DISTRICT

| 1000 | C203PCD | Mercedes-Benz L608D | Alexander AM | B20F | 1986 | Ex Brighton & Hove, 1990 |

| *1001-1038* | | Mercedes-Benz L608D | Rootes | B20F | 1986 | |

1001	C201EKJ	1008	C208EKJ	1015	C215EKJ	1022	D22KKP	1032	D32KKP
1002	C202EKJ	1009	C209EKJ	1016	C216EKJ	1023	D23KKP	1034	D34KKP
1003	C203EKJ	1010	C210EKJ	1017	C217EKJ	1024	D24KKP	1035	D35KKP
1004	C204EKJ	1011	C211EKJ	1018	C218EKJ	1025	D25KKP	1036	D36KKP
1005	C205EKJ	1012	C212EKJ	1019	C219EKJ	1027	D27KKP	1037	D37KKP
1006	C206EKJ	1013	C213EKJ	1020	C220EKJ	1028	D28KKP	1038	D38KKP
1007	C207EKJ	1014	C214EKJ	1021	C221EKJ	1030	D30KKP		

| 1040 | D441RKE | Mercedes-Benz 609D | Reeve Burgess | B20F | 1987 | Ex Marinair, Canterbury, 1988 |

| *1041-1087* | | Mercedes-Benz 609D | Reeve Burgess | B20F* | 1987-90 | * 1077/8 are DP19F |

1041	E41UKL	1050	E50UKL	1059	E59UKL	1069	G69PKR	1078	G78SKR
1042	E42UKL	1051	E51UKL	1060	E60UKL	1070	G70PKR	1079	G79SKR
1043	E43UKL	1052	E52UKL	1061	E61UKL	1071	G71PKR	1080	G80SKR
1044	E44UKL	1053	E53UKL	1062	E62UKL	1072	G72PKR	1082	G82SKR
1045	E45UKL	1054	E54UKL	1063	E63UKL	1073	G73PKR	1084	G84SKR
1046	E46UKL	1055	E55UKL	1064	E64UKL	1074	G74PKR	1085	G85SKR
1047	E47UKL	1056	E56UKL	1065	E65XKE	1075	G75PKR	1086	G86SKR
1048	E48UKL	1057	E57UKL	1066	F66BKK	1076	G76PKR	1087	G87SKR
1049	E49UKL	1058	E58UKL	1067	F67BKK	1077	G77PKR		

1200	E980NMK	Mercedes-Benz 709D	Reeve Burgess	B20F	1988	Ex Biss, Bishops Stortford, 1990
1201	G201RKK	Mercedes-Benz 709D	Reeve Burgess Beaver	B25F	1989	
1202	G202RKK	Mercedes-Benz 709D	Reeve Burgess Beaver	B25F	1989	
1203	G203RKK	Mercedes-Benz 709D	Reeve Burgess Beaver	B25F	1989	
1204	H204EKO	Mercedes-Benz 709D	Carlyle	B25F	1991	
1205	M205SKE	Mercedes-Benz 709D	Plaxton Beaver	B23F	1995	
1206	M206SKE	Mercedes-Benz 709D	Plaxton Beaver	B23F	1995	

| *1207-1217* | | Mercedes-Benz 709D | Plaxton Beaver | B27F | 1996 | |

1207	N207CKP	1210	N210CKP	1213	N213CKP	1216	N216CKP
1208	N208CKP	1211	N211CKP	1214	N214CKP	1217	N217CKP
1209	N209CKP	1212	N212CKP	1215	N215CKP		

1301	H301FKL	Mercedes-Benz 709D	Reeve Burgess Beaver	DP25F	1991	Ex New Enterprise, 1996
1302	G702NGR	Mercedes-Benz 811D	Scott	DP25F	1990	Ex Kentish Bus, 1995
1351	N351YKE	Mercedes-Benz 709D	Plaxton Beaver	DP16FL	1995	
1352	N352BKK	Mercedes-Benz 709D	Plaxton Beaver	DP16FL	1995	
1713	L287EKK	Iveco Daily 59.12	Dormobile Routemaker	B25F	1994	Ex Kentish Bus, 1996
1714	L714EKO	Iveco Daily 59.12	Dormobile Routemaker	B25F	1994	Ex Kentish Bus, 1996
1862	F862LCU	MCW Metrorider MF158/15	Metro-Cammell-Weymann	B31F	1988	Ex Kentish Bus, 1996
1863	F863LCU	MCW Metrorider MF158/15	Metro-Cammell-Weymann	B31F	1988	Ex Kentish Bus, 1996
2167	CKE167Y	Leyland Leopard PSU3G/4R	Eastern Coach Works B51	C49F	1982	
2168	CKE168Y	Leyland Leopard PSU3G/4R	Eastern Coach Works B51	C49F	1982	
2169	CKE169Y	Leyland Leopard PSU3G/4R	Eastern Coach Works B51	C49F	1982	
2170	CKE170Y	Leyland Leopard PSU3G/4R	Eastern Coach Works B51	C49F	1982	
2171	YSU894	Leyland Tiger TRCTL11/2R	Plaxton Paramount 3200ExpC53F		1983	Ex Kentish Bus, 1990
2173	YSU896	Leyland Tiger TRCTL11/2R	Plaxton Paramount 3200ExpC53F		1983	Ex London Country NE, 1990
2174	YSU897	Leyland Tiger TRCTL11/2R	Plaxton Paramount 3200ExpC53F		1983	Ex Kentish Bus, 1990
2175	TSU646	Leyland Tiger TRCTL11/3R	Plaxton Paramount 3200ExpC53F		1983	

| *2176-2185* | | Leyland Tiger TRCTL11/3R | Duple Laser Express | C53F* | 1983 | |
| | | | | | | * 2176-8 are C50F; 2176 on extended loan to Kentish Bus |

2176	YLK281	2178	681CXM	2180	YOT607	2183	TSU636
2177	445YMU	2179	869SVX	2182	VAY879	2185	648WHK

2186	YSU870	Leyland Tiger TRCTL11/3ARZA	Plaxton Paramount 3500 3	C53F	1988	
2187	YSU871	Leyland Tiger TRCTL11/3ARZA	Plaxton Paramount 3500 3	C53F	1988	
2188	F188HKK	Leyland Tiger TRCTL10/3RZA	Duple 340	C53F	1989	
2189	F189HKK	Leyland Tiger TRCTL10/3RZA	Duple 340	C53F	1989	
2190	ESK987	Leyland Tiger TRCTL11/3R	Duple Caribbean 2	C50F	1985	Ex Brighton & Hove, 1992
2191	ESK988	Leyland Tiger TRCTL11/3R	Duple Caribbean 2	C50F	1985	Ex Brighton & Hove, 1992
2192	YSU872	Leyland Tiger TRCTL11/3RZ	Duple 320	C53F	1989	Ex Park, Hamilton, 1993
2193	YSU873	Leyland Tiger TRCTL11/3RZ	Duple 320	C53F	1989	Ex Park, Hamilton, 1993

Following the closure of Luton (Chatham) depot in November 1995, M&D's Gillingham depot became responsible for almost half of the fleet. Leyland Olympian 5905, with Northern Counties bodywork, leaves Chatham on its way to Gravesend. Unusually, M&D have opted to retain the NBC shade of green as the main element of their modern livery. Richard Godfrey

The newest full-size single-deckers in the M&D fleet are Volvo B6s with Plaxton bodywork. No.3602, new in 1994, stands at Monson Road, Tunbridge Wells, showing the flying sash livery applied to this type of vehicle. Gerald Mead

In the 1995 delivery of nine Volvo B6s, the first three received Maidstone Park & Ride livery. No.3611 was caught on Yalding bridge early one morning in June 1995 working a KCC trip prior to taking up its main daytime duty. Eric Baldock

In May 1996, M&D took over the local routes formerly operated by Grey-Green after a brief period of operation by London Coaches (Kent). Leyland Lynx 3040 had originated with Merthyr Tydfil, but when found at Chatham in July 1996 had received full M&D livery. Eric Baldock

Two Iveco Daily vehicles with Dormobile bodywork joined the M&D fleet from Kentish Bus in the spring of 1996 to assist with an increased requirement at Sittingbourne, where No.1714 was caught in June 1996 on local service. Eric Baldock

2194	J25UNY	Leyland Tiger TRCL10/3ARZM	Plaxton 321		C53F	1992	Ex Bebb, Llantwit Fardre, 1993
2195	J26UNY	Leyland Tiger TRCL10/3ARZM	Plaxton 321		C53F	1992	Ex Bebb, Llantwit Fardre, 1993
2196	J27UNY	Leyland Tiger TRCL10/3ARZM	Plaxton 321		C53F	1992	Ex Bebb, Llantwit Fardre, 1993

2585-2590 Dennis Javelin 12SDA2146   Caetano Algarve II   C51FT 1996 Ex London & Country, 1996

2585	N585GBW	**2587**	N587GBW	**2589**	N589GBW
2586	N586GBW	**2588**	N588GBW	**2590**	N590GBW

2842	G546NKJ	Volvo B10M-60	Caetano Algarve	C53F	1989	Ex Londoners, London SE15, 1996
2843	G998RKN	Volvo B10M-60	Caetano Algarve	C49FT	1990	Ex Londoners, London SE15, 1996
2844	TIB5901	Volvo B10M-60	Plaxton Paramount 3500 3	C50F	1988	Ex Kentish Bus, 1996
2845	A14GTA	Volvo B10M-60	Plaxton Paramount 3500 3	C49FT	1990	Ex Kentish Bus, 1996
2846	H846AHS	Volvo B10M-60	Plaxton Paramount 3500 3	C49FT	1991	Ex Express Travel, Speke, 1995
2847	H847AHS	Volvo B10M-60	Plaxton Paramount 3500 3	C49FT	1991	Ex Express Travel, Speke, 1995
2848	H616UWR	Volvo B10M-60	Plaxton Paramount 3500 3	C50F	1991	Ex Wallace Arnold, 1996
2849	H618UWR	Volvo B10M-60	Plaxton Paramount 3500 3	C50F	1991	Ex Wallace Arnold, 1996
2850	H637UWR	Volvo B10M-60	Plaxton Paramount 3500 3	C50F	1991	Ex Westbus, Hounslow, 1996
3002	TSJ77S	Leyland Leopard PSU3D/4R	Alexander AY	B53F	1978	Ex Western Scottish, 1993
3040	D108NDW	Leyland Lynx LX112TL11ZR1	Leyland	B49F	1987	Ex London Coaches (Kent), 1996
3041	E885KYW	Leyland Lynx LX112TL11ZR1	Leyland	B49F	1987	Ex London Coaches (Kent), 1996
3042	E886KYW	Leyland Lynx LX112TL11ZR1	Leyland	B47F	1987	Ex London Coaches (Kent), 1996
3043	E887KYW	Leyland Lynx LX112TL11ZR1	Leyland	B47F	1987	Ex London Coaches (Kent), 1996
3044	E890KYW	Leyland Lynx LX1126LXCTR1	Leyland	B47F	1987	Ex London Coaches (Kent), 1996
3045	F45ENF	Leyland Lynx LX112L10ZR1R	Leyland	B49F	1988	Ex Shearings, 1991
3046	F46ENF	Leyland Lynx LX112L10ZR1R	Leyland	B49F	1988	Ex Shearings, 1991
3047	F47ENF	Leyland Lynx LX112L10ZR1R	Leyland	B49F	1988	Ex Shearings, 1991
3048	F48ENF	Leyland Lynx LX112L10ZR1R	Leyland	B49F	1988	Ex Shearings, 1991
3049	H256YLG	Leyland Lynx 2 LX2R11V18Z4R	Leyland	B49F	1990	Ex Cherry, Bootle, 1995
3050	G45VME	Leyland Lynx LX2R11C15Z4S	Leyland	B49F	1989	Ex Kentish Bus, 1995
3461	G218LGK	Dennis Dart 9SDL3002	Duple/Carlyle	B36F	1990	Ex Kentish Bus. 1996
3462	G122RGT	Dennis Dart 9SDL3002	Duple/Carlyle	B36F	1990	Ex R&I Tours, London NW10, 1995
3463	J463MKL	Dennis Dart 9SDL3012	Plaxton Pointer	B40F	1991	
3464	J464MKL	Dennis Dart 9SDL3012	Plaxton Pointer	B40F	1991	
3465	J465MKL	Dennis Dart 9SDL3012	Plaxton Pointer	B40F	1991	

3466-3471 Dennis Dart 9SDL3017   Plaxton Pointer   B40F 1992   3470 was rebodied 1995

3466	J466OKP	**3468**	J468OKP	**3470**	K470SKO
3467	J467OKP	**3469**	K469SKO	**3471**	K471SKO

3474	M100CBB	Dennis Dart 9.8SDL3040	Plaxton Pointer	B40F	1995	Ex Cardiff Bluebird, 1996
3475	M200CBB	Dennis Dart 9.8SDL3040	Plaxton Pointer	B40F	1995	Ex Cardiff Bluebird, 1996

3601-3618 Volvo B6   Plaxton Pointer   B40F 1994/5

3601	L601EKM	**3605**	L605EKM	**3609**	L609EKM	**3613**	M613PKP	**3617**	M617PKP
3602	L602EKM	**3606**	L606EKM	**3610**	L610EKM	**3614**	M614PKP	**3618**	M618PKP
3603	L603EKM	**3607**	L607EKM	**3611**	M611PKP	**3615**	M615PKP		
3604	L604EKM	**3608**	L608EKM	**3612**	M612PKP	**3616**	M616PKP		

5105	KKO105P	Bristol VRT/SL3/501	Eastern Coach Works	H43/31F	1975

5107-5116 Bristol VRT/SL3/6LXB   Eastern Coach Works   H43/31F 1976

5107	PKM107R	**5109**	PKM109R	**5111**	PKM111R	**5113**	PKM113R	**5116**	PKM116R
5108	PKM108R	**5110**	PKM110R	**5112**	PKM112R	**5114**	PKM114R		

5120	PKP120R	Bristol VRT/SL3/501	Eastern Coach Works	H43/31F	1977

5125-5138 Bristol VRT/SL3/6LXB   Eastern Coach Works   H43/31F 1977-78

5125	WKO125S	**5127**	WKO127S	**5132**	WKO132S	**5135**	WKO135S	**5138**	WKO138S
5126	WKO126S	**5128**	WKO128S	**5133**	WKO133S	**5137**	WKO137S		

5201-5210 MCW Metrobus 2 DR102/42   Metro-Cammell-Weymann H45/31F 1984

5201	A201OKJ	**5203**	A203OKJ	**5205**	A205OKJ	**5208**	A208OKJ	**5210**	A210OKJ
5202	A202OKJ	**5204**	A204OKJ	**5207**	A207OKJ	**5209**	A209OKJ		

5441	GKE441Y	Leyland Olympian ONTL11/2R	Eastern Coach Works	CH45/28F	1983

5721-5735 Leyland Atlantean AN68A/1R   Northern Counties   H43/32F   1976-77 Ex GM Buses, 1987-88

5721 LJA621P	5724 LJA650P	5728 SRJ746R	5731 LJA635P	5734 ONF654R
5722 LJA626P	5726 ONF680R	5729 SRJ751R	5732 LJA648P	5735 ONF655R
5723 LJA644P	5727 SRJ743R	5730 UNA798S	5733 LJA652P	

5738	KPJ280W	Leyland Atlantean AN68B/1R	Roe	H43/30F	1981	Ex Luton & District, 1991
5742	XPG164T	Leyland Atlantean AN68A/1R	Park Royal	H43/30F	1978	Ex Luton & District, 1991
5743	KPJ275W	Leyland Atlantean AN68B/1R	Roe	H43/30F	1981	Ex Kentish Bus, 1996
5826	URB166S	Bristol VRT/SL3/6LXB	Eastern Coach Works	H43/31F	1977	Ex Bluebird Northern, 1993
5827	WRC833S	Bristol VRT/SL3/501	Eastern Coach Works	H43/31F	1978	Ex Trent, 1993
5828	BRC834T	Bristol VRT/SL3/6LXB	Eastern Coach Works	H43/31F	1979	Ex Trent, 1993
5829	BRC835T	Bristol VRT/SL3/6LXB	Eastern Coach Works	H43/31F	1979	Ex Trent, 1993
5830	BRC837T	Bristol VRT/SL3/6LXB	Eastern Coach Works	H43/31F	1979	Ex Trent, 1993

5831-5886 Bristol VRT/SL3/6LXB   Eastern Coach Works   H43/31F   1978-81 5870 ex West Riding, 1995

5831 BKE831T	5842 BKE842T	5855 BKE855T	5869 FKM869V	5880 FKM880V
5832 BKE832T	5843 BKE843T	5856 BKE856T	5870 ODC470W	5881 FKM881V
5833 BKE833T	5845 BKE845T	5857 BKE857T	5873 FKM873V	5882 FKM882V
5835 BKE835T	5846 BKE846T	5863 FKM863V	5874 FKM874V	5883 HKM883V
5837 BKE837T	5847 BKE847T	5864 FKM864V	5875 FKM875V	5884 HKM884V
5838 BKE838T	5848 BKE848T	5865 FKM865V	5876 FKM876V	5885 HKM885V
5839 BKE839T	5852 BKE852T	5866 FKM866V	5877 FKM877V	5886 HKM886V
5840 BKE840T	5853 BKE853T	5867 FKM867V	5878 FKM878V	
5841 BKE841T	5854 BKE854T	5868 FKM868V	5879 FKM879V	

5888	A888PKR	Leyland Olympian ONLXB/1R	Eastern Coach Works	DPH42/27F	1984
5889	A889PKR	Leyland Olympian ONLXB/1R	Eastern Coach Works	DPH42/27F	1984
5890	A890PKR	Leyland Olympian ONLXB/1R	Eastern Coach Works	DPH42/27F	1984

5891-5900 Leyland Olympian ON6LXB/1RH   Northern Counties   H45/30F   1988

5891 E891AKN	5893 F893BKK	5895 F895BKK	5897 F897DKK	5899 F899DKK
5892 E892BKK	5894 F894BKK	5896 F896DKK	5898 F898DKK	5900 F900DKK

5901-5905 Leyland Olympian ON2R50G13Z4 Northern Counties   H45/30F   1990

5901 G901SKP	5902 G902SKP	5903 G903SKP	5904 G904SKP	5905 G905SKP

5906-5910 Leyland Olympian ON2R50C13Z4 Northern Counties
Countybus Palatine   H47/30F   1993

5906 K906SKR	5907 K907SKR	5908 K908SKR	5909 K909SKR	5910 K910SKR

5911-5920 Volvo Olympian YN2RC16Z4   Northern Counties
Countybus Palatine   H47/30F   1994*   * 5913 rebodied 1995

5911 M911MKM	5913 M913MKM	5915 M915MKM	5917 M917MKM	5919 M919MKM
5912 M912MKM	5914 M914MKM	5916 M916MKM	5918 M918MKM	5920 M920MKM

5921-5925 Volvo Olympian YN2RC16Z4   Northern Counties
Countybus Palatine I   H47/30F   1995

5921 M921PKN	5922 M922PKN	5923 M923PKN	5924 M924PKN	5925 M925PKN

Special liveries
Kent Karrier: 1351/2
Green Line: 2175-80/2/3/5-96, 2843/4/6-9
Gatwick Direct: 2850
Maidstone Park-and-Ride: 3045-50, 3611-3
Londoners: 2842
White: 2845
Overall advertisements: 1050, 3461/2, 5203/728/31/2/853-5/66-8/76/7/86/91

During the 1995/6 academic year, M&D and Kentish Bus provided a service between Dartford and Gillingham to link University of Greenwich sites, using two Dennis Darts acquired from R&I Tours. Owned by Kentish Bus when photographed, G218LGK became M&D 3461 when they took over the whole service in June 1996 shortly before its withdrawal. Laurie Rufus

The withdrawal of Kent County Council in 1995 from providing vehicles for specialist contract routes led to the arrival of two Mercedes-Benz 709D with Plaxton bodies painted in this special Kent Karrier livery. No.1352 was caught in Tunbridge Wells in April 1996 on a local route which is interworked with a social centre service. Terry Blackman

The rebranding of Green Line services in Kent during 1995 included the former Invictaway network operated by M&D since 1980. No.2179, a Leyland Tiger with Duple Laser coachwork, shows the dedicated lettering applied to the Medway Towns services as it passes through Gravesend on ordinary bus work in June 1996. Laurie Rufus

Previously in the M&D coaching fleet, New Enterprise No.7033 is a Leyland Leopard with Plaxton coachwork, found at Hildenborough in July 1996 on a Kent contract route. The new livery introduced for this subsidiary fleet in the past year will be noted – as will the fleet number, not yet altered following the renumbering of the New Enterprise fleet within the Invictaway group at the end of 1995. Richard Godfrey

New Enterprise also operated the last two survivors of M&D's batch of MCW Metrobuses purchased for NBC evaluatory trials in 1980. No.7057 was on its regular school trip in Hildenborough in July 1996. Richard Godfrey

Mercury Passenger Services is another operator to have invested in personalised registrations. No.1020 is a Dennis Dart with Marshall C37 bodywork. Seen at Maidstone Hospital in February 1995, this was a Kent Sunday contract working which has now passed back to Maidstone & District. Richard Godfrey

M&D have started to renew their first generation of minibuses with Mercedes-Benz 709D vehicles fitted with Plaxton bodywork. No.1208, new in 1996, was photographed in Sittingbourne on a KCC contract service gained from another operator in the 1996 retendering round. Eric Baldock

New Enterprise fleet

7003	M619PKP	Volvo B6	Plaxton Pointer	B40F	1995	Ex Maidstone & District, 1996
7006	F68BKK	Mercedes-Benz 609D	Reeve Burgess	DP19F	1988	Ex Maidstone & District, 1993
7008	MPL134W	Leyland Leopard PSU3E/4R	Duple DominantIVExp	C53F	1981	Ex Barrie, Alexandria, 1988
7012	JKM166V	Leyland Leopard PSU5C/4R	Duple Dominant II	C53F	1980	Ex Maidstone & District, 1988
7016	CVA110V	Bedford YMT	Plaxton Supreme IV	C45F	1980	Ex Young, Rampton, 1985
7018	LSK643	Bedford YNV	Plaxton Paramount 3200 2	C49F	1986	Ex Excelsior, Bournemouth, 1988
7023	TSU645	Leyland Tiger TRCTL11/3R	Plaxton Paramount 3200Exp	C53F	1983	Ex Maidstone & District, 1990
7024	494WYA	Leyland Tiger TRCTL11/3R	Plaxton Paramount 3500	C57F	1984	Ex PMT, 1990
7025	LSK641	Leyland Tiger TRCTL11/3R	Plaxton Paramount 3200	C53F	1983	Ex Mercer, Preston, 1991
7026	NTK611	Leyland Tiger TRCTL11/3R	Duple Laser Express	C53F	1983	Ex Maidstone & District, 1996
7027	544XVW	Leyland Tiger TRCTL11/3R	Duple Laser Express	C53F	1983	Ex Maidstone & District, 1996
7030	A222DRM	Bedford YNT	Plaxton Paramount 3200	C57F	1984	Ex DJ Clarke, Elmswell, 1994
7031	UJI2338	Scania K113CRB	Plaxton Paramount 3500 3	C49FT	1990	Ex Happy Days, Woodseaves, 1994
7032	YKP975X	Leyland Leopard PSU3E/4R	Duple DominantII	C53F	1981	Ex Maidstone & District, 1995
7033	GGM69W	Leyland Leopard PSU3F/4R	Plaxton SupremeIV Express	DP53F	1981	Ex Maidstone & District, 1995
7034	UJI2339	Leyland Tiger TRCTL11/3RH	Plaxton Paramount 3500 2	C49FT	1985	Ex Kentish Bus, 1995
7035	UJI2337	Leyland Tiger TRCTL11/3RH	Plaxton Paramount 3500 2	C49FT	1985	Ex Kentish Bus, 1995
7059	WKO139S	Bristol VRT/SL3/6LXB	Eastern Coach Works	H43/31F	1978	Ex Maidstone & District, 1994
7060	VCA461W	Bristol VRT/SL3/6LXB	Eastern Coach Works	H43/31F	1980	Ex Crosville Wales, 1996
7061	YNW401S	Bristol VRT/SL3/6LXB	Eastern Coach Works	H43/31F	1978	Ex Southend, 1996
7062	YUM515S	Bristol VRT/SL3/6LXB	Eastern Coach Works	H43/31F	1978	Ex Southend, 1996

Mercury fleet

1020	M20MPS	Dennis Dart 9.8SDL3054	Marshall C37	B40F	1994	
1023	XRF23S	Dennis Dominator DD101A	East Lancs	H43/32F	1978	Ex Maidstone & District, 1995
1030	M30MPS	Dennis Dart 9.8SDL3054	Marshall C37	DP40F	1995	
1040	M40MPS	Iveco Daily 59.12	Marshall C31	B26FL	1995	
1060	J60MPS	Mercedes-Benz 811D	PMT Ami	DP33F	1992	Ex Flights, Birmingham, 1995
1070	L70MPS	Talbot Pullman	TBP	B22F	1993	Ex Kelvin Central, 1995
1080	L80MPS	Talbot Pullman	TBP	B22FL	1993	Ex Kelvin Central, 1995
1162	D162TYJ	Ford Transit	Dormobile	B14FL	1986	Ex East Sussex County Council (npsv), 1995
1204	F204YKG	Freight Rover Sherpa 405D	Carlyle	B20F	1988	Ex Red & White, 1994
1207	F207AKG	Freight Rover Sherpa 405D	Carlyle	B20F	1988	Ex Red & White, 1995
1749	LHS749V	Volvo Ailsa AB55-10	Alexander AV	H44/35F	1979	Ex Kelvin Central, 1996
1813	D813KWT	Freight Rover Sherpa 374D	Dormobile	DP16F	1987	Ex West Riding, 1991
1886	SJI1886	Toyota BB30R	Caetano Optimo	C21F	1987	Ex Dickson, Normandy, 1992
2190	LDS190A	Bristol VRT/SL3/501	Eastern Coach Works	CH41/29F	1978	Ex Merseyrider, 1995
	LRR689W	Leyland Atlantean AN68A/1R	Northern Counties	H47/33D	1980	Ex Nottingham, 1996
	GHB84W	Bristol VRT/SL3/6LXB	East Lancs	H44/32F	1981	Ex Merseyrider, 1994

Previous registrations

A14GTA	G89RGG	VAY879	A182MKE
ESK987	B812JPN	YKP975X	XGS771X, YSU873
ESK988	B815JPN	YLK281	A176MKE
J60MPS	J10FTG	YOT607	A180MKE
LDS190A	JPT906T, 449CLT	YSU870	E186XKO
LSK641	KGS494Y	YSU871	E187XKO
LSK643	C112AFX	YSU872	G795RNC
L70MPS	L464DOA	YSU873	G796RNC
L80MPS	L140FOJ	YSU894	A107EPA
NTK611	A181MKE	YSU896	A135EPA
SJI1886	D315HYN	YSU897	A140EPA
TIB5901	E301UUB, HIL2280,	681CXM	A178MKE
	E848WWU	869SVX	A179MKE
TSU636	A183MKE	438UHT	WFJ931X, HHF15
TSU645	FKL173Y	648WHK	A185MKE
TSU646	FKL175Y	494WYA	A268MEH, 507EXA,
UJI2337	C204PPE, XSV691, C895YKJ		A420HND
UJI2338	G897DEH	544XVW	A184MKE
UJI2339	C202PPE, XSV689, C894YKJ	445YMU	A177MKE

M TRAVEL

Redbeam Ltd, Bowling Green Lane, Newport, Isle of Wight, PO30 1RR

The bus operations of M Travel commenced with minibus work franchised from Southern Vectis. More recently, other routes have been introduced on an independent basis. An unusual feature is a Ford Transit converted to open-top use on the Ventnor & District tour.

M TRAVEL

B259MDL	Ford Transit	Carlyle	B16F	1985	Ex Southern Vectis, 1991
B260MDL	Ford Transit	Carlyle	B16F	1985	Ex Southern Vectis, 1991
B261MDL	Ford Transit	Carlyle	OB16F	1985	Ex Southern Vectis, 1991
C450SJU	Ford Transit	Robin Hood	B16F	1985	Ex Midland Fox, 1994
C476TAY	Ford Transit	Robin Hood	B16F	1985	Ex Midland Fox, 1994
C525BFB	Ford Transit	Dormobile	B16F	1985	Ex Badgerline, 1994
C534BHY	Ford Transit	Dormobile	B16F	1986	Ex Badgerline, 1994
D75KRL	Ford Transit	Dormobile	B16F	1986	Ex Badgerline, 1995
D81KRL	Ford Transit	Dormobile	B16F	1986	Ex Badgerline, 1995
F352DVR	Ford Transit	Mellor	B16F	1988	Ex Garnett, Ainsdale, 1996
OIW6793	Toyota Coaster HB31R	Caetano Optimo	C18F	1988	Ex Tellings-Golden Miller, Byfleet, 1993
H224EDL	Ford Transit	Dormobile	B18F	1991	

Previous registrations
OIW6793 F864TNH

Special liveries
Ventnor Buggy: B261MDL
White: OIW6793

The youngest vehicle operated by M Travel, and the only one new to the fleet, H224EDL is a Ford Transit of 1991 with Dormobile bodywork, here seen in Newport during September 1995. Richard Godfrey

MIDHURST & DISTRICT

Richardson Travel Ltd, Suite 2, Russell House, Bepton Road, Midhurst, West Sussex, GU29 9RA

Midhurst & District operate a small network of routes in West Sussex, alongside specialist trips for educational establishments. The fleet is housed at a depot in Pitsham Lane, Midhurst.

MIDHURST & DISTRICT

206	USU638	Leyland Tiger TRCTL11/3R	Plaxton Paramount 3200	C53F	1983	Ex Richardson, Sheffield, 1990
538	BTU371S	Bristol VRT/SL3/501	Eastern Coach Works	H43/31F	1978	Ex Northern, Anston, 1990
						(since converted to Gardner 6LX engine)
	NCD552M	Bristol VRT/SL2/6LX	Eastern Coach Works	H43/31F	1973	Ex Weller, Midhurst, 1989
	GTA52N	Bristol VRT/SL2/6LX	Eastern Coach Works	H43/32F	1975	Ex Weller, Midhurst, 1989
	CBV122S	Leyland Atlantean AN68A/1R	East Lancs	H45/31F	1978	Ex Blackburn, 1995
	VUD149X	Leyland Tiger TRCTL11/3R	Plaxton Supreme V	C53F	1982	Ex Cottrell, Mitcheldean, 1994
	D456ERF	Volvo B10M-61	Plaxton Paramount 3500 3	C57F	1987	Ex Durber, Burslem, 1996
	G341FFX	Volvo B10M-60	Plaxton Paramount 3500 3	C49FT	1990	Ex Dorset Travel, 1995
	L741YGE	Volvo B10M-62	Jonckheere Deauville	C49FT	1994	Ex Shearings, Wigan, 1996
	M220DWV	Mercedes-Benz 811D	Plaxton Beaver	DP29F	1995	

Previous registrations
USU638 ERF74Y

Found at Midhurst in July 1996, M220DWV is a Mercedes-Benz 811D with Plaxton Dual-purpose bodywork. The AST legend on the front nearside refers to the alternative name of this operator, who also provide academic and specialist tours. Richard Godfrey

NIGHTINGALE

Nightingale Coaches Ltd, 8 Middle Green Trading Estate, Middle Green Road, Langley

In addition to coaching work, Nightingale has developed bus services in the Slough area, using a selection of minibuses, chiefly based on Mercedes-Benz units.

NIGHTINGALE

LIL3063	Ford R1114	Plaxton Supreme	C53F	1977	
LIL3062	Ford R1014	Plaxton Supreme	C35F	1978	Ex Maitland, Bournemouth, 1980
C812KBT	Leyland Cub CU435	Optare	B33F	1986	Ex Yorkshire Rider, 1987
C828HRL	Mercedes-Benz L608D	Dormobile	B20F	1986	Ex Lytham, St Columb, 1986
E897XGK	Mercedes-Benz 609D	Reeve Burgess	C25F	1987	Ex Chivers, Wallington, 1995
E448MMM	Van Hool T815	Van Hool	C41FT	1988	Ex Tellings-Golden Miller, Cardiff, 1991
F336DVR	Mercedes-Benz 811D	Mellor	B31F	1988	
F756HHH	Iveco Daily 49.10	Robin Hood City Nippy	DP21F	1989	
G722RGA	Mercedes-Benz 709D	Dormobile	B23F	1990	Ex McConnachie, Port Glasgow, 1990
K473PNR	Toyota Coaster HDB30R	Caetano Optimo II	C21F	1993	
L387TCR	Mercedes-Benz 811D	WSC Wessex	B31F	1993	
M176BLC	Volvo B10M-62	Plaxton	C53F	1994	
N889NNR	Toyota Coaster HZB50R	Caetano Optimo III	C21F	1995	
N786JBM	Mercedes-Benz 811D	UVG	B31F	1996	

Previous registrations
LIL3062 WLJ209S
LIL3063 SGM100S

Operating in the Slough area, Nightingale's fleet includes C828HRL, a Mercedes-Benz L608D of 1986 with Dormobile conversion. This view was taken in February 1995.
Richard Godfrey

The more modern face of the fleet is represented by F336DVR, an 811D model with Mellor 31-seat bodywork. Loadings appear light in this shot.
Richard Godfrey

NU-VENTURE

Nu-Venture Coaches Ltd, 86 Mill Hall, Aylesford, Maidstone, Kent, ME20 7JN

The long-established local coaching firm of Nu-Venture has operated a number of contracts for Kent County Council since deregulation, and has supplemented these by commercial operations to the west of Maidstone, sometimes taking advantage of what would otherwise be light running between contract work and the home base. From April 1996 additional KCC contracts have been gained in the Maidstone and Tunbridge Wells areas.

Most of the current fleet bears a light blue and white livery with red relief. Some dealer acquisitions are in all-over white.

NU-VENTURE

GNJ573N	Bristol VRT/SL2/6LX	Eastern Coach Works	H43/31F	1974	Ex Eagles & Hughes, Mold, 1994
PRA113R	Leyland Leopard PSU3C/4R	Alexander AT	B53F	1976	Ex Morgan, Biddenden, 1994
PVF361R	Leyland National 11351A/1R		B49F	1976	Ex Rodemark, Herstmonceux, 1996
PAU209R	Daimler Fleetline CRG6LX	Northern Counties	H47/30D	1976	Ex Darlington, 1995
AYR345T	Leyland National 10351A/2R		B36D	1979	Ex Boro'line Maidstone, 1992
8421RU	Leyland Tiger TRCTL11/2R	Duple Laser	C53F	1984	Ex Shearings, Wigan, 1991
E966TEW	Scania K112CRB	Van Hool Alizée	C55F	1988	Ex Day & Ellwood, Carlisle, 1996
E134NDE	Talbot Pullman	Talbot	B22F	1988	Ex Tenby Bus & Coach, Tenby, 1990
3558RU	Scania K92CRB	Van Hool Alizée	C51FT	1988	Ex Connor, Shenley, 1995
F301GNB	Mercedes-Benz 609D	Made-to-Measure	C24F	1988	Ex Courtney, Binfield, 1995
F100CWG	Scania K92CRB	Van Hool Alizée	C53F	1988	Ex Swallow, Rainham, 1996
G75TKN	Talbot Pullman	Talbot	DP22F	1990	
K200CCC	Scania K113CRB	Van Hool Alizée	C49FT	1993	Ex Cunningham, Corringham, 1996
L866BEA	Iveco Daily 59.12	Marshall C31	B29F	1993	
N254DUR	Mercedes-Benz 709D	Marshall C19	B27F	1995	Ex Delta, Kirkby in Ashfield, 1996
N255DUR	Mercedes-Benz 709D	Marshall C19	B27F	1995	Ex Delta, Kirkby in Ashfield, 1996

Previous registrations

E966TEW	E515YWF, LIB1745	3558RU	E666YDT	8421RU	A157MNE

Special liveries
Tesco: PVF361R

Nu-Venture's fleet includes PAU209R, a Daimler Fleetline with Northern Counties dual-door bodywork formerly in the Nottingham fleet. It was found at Hall Road, Aylesford in May 1995 working a school service. Eric Baldock

OXFORD BUS COMPANY

City of Oxford Motor Services Ltd, Cowley Road, Oxford, OX4 2DJ

The Oxford Bus Company, as it is now marketed, was sold by the NBC to a management-led team on 15th January 1987. The High Wycombe operations of Berks Bucks were absorbed in November 1990 and are now operated as a separate unit; Wycombe Bus has the first Leyland Nationals to be owned by the company. Ownership passed to the Go-Ahead Group on 1st March 1994.

Operations are largely confined to the areas around Oxford and High Wycombe, other routes having been transferred to the offshoot South Midland company which in turn was taken over by Thames Transit in December 1988. There is a frequent City Link service along the M40 to London, together with a similar facility direct to Heathrow and Gatwick Airports. Another interesting operation is the Park-and-Ride network between outlying car parks and the city centre.

Oxford caused some interest by purchasing redundant Leyland Titans from London Buses Ltd These ousted the older examples of the Bristol VRT type. Four electric Optare Metroriders were taken into stock in 1993.

The livery is red and white with blue skirt (formerly dark red with white roof and black skirt). Park & Ride vehicles carry green and white with blue skirt. City Link vehicles carry dark blue, deep yellow and white, applied in NBC-derived style. The fleet is garaged at the main address and in High Wycombe.

Replacement of double-deckers by single-deckers has occurred in the form of Volvo B10Ms with Plaxton Verde bodywork. No.611 is one of twenty-eight such vehicles to have joined the fleet within a year, and was found at Headington in July 1996. Capital Transport

Oxford may have taken a leaf out of Thames Transit's book in purchasing twenty dual-door single-deckers for local routes in 1995. No.515 is a 9.8-metre Dennis Dart with Marshall bodywork, seen in July 1996. Capital Transport

Five Leyland Lynxes were acquired from The Bee Line in 1990, when they were just two years old. No.301 (then numbered 1401) was photographed in High Wycombe. Colin Lloyd

OXFORD BUS COMPANY

50-55
Dennis Javelin 12SDA2118 · Plaxton Première 320 · C53F · 1992

50	K750UJO	52	K752UJO	54	K754UJO
51	K751UJO	53	K753UJO	55	K755UJO

130-134
DAF MB230LT615 · Plaxton Paramount 3500 3 · C53F · 1988

130	E130YUD	131	E131YUD	132	E132YUD	133	E133YUD	134	E134YUD

135-139
DAF SB3000DKV601 · Plaxton Paramount 3500 3 · C53F · 1989

135	F135LJO	136	F136LJO	137	F137LJO	138	F138LJO	139	F139LJO

140	J140NJO	DAF SB2305DHS585	Plaxton Paramount 3200 3	C53F	1991
141	J141NJO	DAF SB2305DHS585	Plaxton Paramount 3200 3	C53F	1991

150-158
Volvo B10M-62 · Plaxton Première 350 · C53F · 1993/95

150	L150HUD	152	L152HUD	154	L154HUD	156	N156BFC	158	N158BFC
151	L151HUD	153	L153HUD	155	L155HUD	157	N157BFC		

159-163
Volvo B10M-60 · Plaxton Première 350 · C51F · 1991 · Ex Shearings, Wigan, 1995

159	UJI1759	160	UJI1760	161	UJI1761	162	UJI1762	163	UJI1763

201-224
Leyland Olympian ONLXB/1R · Eastern Coach Works · H45/28D* · 1982-83 · *218 is H47/25D

201	VJO201X	206	VJO206X	211	WWL211X	216	BBW216Y	221	CUD221Y
202	VJO202X	207	WWL207X	212	WWI 212X	217	BBW217Y	222	CUD222Y
203	VJO203X	208	WWL208X	213	BBW213Y	218	BBW218Y	223	CUD223Y
204	VJO204X	209	WWL209X	214	BBW214Y	219	CUD219Y	224	CUD224Y
205	VJO205X	210	WWL210X	215	BBW215Y	220	CUD220Y		

225-229
Leyland Olympian ONLXB/1RH · Alexander RL · H47/26D · 1988

225	E225CFC	226	E226CFC	227	E227CFC	228	E228CFC	229	E229CFC

230-235
Leyland Olympian ON2R50G16Z4 · Alexander RL · H47/30F · 1990

230	G230VWL	232	G232VWL	234	G234VWL
231	G231VWL	233	G233VWL	235	G235VWL

236	FWL778Y	Leyland Olympian ONLXB/1R	Eastern Coach Works	H45/32F	1983	Ex UKAEA, Harwell, 1991
237	FWL779Y	Leyland Olympian ONLXB/1R	Eastern Coach Works	H45/32F	1983	Ex UKAEA, Harwell, 1991
238	FWL780Y	Leyland Olympian ONLXB/1R	Eastern Coach Works	H45/32F	1983	Ex UKAEA, Harwell, 1991
239	FWL781Y	Leyland Olympian ONLXB/1R	Eastern Coach Works	H45/32F	1983	Ex UKAEA, Harwell, 1991
240	D822UTF	Leyland Olympian ONLXB/1RH	Eastern Coach Works	CH39/21F	1986	Ex The Bee Line, 1990
241	D823UTF	Leyland Olympian ONLXB/1RH	Eastern Coach Works	CH39/21F	1986	Ex The Bee Line, 1990
242	D824UTF	Leyland Olympian ONLXB/1RH	Eastern Coach Works	CH39/21F	1986	Ex The Bee Line, 1990

301-305
Leyland Lynx LX112L10ZR1S · Leyland · B49F · 1988 · Ex The Bee Line, 1990

301	F556NJM	302	F557NJM	303	F558NJM	304	F559NJM	305	F560NJM

377	THX177S	Leyland National 10351A/2R		DP41F	1978	Ex London Buses, 1993
384	VPF296S	Leyland National 11351A/1R		B49F	1978	Ex The Bee Line, 1990
385	JWV127W	Leyland National 2 NL116L11/1R		B52F	1980	Ex Brighton & Hove, 1996
386	JWV128W	Leyland National 2 NL116L11/1R		B52F	1980	Ex Brighton & Hove, 1996
443	SNJ592R	Bristol VRT/SL3/6LXB	Eastern Coach Works	H43/31F	1977	Ex Brighton & Hove, 1995
444	AAP651T	Bristol VRT/SL3/6LXB	Eastern Coach Works	H43/31F	1978	Ex Brighton & Hove, 1995
446	EAP989V	Bristol VRT/SL3/6LXB	Eastern Coach Works	H43/31F	1980	Ex Brighton & Hove, 1995
447	EAP999V	Bristol VRT/SL3/6LXB	Eastern Coach Works	H43/31F	1980	Ex Brighton & Hove, 1995
448	MRJ8W	Bristol VRT/SL3/6LXB	Eastern Coach Works	DPH41/29F	1980	Ex Mayne, Manchester, 1991
449	MRJ9W	Bristol VRT/SL3/6LXB	Eastern Coach Works	DPH41/29F	1980	Ex Mayne, Manchester, 1991

450-462
Bristol VRT/SL3/6LXB · Eastern Coach Works · H43/31F · 1976 · Ex The Bee Line, 1990

450	GGM110W	453	HJB453W	456	HJB456W	459	HJB459W		
451	HJB451W	454	HJB454W	457	HJB457W	461	HJB461W		
452	HJB452W	455	HJB455W	458	HJB458W	462	HJB462W		

501-520   Dennis Dart 9.8SDL3054   Marshall C37   B36D   1995

501	M501VJO	505	M505VJO	509	M509VJO	513	M513VJO	517	M517VJO
502	M502VJO	506	M506VJO	510	M510VJO	514	M514VJO	518	M518VJO
503	M503VJO	507	M507VJO	511	M511VJO	515	M515VJO	519	M519VJO
504	M504VJO	508	M508VJO	512	M512VJO	516	M516VJO	520	M520VJO

521-527   Dennis Dart SLF 10m   Plaxton Pointer   B37F   1996

| 521 | N521MJO | 523 | N523MJO | 525 | P525YJO | 527 | P527YJO |
| 522 | N522MJO | 524 | N524MJO | 526 | P526YJO | | |

601-628   Volvo B10B-58   Plaxton Verde   B51F   1995/6

601	N601FJO	607	N607FJO	613	N613FJO	619	N619FJO	625	N413NRG
602	N602FJO	608	N608FJO	614	N614FJO	620	N620FJO	626	N414NRG
603	N603FJO	609	N609FJO	615	N615FJO	621	N621FJO	627	N415NRG
604	N604FJO	610	N610FJO	616	N616FJO	622	N622FJO	628	N416NRG
605	N605FJO	611	N611FJO	617	N617FJO	623	N623FJO		
606	N606FJO	612	N612FJO	618	N618FJO	624	N624FJO		

701	G621XLO	Mercedes-Benz 811D	Reeve Burgess Beaver	B29F	1989	Ex London Central, 1995
702	G222KWE	Mercedes-Benz 811D	Reeve Burgess Beaver	B26F	1989	Ex London Central, 1995
703	H189RWF	Mercedes-Benz 811D	Reeve Burgess Beaver	B29F	1990	Ex London Central, 1995
704	H191RWF	Mercedes-Benz 811D	Reeve Burgess Beaver	B29F	1990	Ex London Central, 1995
709	G109PGT	Mercedes-Benz 811D	Alexander AM	B28F	1990	Ex London General, 1996
710	G110PGT	Mercedes-Benz 811D	Alexander AM	B28F	1990	Ex London General, 1996
714	G114PGT	Mercedes-Benz 811D	Alexander AM	B28F	1990	Ex London General, 1996
715	G115PGT	Mercedes-Benz 811D	Alexander AM	B28F	1990	Ex London General, 1996
717	G117PGT	Mercedes-Benz 811D	Alexander AM	B28F	1990	Ex London General, 1996
724	G124PGT	Mercedes-Benz 811D	Alexander AM	B28F	1990	Ex London General, 1996
750	D750SJO	MCW Metrorider MF150/13	Metro-Cammell-Weymann	B25F	1987	

751-757   MCW Metrorider MF150/26   Metro-Cammell-Weymann   B25F   1987

| 751 | E751VJO | 753 | E753VJO | 755 | E755VJO | 757 | E757VJO |
| 752 | E752VJO | 754 | E754VJO | 756 | E756VJO | | |

758-762   MCW Metrorider MF150/51   Metro-Cammell-Weymann   B25F   1987

| 758 | E758XWL | 759 | E759XWL | 760 | E760XWL | 761 | E761XWL | 762 | E762XWL |

763	F763LBW	MCW Metrorider MF150/114	Metro-Cammell-Weymann	B25F	1989	
764	F501ANY	MCW Metrorider MF150/109	Metro-Cammell-Weymann	B23F	1989	Ex Merthyr Tydfil, 1989
765	F502ANY	MCW Metrorider MF150/109	Metro-Cammell-Weymann	B23F	1989	Ex Merthyr Tydfil, 1989
766	F503ANY	MCW Metrorider MF150/109	Metro-Cammell-Weymann	B23F	1989	Ex Merthyr Tydfil, 1989
767	F504ANY	MCW Metrorider MF150/109	Metro-Cammell-Weymann	B23F	1989	Ex Merthyr Tydfil, 1989
768	F505CBO	MCW Metrorider MF150/105	Metro-Cammell-Weymann	B25F	1989	Ex Merthyr Tydfil, 1989

769-783   Optare MetroRider   Optare   B28F   1990

769	G769WFC	772	G772WFC	775	G775WFC	778	G778WFC	781	G781WFC
770	G770WFC	773	G773WFC	776	G776WFC	779	G779WFC	782	G782WFC
771	G771WFC	774	G774WFC	777	G777WFC	780	G780WFC	783	G783WFC

801	L801HJO	Optare MetroRider MREL	Optare	B18F	1993
802	L802HJO	Optare MetroRider MREL	Optare	B18F	1993
803	L803HJO	Optare MetroRider MREL	Optare	B18F	1993
804	L804HJO	Optare MetroRider MREL	Optare	B18F	1993

950-975   Leyland Titan TNLXB2RR   Leyland   H44/26D 1981-83 Ex London Buses, 1993/4

950	GYE280W	955	KYV452X	960	OHV711Y	965	OHV783Y	970	KYN308X
951	KYV516X	956	KYV519X	961	KYV524X	966	KYV381X	971	KYV457X
952	KYN300X	957	KYN291X	962	KYV530X	967	KYV392X	973	KYV493X
953	KYV317X	958	KYV370X	963	OHV727Y	968	NUW661Y	974	NUW635Y
954	KYV328X	959	NUW667Y	964	OHV745Y	969	KYV510X	975	A869SUL

| 999 | PWL999W | Leyland Olympian B45/TL11/2R Alexander RL | H50/34D | 1980 | Ex Singapore Bus (Leyland demonstrator),1987 |

Previous registrations
UJI1759-1763   H959/954/957/960/958DRJ

Special liveries
Park and Ride: 211/3/5/6/8/9/25-9, 950/1/4/8/71/99
Citylink: 50-5, 130-41/50-63
Overall advertisements: 223/34/9/42, 303/84

This striking new livery is being applied to vehicles used on Park & Ride services, and must be one of the more spectacular schemes carried by a Leyland Titan. No.951 was caught in June 1996. Terry Blackman

In the 1980s, Oxford turned to Leyland Olympians for fleet replacement. No.227 comes from a batch of five delivered in 1988 with Alexander bodywork, and is also painted in Park & Ride livery. Capital Transport

The first of more than thirty MCW Metroriders to reach the Oxford fleet in the late 1980s, No.750 is seen on the Jericho service.
Tony Smethers

In 1993, Oxford took delivery of four Optare MetroRiders powered by stored electricity. No.802 shows the dedicated livery which is applied in recognition of this fact, the fleet identity only being apparent in the plate on the front radiator grille.
Malcolm King

The Citylink services have been regularly upgraded. No.158, a Volvo B10M-62 of 1995 with Plaxton Première coachwork, demonstrates the latest form of livery as applied to the service linking Oxford with Heathrow and Gatwick airports in this shot at Heathrow in September 1995.
Ivor Norman

POYNTER'S

R.J. & B.J. Poynter, Sunray, Churchfield Way, Wye, Ashford, Kent, TN25 5EQ

Poynter's have developed a stake in Kent County Council contract work on rural routes in the Ashford and Canterbury areas since deregulation. Although there was something of a setback when routes were lost in the 1992 tendering round at Ashford, there have been subsequent gains in the Canterbury area and from the withdrawal of Westbus from their Ashford base in the autumn of 1993. There is also a strong presence on local works and schools contracts.

The fleet carries a livery of cream with yellow and orange.

POYNTER'S

Reg	Type	Body	Seating	Year	History
NFM831M	Leyland National 1151/1R/0405		DP49F	1973	Ex Seabrook Coach, Hythe, 1991
GVV887N	Leyland National 11351/1R		B49F	1975	Ex PMT, 1993
KRE279P	Leyland National 11351/1R		B52F	1975	Ex PMT, 1993
KDW339P	Leyland National 11351/1R		B49F	1975	Ex Westbus, Ashford, 1993
MFN117R	Leyland National 11351A/1R		B49F	1976	Ex Constable, Long Melford, 1995
HMA562T	Leyland National 10351B/1R		B44F	1978	Ex Crosville Wales, 1991
GMB665T	Leyland National 10351B/1R		B44F	1978	Ex Crosville Wales, 1991
MCA674T	Leyland National 10351B/1R		B44F	1979	Ex PMT, 1993
FGE424X	Dennis Dominator DD137B	Alexander RL	H45/34F	1982	Ex Delta, Kirkby in Ashfield, 1996
FGE437X	Dennis Dominator DD137B	Alexander RL	H45/34F	1982	Ex Delta, Kirkby in Ashfield, 1996
A794SKL	DAF SB2300DHS585	Berkhof Esprite 340	C49FT	1984	Ex UMBH, Southend, 1990
RJI6569	Kässbohrer Setra S228DT	Kässbohrer Imperial	CH54/20CT	1984	Ex Warren, Alton, 1994
2448UE	DAF SB2300DHS585	Berkhof Esprite 340	C57F	1985	Ex Travelfar, Henfield, 1991
3318VU	DAF SB2300DHS585	LAG Galaxy	C53F	1985	Ex D Coaches, Morriston, 1992
C424AHT	Ford Transit 190	Carlyle	B16F	1986	Ex Pickford, Grittleton, 1991
C634BEX	Freight Rover Sherpa 365	Dormobile	B16F	1986	Ex Spratt, Wreningham, 1995
8465LJ	LAG Panoramic	LAG	C49FT	1988	Ex Express Travel, Speke, 1994
6769FM	LAG Panoramic	LAG	C49FT	1988	Ex Express Travel, Speke, 1994

Previous registrations
A794SKL	A166OHJ, 6769FM
RJI6569	A848UGB, WLO471, A409JPB
2448UE	B688BTW
3318VU	C770FEP
6769FM	F617VNH
8465LJ	F102UNV

Poynter's local bus services are in the hands of Leyland Nationals, the more recent of which are to 10.3-metre specification. GMB665T came from Crosville Wales in 1995. Martin Smith

PRESTWOOD TRAVEL

P & G L Baird, 152 Wrights Lane, Prestwood, Great Missenden, Buckinghamshire, HP16 0LG

Prestwood Travel couples coaching work with a number of routes in the Aylesbury and High Wycombe area. Much of the bus network is resourced by AEC Reliances which started their lives as Green Line vehicles.

    The fleet is based at Binders Industrial Estate, Cryers Hill, High Wycombe.

PRESTWOOD TRAVEL

WRO438S	AEC Reliance 6U3ZR	Plaxton Supreme	C53F	1978	Ex Smith, Chesham, 1995
APM111T	AEC Reliance 6U2R	Plaxton Supreme IV Exp	C53F	1979	Ex London Country, 1985
APM117T	AEC Reliance 6U2R	Plaxton Supreme IV Exp	C49F	1979	Ex London Country, 1985
EPM140V	AEC Reliance 6U2R	Plaxton Supreme IV Exp	C53F	1979	Ex Marchant, Cheltenham, 1990
EPM144V	AEC Reliance 6U2R	Plaxton Supreme IV Exp	C53F	1979	Ex London Country, 1986
EPM146V	AEC Reliance 6U2R	Plaxton Supreme IV Exp	C53F	1979	Ex London Country, 1986
PPJ162W	Leyland Leopard PSU5D/5R	Wadham Stringer Vanguard	B54F	1981	Ex Ministry of Defence, 1995
CPE480Y	Leyland Leopard PSU5D/5L	Wadham Stringer Vanguard	B54F	1982	Ex Ministry of Defence, 1995
RJI4670	Bova Europa EL25/581	Bova	C52F	1981	Ex Warren, Alton, 1992
RJI4668	Bova Europa EL26/581	Bova	C53F	1983	Ex Pan Atlas, London W3, 1987
RJI4669	Bova Europa EL26/581	Bova	C53F	1983	Ex Pan Atlas, London W3, 1987
8726FH	Bova Europa EL26/581	Bova	C53F	1983	Ex McAndrew, Leamington, 1990
E901LVE	Volkswagen LT55	Optare City Pacer	B25F	1987	Ex Cambus, 1993
E902LVE	Volkswagen LT55	Optare City Pacer	B25F	1987	Ex Cambus, 1993
E48TYG	Leyland Royal Tiger	Leyland Doyen	C53F	1988	Rx Holmeswood, Rufford, 1995

Previous registrations

CPE480Y	51 AC 05	RJI4669	DOY134Y
PPJ162W	50 AC 03	RJI4670	997GAT, VPG339X
RJI4668	DOY133Y	8726FH	CLX573Y

Prestwood's E901LVE is an Optare City Pacer new in 1987, acquired from Cambus in 1993. This view was taken on 31st July 1995 in High Wycombe. The Roman lettering in the fleetname makes an interesting contrast with the modernity of the vehicle. Dave Stewart

PROVINCIAL

Provincial Bus Co. Ltd, Gosport Road, Hoeford, Fareham, Hampshire, PO16 0ST

Provincial was the successor to the Provincial Tramways Company Ltd. This started horse tramways in Portsmouth in 1873, and a subsidiary operation followed in Gosport in 1884. The Portsmouth operation passed to Portsmouth Corporation Tramways Department, but the Gosport tramway continued until electrification in 1905. Motor-buses were introduced in 1910 and the tramway was eventually replaced in 1929 when the title of the company was changed to Gosport & Fareham Omnibus Company, when the Provincial fleetname was introduced. The company became part of the National Bus Company in 1970, and was augmented by the addition of the Fareham depots and operations of Hants & Dorset in 1983.

With the sale by the government of the NBC subsidiaries, Provincial became an employee co-ownership scheme, the only NBC fleet to have been sold in this way. In 1988 day-time operations were extended into Portsmouth, and since then Hampshire County Council contracts have been secured.

Blue Admiral and Red Admiral, part of the Thames Transit group, commenced trading in Portsmouth on 25th May 1991. This followed the introduction of Thames Transit operations in that area on 20th January 1991 as a result of the Monopolies & Mergers Commission directive to Stagecoach Holdings to divest itself of its Portsmouth activities.

In April 1996 the sale of both Provincial and Blue/Red Admiral to the Firstbus group was completed. The Red Admiral fleet was immediately absorbed into that of Blue Admiral, which was in turn absorbed by Provincial on 26th May 1996. A new livery of County cream and Post Office red is being introduced. Depots are at Fareham, Havant and Hoeford.

The needs of busier routes were addressed in 1995 with the arrival of seven full-length Dennis Darts with Wadham Stringer bodywork. No.604 was photographed in June 1996. Malc McDonald

Several Bristol VRTs with Eastern Coach Works bodies have been acquired from larger operators in recent years. No.520 (now renumbered 512), a late dual-door example, was new in 1980 and came from Bristol in 1994.
Malc McDonald

The Blue Admiral and Red Admiral fleets at Portsmouth were absorbed into Provincial during the spring of 1996. Now numbered 250, this former Admiral Iveco Daily shows its dual-door Mellor bodywork to good effect in June 1996. Note the Provincial fleetnames on Admiral livery.
Eric Baldock

The green-and-cream livery of Provincial No.192 will disappear in the coming months. This is one of a substantial series of Iveco Daily vehicles with Marshall C31 bodywork delivered from 1993 to 1995.
Gerald Mead

PROVINCIAL

101	D937ECR	Iveco Daily 49.10	Robin Hood City Nippy	B19F	1986	Ex Blue Admiral, 1996
102	D939ECR	Iveco Daily 49.10	Robin Hood City Nippy	B19F	1986	Ex Blue Admiral, 1996

103-117 Iveco Daily 49.10 Robin Hood City Nippy B23F 1988 Ex Blue Admiral, 1996

103	E959LPX	**106**u	E962LPX	**109**	E965LPX	**112**u	E968LPX	**115**u	E971LPX
104u	E960LPX	**107**	E963LPX	**110**u	E966LPX	**113**	E969LPX	**116**	E972LPX
105u	E961LPX	**108**u	E964LPX	**111**u	E967LPX	**114**u	E970LPX	**117**u	E973LPX

118	D118DRV	Iveco Daily 49.10	Robin Hood City Nippy	B19F	1986	
119	D119DRV	Iveco Daily 49.10	Robin Hood City Nippy	B19F	1986	
120	D120DRV	Iveco Daily 49.10	Robin Hood City Nippy	B19F	1986	
121u	D618BCK	Iveco Daily 49.10	Robin Hood City Nippy	B21F	1987	Ex Blue Admiral, 1996
122	D122DRV	Iveco Daily 49.10	Robin Hood City Nippy	B19F	1986	
123	D123DRV	Iveco Daily 49.10	Robin Hood City Nippy	B19F	1986	
124	F24PSL	Iveco Daily 49.10	Robin Hood City Nippy	B23F	1989	Ex Blue Admiral, 1996
127	D127FRV	Iveco Daily 49.10	Robin Hood City Nippy	B21F	1986	

128-139 Iveco Daily 49.10 Phoenix B24F 1992

128	F128SBP	**130**	F130SBP	**132**	F132TCR	**135**	F135TCR	**138**	G138WOW
129	F129SBP	**131**	F131SBP	**134**	F134TCR	**137**	G137WOW	**139**	G139WOW

140-146 Iveco Daily 49.10 Marshall C31 B23F 1992

140	J140KPX	**142**	J142KPX	**144**	J144KPX	**146**	J146KPX
141	J141KPX	**143**	J143KPX	**145**	J145KPX		

147	H463GTM	Iveco Daily 49.10	Mellor	B19F	1991	Ex Blue Admiral, 1996

160-165 Iveco Daily 59.12 Wadham Stringer B27F 1993

160	K160PPO	**162**	K162PPO	**164**	K164PPO
161	K161PPO	**163**	K163PPO	**165**	K165PPO

166-207 Iveco Daily 59.12 Marshall C31 B27F 1993-5

166	L166TRV	**175**	L175TRV	**184**	M184XTR	**193**	M193XTR	**203**	M203XTR
167	L167TRV	**176**	L176TRV	**185**	M185XTR	**194**	M194XTR	**204**	M204BPO
168	L168TRV	**177**	L177TRV	**186**	M186XTR	**195**	M195XTR	**205**	M205BPO
169	L169TRV	**178**	L178TRV	**187**	M187XTR	**196**	M196XTR	**206**	M206BPO
170	L170TRV	**179**	M179XTR	**188**	M188XTR	**197**	M197XTR	**207**	M207BPO
171	L171TRV	**180**	M180XTR	**189**	M189XTR	**198**	M198XTR		
172	L172TRV	**181**	M181XTR	**190**	M190XTR	**199**	M199XTR		
173	L173TRV	**182**	M182XTR	**191**	M191XTR	**201**	M201XTR		
174	L174TRV	**183**	M183XTR	**192**	M192XTR	**202**	M202XTR		

208-213 Iveco Daily 59.12 Marshall C31 B26D 1994 Ex Blue Admiral, 1996

208	M642HDV	**210**	M644HDV	**212**	M646HDV
209	M643HDV	**211**	M645HDV	**213**	M647HDV

221-271 Iveco Daily 59.12 Mellor Duet B26D 1992-4 Ex Blue Admiral, 1996

221	K701UTT	**232**	K716UTT	**243**	K633XOD	**254**	K922VDV	**265**	L316BOD
222	K703UTT	**233**	K723UTT	**244**	K911VDV	**255**	K923VDV	**266**	L317BOD
223	K704UTT	**234**	K728UTT	**245**	K912VDV	**256**	K928VDV	**267**	L319BOD
224	K705UTT	**235**	K729UTT	**246**	K914VDV	**257**	K929VDV	**268**	L320BOD
225	K706UTT	**236**	K801WFJ	**247**	K915VDV	**258**	K930VDV	**269**	L322BOD
226	K707UTT	**237**	K802WFJ	**248**	K916VDV	**259**	K931VDV	**270**	L323BOD
227	K708UTT	**238**	K819WFJ	**249**	K917VDV	**260**	L311BOD	**271**	L324BOD
228	K709UTT	**239**	K619XOD	**250**	K918VDV	**261**	L312BOD		
229	K710UTT	**240**	K621XOD	**251**	K919VDV	**262**	L313BOD		
230	K712UTT	**241**	K622XOD	**252**	K920VDV	**263**	L314BOD		
231	K715UTT	**242**	K623XOD	**253**	K921VDV	**264**	L315BOD		

301	NPD146L	Leyland National 1151/1R/0402		B49F	1973	Ex London Country, 1983

302-309 Leyland National 1151/2R/0403 B44D 1972/3

| 302 | HOR414L | 304 | HOR416L | 308 | PCG921M |
| 303 | HOR415L | 307 | PCG920M | 309 | PCG922M |

310-315 Leyland National 11351/2R B44D 1974-75

| 310 | GCR727N | 312 | JBP129P | 314 | JBP132P |
| 311 | GCR728N | 313 | JBP131P | 315 | JBP133P |

316	MJT880P	Leyland National 11351/1R	B49F	1976	Ex Hants & Dorset, 1983
317	RUF37R	Leyland National 11351A/2R	B49F	1977	Ex Rennie, Dunfermline, 1988
318	SPR39R	Leyland National 11351A/1R	B49F	1977	Ex Hants & Dorset, 1983
319	SPR40R	Leyland National 11351A/1R	B49F	1977	Ex Hants & Dorset, 1983
321	RJT147R	Leyland National 11351A/1R	B49F	1977	Ex Hants & Dorset, 1983
322	RJT148R	Leyland National 11351A/1R	B49F	1977	Ex Hants & Dorset, 1983
323	LTP634P	Leyland National 11351A/2R	B44D	1976	
324	MOW636R	Leyland National 11351A/2R	B44D	1977	
325	MOW637R	Leyland National 11351A/2R	B44D	1977	
326u	NOE561R	Leyland National 11351A/1R	B49F	1976	Ex Midland Red East, 1983
327	PTR238S	Leyland National 11351A/2R	B44D	1978	
328	WFX253S	Leyland National 11351A/1R	DP48F	1978	Ex Hants & Dorset, 1983
329	WFX257S	Leyland National 11351A/1R	DP48F	1978	Ex Hants & Dorset, 1983
330	SBK740S	Leyland National 11351A/2R	B44D	1978	
331	UFX847S	Leyland National 11351A/1R	B49F	1977	Ex Hants & Dorset, 1983
332	UFX848S	Leyland National 11351A/1R	B49F	1977	Ex Hants & Dorset, 1983
333	VFX980S	Leyland National 11351A/1R	B49F	1978	Ex Hants & Dorset, 1983
334	TPX41T	Leyland National 11351A/2R	B44D	1978	
335	TPX42T	Leyland National 11351A/2R	B44D	1978	
336	UPO443T	Leyland National 11351A/2R	B44D	1979	
337	UPO444T	Leyland National 11351A/2R	B44D	1979	
338	EEL893V	Leyland National 11351A/1R	DP52F	1979	Ex Hants & Dorset, 1983

350-362 Leyland National 10351A/2R B36D 1976-79 Ex London Buses, 1991

350	KJD511P	353	THX131S	356	THX248S	359	AYR331T	362	BYW415V
351	KJD528P	354	THX234S	357	YYE276T	360	AYR341T		
352	THX115S	355u	THX242S	358	YYE278T	361	AYR344T		

401	A301KJT	Leyland National 2 NL116L11/1R	DP47F	1984	
402	A302KJT	Leyland National 2 NL116L11/1R	DP47F	1984	

403-410 Leyland National 2 NL116L11/1R B52F 1980 Ex Kelvin Central, 1996

| 403 | MDS855V | 405 | MDS857V | 407 | MDS864V | 409 | WAJ766V |
| 404 | MDS856V | 406 | MDS863V | 408 | MDS867V | 410 | SNS827W |

411	YFS306W	Leyland National 2 NL116L11/1R	B52F	1981	Ex Kelvin Central, 1996
412	MSO12W	Leyland National 2 NL106L11/1R	B41F	1980	Ex Kelvin Central, 1996

413-418 Leyland National 2 NL116L11/1R B49F 1981 Ex Kelvin Central, 1996

| 413 | AST151W | 415 | AST154W | 417 | AST158W |
| 414 | AST153W | 416 | AST156W | 418 | AST159W |

419	SWX534W	Leyland National 2 NL116AL11/R		B52F	1981	Ex Kelvin Central, 199
420	UMY66Y	Leyland National 2 NL116AL11/1R		B52F	1981	Ex Kelvin Central, 1996
501	SFJ101R	Bristol VRT/SL3/6LXB	Eastern Coach Works	H43/31F	1977	Ex Western National, 1993
502	NTC573R	Bristol VRT/SL3/6LXB	Eastern Coach Works	H43/27D	1977	Ex Bristol, 1994
503	RHT503S	Bristol VRT/SL3/6LXB	Eastern Coach Works	H43/27D	1978	Ex Bristol, 1994
504	RHT504S	Bristol VRT/SL3/6LXB	Eastern Coach Works	H43/27D	1978	Ex Bristol, 1994
505	RHT512S	Bristol VRT/SL3/6LXB	Eastern Coach Works	H43/27D	1978	Ex Bristol, 1994
506	UVX2S	Bristol VRT/SL3/6LXB	Eastern Coach Works	H39/31F	1977	Ex Badgerline, 1994
507	UTO836S	Bristol VRT/SL3/501	Eastern Coach Works	H43/31F	1977	Ex Western National, 1993
508	TWS908T	Bristol VRT/SL3/6LXB	Eastern Coach Works	H43/27D	1979	Ex Bristol, 1994
509	AFJ748T	Bristol VRT/SL3/6LXB	Eastern Coach Works	H43/31F	1979	Ex Western National, 1993
510	AFJ752T	Bristol VRT/SL3/6LXB	Eastern Coach Works	H43/31F	1979	Ex Western National, 1993
511	AFJ763T	Bristol VRT/SL3/6LXB	Eastern Coach Works	H43/31F	1979	Ex Western National, 1993
512	AHU514V	Bristol VRT/SL3/6LXB	Eastern Coach Works	H39/31D	1980	Ex Bristol, 1994
513	LWU471V	Bristol VRT/SL3/6LXB	Eastern Coach Works	H43/31F	1980	Ex Rider (York), 1994
591	NFX130P	Daimler Fleetline CRL6-30 Alexander AD		CO43/31F	1976	Ex Bournemouth, 1991

592	NFX131P	Daimler Fleetline CRL6-30	Alexander AD	CO43/31F	1976	Ex Bournemouth, 1991
594	MOD571P	Bristol VRT/SL3/6LXB	Eastern Coach Works	CO43/31F	1979	Ex Western National, 1993
600	H523CTR	ACE Cougar	Wadham Stringer	B41F	1990	

601-607   Dennis Dart 9.8SDL3054   UVG Urban Star   B40F   1995

| 601 | N601EBP | 603 | N603EBP | 605 | N605EBP | 607 | N607EBP |
| 602 | N602EBP | 604 | N604EBP | 606 | N606EBP | | |

701-708   Mercedes-Benz 709D   Reeve Burgess   DP25F   1988   Ex Blue Admiral, 1996

| 701 | F712FDV | 703 | F721FDV | 705 | F727FDV | 707 | F749ADV |
| 702 | F713FDV | 704 | F725FDV | 706 | F739FDV | 708 | F761FDV |

710-729   Mercedes-Benz 709D   Plaxton Beaver   B27F   1996

710	N710GRV	714	N714GRV	718	N718GRV	722	P722KCR	726	P726KCR
711	N711GRV	715	N715GRV	719	N719GRV	723	P723KCR	727	P727KCR
712	N712GRV	716	N716GRV	720	N720GRV	724	P724KCR	728	P728KCR
713	N713GRV	717	N717GRV	721	N721GRV	725	P725KCR	729	P729KCR

801-822   Mercedes-Benz 811D   Carlyle   B29F   1991   Ex Blue Admiral, 1996

801	H171GTA	806	H176GTA	811	H783GTA	817	H992FTT	822	H997FTT
802	H172GTA	807	H177GTA	812	H787GTA	818	H993FTT		
803	H173GTA	808	H178GTA	813	H788GTA	819	H994FTT		
804	H174GTA	809	H179GTA	815	H990FTT	820	H995FTT		
805	H175GTA	810	H782GTA	816	H991FTT	821	H996FTT		

| 965 | BDL65T | Bedford YMT | Plaxton Supreme IV | C53F | 1979 | Ex Solent Blue Line, 1993 |

Special liveries

Overall advertisements: 160-4/6/7, 302/3/19/21/2/6/31/60/1

Recently converted to open-top and receiving the new livery with lettering for a tourist-based service, No.594 is a standard Bristol VRT with Eastern Coach Works body photographed in June 1996 at Portsmouth Harbour. Eric Baldock

RAMBLER

M. & C. Rowland and J. Goodwin, West Ridge Manor, Whitworth Road, St Leonards-on-Sea

The business was founded in 1924 by R.G. Rowland. Local bus operations started with an East Sussex County Council service between Bexhill and Hooe from 1980 to 1982. Since May 1986 Rambler has operated several journeys of the East Sussex County Rider scheme in the Battle and Bexhill areas, and from July 1987 took over a cross-Hastings service between St Leonards and Hollington. In October 1990 this work was lost, but simultaneously a new Sunday service was gained covering part of the route and a commercial service began in Hastings. From September 1991 coastal route 44 between Hastings and Rye via Fairlight commenced under ESCC contract. Commercial services have now been withdrawn and bus operation is limited to the 44 and a few odd contracts. Vehicles used on bus services carry a Ramblerbus name.

Fleet livery is green, black and cream with pale green relief. The present garage was opened in May 1980, and the head office moved there in January 1990.

Rare both in chassis and body is Rambler's No.14, a Bedford YMQS with Lex Maxeta bodywork new in 1981. When photographed at Ore, it was working an East Sussex winter Sunday contract which is covered commercially by South Coast Buses during the summer.
Terry Blackman

One of the more recent arrivals is No.01, a Mercedes-Benz 609D with Made-to-Measure coachwork. Found at Hastings Station in January 1996 on the coastal route from Rye, the advertised combination of executive travel without fares increase is an evident marketing ploy.
Richard Godfrey

RAMBLER

01	HDY565	Mercedes-Benz 609D	Made-to-Measure	C24F	1990	Ex Whitehead, Rochdale, 1995
02	TDY388	Volvo B10M-61	Jonckheere Jubilee P599	C49FT	1988	Ex Abridge, Hadleigh, 1995
03	VDY468	Volvo B10M-61	Jonckheere Jubilee P599	C49FT	1988	Ex Abridge, Hadleigh, 1995
04	NDY962	Bedford YNT	Plaxton Paramount 3200 2	C55F	1985	Ex Wilson, Dalkeith, 1994
05	HKX553V	Bedford JJL	Marshall	B24F	1979	Ex Holloway, Denham (npsv), 1993
06	PKO260W	Bedford YMT	Duple Dominant II	C53F	1981	Ex Moore & Verge, Cliftonville, 1992
07	C203GKR	Bedford YMT	Wright TT	DP53F	1986	Ex Evans, Tregaron, 1995
11	NDY820	Bedford YMT	Wright TT	DP53F	1982	Ex Boro'line Maidstone, 1992
12	MUY41X	Bedford YMQ	Wright TT	B45F	1982	Ex Perry, Bromyard, 1992
14	WNH52W	Bedford YMQS	Lex Maxeta	B33F	1981	Ex Milton Keynes City Bus, 1987
15	TDY946	Mercedes-Benz 609D	Whittaker	C24F	1989	Ex Williams, St Albans, 1993
16	K16ADY	DAF Sherpa 400	Crystals	C16F	1992	
17	MDY397	Volvo B10M-61	Van Hool Alizée	C49FT	1988	Ex Excelsior, Bournemouth, 1993
18	LDY173	Volvo B10M-61	Van Hool Alizée	C51FT	1988	
19	SDY788	Volvo B10M-61	Van Hool Alizée	C53F	1987	Ex Shearings, Wigan, 1992
20	910OCV	Bedford YMT	Duple Dominant II	C53F	1977	Ex Coliseum, West End, 1990
21	ODY395	Bedford YMT	Plaxton Paramount 3200Exp	C53F	1984	Ex Sheffield United Transport, 1993
22	NCF715	Bedford YMT	Plaxton Supreme IV	C53F	1979	Ex Portrest, Southam, 1989
23	PDY42	Bedford YNV	Plaxton Paramount 3200 3	C55F	1988	Ex Banstead Coaches, Banstead, 1995
24	PDY272	Bedford YNT	Plaxton Paramount 3200	C53F	1985	Ex Cleverly, Cwmbran, 1994
25	GDY493	Bedford YNT	Plaxton Paramount 3200	C51F	1984	Ex Hil-Tech, Hillingdon, 1993
26	FDY383	Bedford YNT	Plaxton Paramount 3200	C51F	1984	Ex Hil-Tech, Hillingdon, 1993
27	M222CDY	Scania K113CRB	Van Hool Alizée	C51FT	1995	
28	M222DDY	Scania K113CRB	Van Hool Alizée	C51FT	1995	
29	WUF44	Bedford YNT	Plaxton Paramount 3200	C53F	1983	Ex Hodson, Navenby, 1993
30	ODY607	Bedford YNT	Plaxton Paramount 3200	C53F	1984	Ex Associated, Worcester, 1993
31	1924RH	Bedford YNT	Plaxton Paramount 3200	C53F	1983	Ex Taylor, Meppershall, 1991
32	FDY83	Bedford YNT	Plaxton Paramount 3200	C53F	1984	Ex Barnes, Aldbourne, 1993
33	UDY910	Bedford YMPS	Plaxton Paramount 3200 3	C33F	1987	
34	RDY155	Bedford YMPS	Plaxton Paramount 3200 3	C33F	1987	
35	DDY222	Volvo B10M-62	Jonckheere Deauville	C51FT	1994	Ex Shearings, Wigan, 1995
36	KDY814	Volvo B10M-60	Plaxton Paramount 3500 3	C53F	1991	Ex Wallace Arnold, Leeds, 1994
37	HDY405	Volvo B10M-61	Plaxton Paramount 3500 3	C53F	1987	
38	N222EDY	Volvo B10M-62	Van Hool Alizée	C51FT	1996	
	H170EJF	Toyota HDB30R	Caetano Optimo II	C21F	1991	Ex Munro, Uddingston, 1996

Previous registrations

DDY222	L571FVU
FDY83	A440HJF
FDY383	A68NPP, 8876FN
GDY493	A67NPP
HDY405	D137VJK
HDY565	G48VVM
KDY814	H631UWR
LDY173	E184XJK
MDY397	AYU763 (Belgium), F450WFX, XEL941, F507MAA
MUY41X	ABH760X, 851PKJ
NCF715	YEB105T
NDY820	CKN143Y
NDY962	C345RSG
ODY395	A627YWF
ODY607	A383BNP
PDY42	E232GPH
PDY272	B930AAX
RDY155	D134VJK, TYW50
SDY788	D558MVR
TDY388	E697NNH, HSK834
TDY946	F609EHE
UDY910	D133VJK
VDY468	E696NNH, HSK835
WUF44	A244KFJ
910OCV	OTR412S
1924RH	JNM744Y, 617MUR, KUR585Y

RDH SERVICES

R D & D P Hunnisett & T M Hawthorne, Westcroft, Plumpton Lane, Plumpton, East Sussex.

RDH Services operates a number of East Sussex County Council contract services, which for some time used vehicles supplied from the County Council's stock of County Rider vehicles. Significant gains were achieved in the 1993 tendering round in the Lewes area. A small coach fleet is also held for contract purposes. Livery is white with orange and brown relief.

RDH SERVICES

Reg	Chassis	Body	Seating	Year	History
KJD433P	Bristol LH6L	Eastern Coach Works	B39F	1976	Ex Wright, Rainham, 1994
SRN6P	Leyland Leopard PSU3D/4R	Duple Dominant	C53F	1976	Ex Poole, Chislehurst, 1994
LIL4349	Leyland Leopard PSU3C/4R	Duple Dominant	C51F	1976	Ex Cook, Biggleswade, 1995
OJD79R	Bristol LH6L	Eastern Coach Works	B39F	1977	Ex Wright, Rainham, 1994
LIL4309	Leyland Leopard PSU3E/4R	Plaxton	C53F	1977	Ex Walker, Brighton, 1994
JIL9268	MAN SR240	MAN	C53F	1981	Ex Jenkins, Seaford, 1992
TIB4922	Mercedes-Benz L508DG	Robin Hood	B16FL	1982	Ex Hailsham Town Bus, 1989
JIL9269	Leyland Tiger TRCTL11/3R	Van Hool Alizée	C53F	1983	Ex Lodge, High Easter, 1995
B549DWJ	Mercedes-Benz L608D	Reeve Burgess	B16FL	1984	Ex East Sussex County Council, 1996
JAZ6920	Bedford YMP	Plaxton	C33F	1985	Ex Brown, Helperby, 1996
C551NWV	Mercedes-Benz L608D	Reeve Burgess	DP19F	1985	Ex East Sussex County Council, 1995
LIL6796	Bedford YMP	Plaxton Paramount 3200 2	C35F	1986	Ex Alexcars, Cirencester, 1995
D171NON	Freight Rover Sherpa 395D	Carlyle	B18F	1987	Ex C-Line, Chester, 1991
F438OTP	Leyland Swift LBM6N/1RS	Wadham Stringer Vanguard	B26FL	1988	Ex East Sussex County Council, 1992
JIL5226	Mercedes-Benz 609D	Reeve Burgess	B20F	1989	Ex Walsh, Middleton, 1995
JIL5228	Mercedes-Benz 609D	Reeve Burgess	B20F	1989	Ex Walsh, Middleton, 1995
H751DKL	Talbot Freeway	Talbot	B16F	1990	Ex East Sussex County Council, 1992
M616MKK	Ford Transit	Ford	B15FL	1994	Ex East Sussex County Council, 1994

Previous registrations

JAZ6920 B730TEL
JIL5226 F138KAO
JIL5228 F131KAO
JIL9268 NFJ375W, XS2210, OUF373W
JIL9269 FWX551Y, 551ALW, JUG389Y

LIL4309 SHM597R
LIL4349 NVD328P
LIL6796 D234TCK, ACH80A, D645GFH
TIB4922 FBP261X

Seen at Tunbridge Wells station, this Mercedes-Benz L608D has dual-purpose Reeve Burgess bodywork, and is normally used as the back-up vehicle for the Groombridge rail replacement service. On this occasion, however, it was covering a shuttle service to East Grinstead.
Terry Blackman

READING BUSES

Reading Transport Ltd, Mill Lane, Reading, Berkshire, RG1 2RW

Reading Transport took over the operations of the Reading Borough Council Transport Department on 26th October 1986. It operated stage services within the borough boundaries and express services to and from London. Following the acquisition of the Reading and Newbury duties of The Bee Line in July 1992 the area of operation has increased.

The fleet remained stable during the latter half of the 1980s, but rapid updating has taken place since then with Leyland Olympians and youthful second-hand MCW Metrobuses from London Buses. Twelve Leyland Titans in the fleet represent the only significant purchase of the type as new in the South of England outside London. The single-deck fleet has been developed by the arrival of midibuses, and the coaching presence has been strengthened by the acquisition, in October 1991, of the London services of The Bee Line, together with some vehicles. Further vehicles came with The Bee Line operations in July 1992. Most recently, DAF and Optare products have formed a major part of the fleet intake.

The livery is cream, burgundy and aquamarine (or green on Newbury-based buses); vehicles on London services are in a three-tone blue livery. Vehicles are based at Mill Lane and Forbury in Reading and at Newbury.

Twenty Optare Deltas on DAF chassis have joined the Reading fleet, ten in 1989 and ten more in the past year. No.514 crosses the river at Dukesbridge in July 1996. Geoff Rixon

Reading was one of the few customers outside London to take the Leyland Titan when it was available on the open market. No.79, built in 1983, is the youngest survivor of the type in the fleet. Malc McDonald

The oldest double-deckers in the fleet are now the MCW Metrobuses, of which No.152 is one of the most senior. Here it is seen passing through the town centre on a circular service. Malc McDonald

Still fairly rare is the Optare Spectra, of which Reading have taken nine specimens. No.705 was new in 1994; its route number seems to be out of proportion with the rest of its appearance. Malcolm King

READING BUSES

11	E911DRD	Leyland Olympian ONLXB/1RH	Optare		H44/26D	1988
12	E912DRD	Leyland Olympian ONLXB/1RH	Optare		H44/26D	1988
13	E913DRD	Leyland Olympian ONLXB/1RH	Optare		H44/26D	1988
14	E914DRD	Leyland Olympian ONLXB/1RH	Optare		H44/26D	1988
15	E915DRD	Leyland Olympian ONLXCT/1RH	Optare		H44/26D	1988
16	E916DRD	Leyland Olympian ONLXCT/1RH	Optare		H44/26D	1988
17	E917DRD	Leyland Olympian ONLXB/1RH	Optare		H44/26D	1988
68	YJB68T	Leyland Titan TNLXB2RRSp	Park Royal		H44/25D	1979
69	YJB69T	Leyland Titan TNLXB2RRSp	Park Royal		H44/25D	1979

70-74   Leyland Titan TNLXB2RR   Leyland   H44/26D   1983

| 70 | SBL70Y | 71 | RMO71Y | 72 | RMO72Y | 73 | RMO73Y | 74 | RMO74Y |

75-79   Leyland Titan TNLXC1RF   Leyland   DPH39/27F 1983

| 75 | RMO75Y | 76 | RMO76Y | 77 | RMO77Y | 78 | RMO78Y | 79 | RMO79Y |

82	D82UTF	Leyland Olympian ONLXCT/1RH	Eastern Coach Works	DPH39/25F	1986
83	D83UTF	Leyland Olympian ONLXCT/1RH	Eastern Coach Works	DPH39/25F	1986
84	D84UTF	Leyland Olympian ONLXCT/1RH	Eastern Coach Works	DPH39/25F	1986
85	F85MJH	Leyland Olympian ONLXCT/1RH	Optare	DPH39/25F	1988
86	F86MJH	Leyland Olympian ONLXCT/1RH	Optare	DPH39/25F	1988
87	F87MJH	Leyland Olympian ONLXCT/1RH	Optare	DPH39/25F	1988

143-149   MCW Metrobus 2 DR102/44   Metro-Cammell-Weymann DPH39/27F 1984

| 143 | A143AMO | 145 | A145AMO | 147 | B147EDP | 149 | B149EDP |
| 144 | A144AMO | 146 | A146AMO | 148 | B148EDP | | |

150-165   MCW Metrobus DR102/8   Metro-Cammell-Weymann H43/27D   1979

150	WRD150T	153	WRD153T	157	WRD157T	160	WRD160T	163	WRD163T
151	WRD151T	154	WRD154T	158	WRD158T	161	WRD161T	164	CJH164V
152	WRD152T	155	WRD155T	159	WRD159T	162	WRD162T	165	CJH165V

166-183   MCW Metrobus DR102/16   Metro-Cammell-Weymann H45/27D   1980-81

166	CJH166V	170	CJH170V	174	HCF174W	178	HCF178W	182	HCF182W
167	CJH167V	171	CJH171V	175	HCF175W	179	HCF179W	183	HCF183W
168	CJH168V	172	CJH172V	176	HCF176W	180	HCF180W		
169	CJH169V	173	HCF173W	177	HCF177W	181	HCF181W		

184-188   MCW Metrobus DR102/25   Metro-Cammell-Weymann H45/28D   1982

| 184 | LMO184X | 185 | LMO185X | 186 | LMO186X | 187 | LMO187X | 188 | LMO188X |

189-193   MCW Metrobus DR102/30   Metro-Cammell-Weymann DPH43/25D 1982

| 189 | LMO189X | 190 | LMO190X | 191 | LMO191X | 192 | LMO192X | 193 | LMO193X |

201-210   Mercedes-Benz 811D   Optare StarRider   B26F   1988-89 Ex The Bee Line, 1992

| 201 | F531NRD | 203 | F533NRD | 205 | F535NRD | 207 | F361SDP | 209 | F363SDP |
| 202 | F532NRD | 204 | F534NRD | 206 | F360SDP | 208 | F362SDP | 210 | F364SDP |

212	E460CGM	Mercedes-Benz 609D	Robin Hood	B20F	1987	Ex The Bee Line, 1992
213	E468CGM	Mercedes-Benz 609D	Robin Hood	B20F	1987	Ex The Bee Line, 1992
214	D939KNW	Volkswagen LT55	Optare City Pacer	B25F	1986	Ex Lancaster, 1992
215	E236VUD	Volkswagen LT55	Optare City Pacer	B25F	1987	Ex Lancaster, 1992
216	WOI3005	MCW Metrorider MF154/1	Metro-Cammell-Weymann	DP26F	1989	Ex Ipswich, 1993
217	H847UUA	Volkswagen LT55	Optare City Pacer	B25F	1991	Ex demonstrator, 1994
220	BUS5X	Scania K113CRB	Van Hool Alizée	C49FT	1989	
234	J786KHD	DAF SB2700DHS585	Van Hool Alizée	C57FT	1992	Ex Chesterfield, 1995
235	J788KHD	DAF SB2700DHS585	Van Hool Alizée	C51F	1992	Ex Hallmark, Luton, 1996
236	J799KHD	DAF SB2700DHS585	Van Hool Alizée	C51F	1992	Ex demonstrator, 1992
244	E451CGM	Hestair Duple 425	Duple 425	C55F	1987	Ex The Bee Line, 1991
247	E454CGM	Hestair Duple 425	Duple 425	C55F	1987	Ex The Bee Line, 1991
251	K505RJX	DAF SB2700DHS585	Van Hool Alizée HE	C55F	1992	
261	G608SGU	Leyland Tiger TRCTL10/3ARZA	Plaxton Paramount 3200 3	C57F	1990	Ex London Buses, 1993
262	G100VMM	Leyland Tiger TRCTL10/3ARZA	Plaxton Paramount 3200 3	C57F	1990	Ex London Buses, 1993
271	L671RUA	Bova FLC12-280	Bova Futura	C53F	1994	Ex demonstrator, 1994
272	M272SBT	Bova FLC12-280	Bova Futura	C53F	1995	
308	NRD145M	Leyland National 1151/1R/0402		B49F	1973	Ex The Bee Line, 1992
314	NRD155M	Leyland National 1151/1R/0402		B49F	1974	Ex The Bee Line, 1992

333	GPC731N	Leyland National 11351/1R		B49F	1974	Ex The Bee Line, 1992
339	GPJ895N	Leyland National 11351/1R		B49F	1975	Ex The Bee Line, 1992
340	GPJ896N	Leyland National 11351/1R		B49F	1975	Ex The Bee Line, 1992
343	KPA355P	Leyland National 11351/1R		B49F	1975	Ex The Bee Line, 1992
344	FNS162T	Leyland National 11351A/1R		B52F	1979	Ex Liyell, Ripley, 1992
345	KRE281P	Leyland National 11351/1R		B52F	1976	Ex PMT, 1993
346	KRE283P	Leyland National 11351/1R		B52F	1976	Ex PMT, 1993
357	NPJ483R	Leyland National 11351A/1R		B49F	1977	Ex The Bee Line, 1992
382	LPF603P	Leyland National 11351/1R/SC		B49F	1976	Ex The Bee Line, 1992

455-469

MCW Metrobus 2 DR102/63   Metro-Cammell-Weymann H45/30F   1987   Ex London Buses, 1991

455	E454SON	458	E458SON	461	E247KCF	464	E464SON	467	E467SON
456	E456SON	459	E459SON	462	E462SON	465	E465SON	468	E468SON
457	E457SON	460	E460SON	463	E463SON	466	E466SON	469	E469SON

501-510

DAF SB220LC550   Optare Delta   B49F*   1989   * 508 is B44F

501	G501XBL	503	G503XBL	505	G505XBL	507	G507XBL	509	G509XBL
502	G502XBL	504	G504XBL	506	G506XBL	508	G508XBL	510	G510XBL

511-520

DAF DE02LTSB220   Optare Delta   B47F   1995/6

511	M511PDP	513	M513PDP	515	N515YTF	517	N517YTF	519	N519YTF
512	M512PDP	514	N514YTF	516	N516YTF	518	N518YTF	520	N520YTF

601-606

MCW Metrorider MF158/8   Metro-Cammell-Weymann B31F   1988

601	E601HTF	603	E603HTF	605	E605HTF
602	E602HTF	604	E603HTF	606	E606HTF

607-613

Optare MetroRider MR07   Optare   B25F   1991

607	J607SJB	609	J609SJB	611	J611SPB	613	H613NJB
608	J608SJB	610	J610SJB	612	J612SPB		

614-623

Optare MetroRider MR17   Optare   B25F   1994

614	M614NRD	616	L616LJM	618	L618LJM	620	L620LJM	622	M622PDP
615	L615LJM	617	L617LJM	619	L619LJM	621	M621PDP	623	M623PDP

623	M23UUA	Optare MetroRider MR17	Optare	B29F	1995	Ex demonstrator, 1995
624	N624ATF	Optare MetroRider	Optare	B25F	1996	CNG-powered
626	M930TYG	Optare MetroRider	Optare	B27F	1995	Ex demonstrator, 1995
652	E222PWY	MCW Metrorider MF150/34	Metro-Cammell-Weymann DP23F	1987	Ex Patel, Leicester, 1995
653	E223PWY	MCW Metrorider MF150/34	Metro-Cammell-Weymann DP23F	1987	Ex Patel, Leicester, 1995
701	MRD1	DAF DB250HS505	Optare Spectra	H43/28F	1992	
702	K702BBL	DAF DB250WB505	Optare Spectra	H44/27F	1992	
703	K703BBL	DAF DB250WB505	Optare Spectra	H44/27F	1992	
704	K170KYG	DAF DB250WB505	Optare Spectra	H44/27F	1992	Ex demonstrator, 1993
705	L705FRD	DAF DB250WS505	Optare Spectra	H46/28F	1994	
706	L706FRD	DAF DB250WS505	Optare Spectra	H46/28F	1994	
707	L707LJM	DAF DB250WS505	Optare Spectra	H46/28F	1994	
751	L751FRD	DAF DB250WS505	Optare Spectra	DPH37/25F	1993	
752	L752FRD	DAF DB250WS505	Optare Spectra	DPH37/25F	1994	
781	F771OJH	Volvo B10M-60	Jonckheere Jubilee P50	C53F	1989	Ex The Bee Line, 1992
784	F774OJH	Volvo B10M-60	Jonckheere Jubilee P50	C53F	1989	Ex The Bee Line, 1992
785	F755OJH	Volvo B10M-60	Jonckheere Jubilee P50	C53F	1989	Ex The Bee Line, 1992
801	K801DCF	MAN 11-180	Optare Vecta	B40F	1993	
802	K802DCF	MAN 11-180	Optare Vecta	B40F	1993	
803	K803DCF	MAN 11-190	Optare Vecta	B41F	1993	
804	K804DCF	MAN 11-190	Optare Vecta	B41F	1993	
805	K805DCF	MAN 11-190	Optare Vecta	B41F	1993	

806-814

MAN 11-190   Optare Vecta   B40F   1994-6 814 ex demonstrator, 1995

806	L806FRD	808	L808FRD	810	M810PDP	812	N812XJH	814	M957VWY
807	L807FRD	809	M809PDP	811	M811PDP	813	N813XJH		

Previous registrations
E247KCF   E475SON, MRD1   BUS5X   F220SDP

Special liveries
Gold Line: 234/5
Londonline: 82, 236/44/7/51/61/2/71/2, 751/2/84
Overall advertisements: 11/5, 72, 85, 185, 208, 508

The acquisition of services at Newbury brought a need for additional single-deckers. Leyland National 346, an 11.3metre model new in 1976, arrived from PMT in 1993. Note the shade of green used to distinguish vehicles based at Newbury. John Grubb

Reading has become a particular disciple of Optare products. No.620 is a MetroRider new in 1994, and was photographed at Hildens Drive, Tilehurst. The publicity for the limited stop service was in reaction to the introduction of a competing service by Reading Mainline. Richard Godfrey

READING MAINLINE

The Greater Reading Omnibus Co, 66 Cardiff Road, Reading, Berkshire, RG1 8LL

Reading Mainline started operations on 23rd July 1994, using Routemasters on cross-town routes from Tilehurst and Oxford Road to Whitley and Northumberland Avenue. This network has since been expanded. The venture is headed by Mike Russell, formerly Operations Manager of Reading Transport. The operating centre is at Cardiff Road, Reading.

READING MAINLINE

1- 7		AEC Routemaster	Park Royal		H36/28R	1959-64	Ex Southend, 1994
1	ALM34B	3	XVS319	5	WLT937	7	VLT44
2	WLT993	4	ALM11B	6	WLT577		

8	YTS973A	AEC Routemaster	Park Royal	H36/28R	1961	Ex Mancunian, Stretford, 1994
9	WLT790	AEC Routemaster	Park Royal	H36/28R	1961	Ex Imperial Engineering, Cheshunt (npsv), 1994
10	WYJ857	AEC Routemaster	Park Royal	H36/28R	1959	Ex Southend, 1994
11	AST416A	AEC Routemaster	Park Royal	H36/28R	1960	Ex Strathtay, 1994
12	AST415A	AEC Routemaster	Park Royal	H36/28R	1959	Ex Strathtay, 1994
13	WTS186A	AEC Routemaster	Park Royal	H36/28R	1962	Ex Strathtay, 1994
14	WLT316	AEC Routemaster	Park Royal	H36/28R	1960	Ex Strathtay, 1994
15	WVS423	AEC Routemaster	Park Royal	H36/28R	1961	Ex preservation, 1994
16	WLT621	AEC Routemaster	Park Royal	H36/28R	1960	Ex Brown, Shaftesbury, 1994
17	859DYE	AEC Routemaster	Park Royal	H36/28R	1964	Ex St John Ambulance Brigade, London SW1 (npsv), 1994
18	PVS828	AEC Routemaster	Park Royal	H36/28R	1961	Ex London General, 1995
19	XVS839	AEC Routemaster	Park Royal	H36/28R	1960	Ex South London, 1995
20	XVS830	AEC Routemaster	Park Royal	H36/28R	1959	Ex London General, 1995
21	CUV201C	AEC Routemaster	Park Royal	H36/28R	1965	Ex London United, 1995
22	XYJ440	AEC Routemaster	Park Royal	H36/28R	1961	Ex London Central, 1995
23	JFO256	AEC Routemaster	Park Royal	H36/28R	1959	Ex London United, 1995
24	MFF580	AEC Routemaster	Park Royal	H36/28R	1961	Ex London United, 1995
25	ALD990B	AEC Routemaster	Park Royal	H36/28R	1964	Ex East Yorkshire, 1995
26	NRH803A	AEC Routemaster	Park Royal	H36/28R	1961	Ex East Yorkshire, 1995
27	WTS102A	AEC Routemaster	Park Royal	H36/28R	1961	Ex Strathtay, 1995
28	XSL220A	AEC Routemaster	Park Royal	H36/28R	1959	Ex Strathtay, 1995
29	ALD948B	AEC Routemaster	Park Royal	H36/28R	1964	Ex CentreWest, 1995
30	ALM37B	AEC Routemaster	Park Royal	H36/28R	1964	Ex preservation, 1996
31	WLT938	AEC Routemaster	Park Royal	H36/28R	1961	Ex preservation, 1996

Previous registrations

AST415A	VLT45	WLT316	WLT316, WTS333A	XVS319	WLT949
AST416A	VLT191	WTS102A	WLT917	XVS830	VLT180
JFO256	VLT23, LGH31T	WTS186A	143CLT	XVS839	VLT244
MFF580	WLT931	WVS423	WLT999	XYJ440	WLT838
NRH803A	WLT871	WYJ857	VLT172	YTS973A	17CLT
PVS828	18CLT	XSL220A	VLT26		

In less than two years, Reading Mainline has assembled a fleet of thirty-one Routemasters (although not all in service yet). No.17 is a little more remarkable for having come back into psv service after a spell with the St John Ambulance Brigade.
Malcolm King

RED ROSE

Red Rose Travel, 2 Brook End, Weston Turville, Buckinghamshire, HP22 5RF

The present Red Rose firm was formed from the previous operation under the same name of T Khan, Aylesbury in February 1995. Several commercial and local authority contract routes are operated in West Hertfordshire and Buckinghamshire. Vehicles carry a livery of pale yellow with red relief.

Q956UOE	Bedford YRT	Willowbrook (1987)	B53F	1976	Ex Sussex Bus, Ford, 1992
WPH132Y	Leyland Tiger TRCTL11/2R	Eastern Coach Works B51	C53F	1982	Ex Darlington, 1995
B63APP	Ford Transit	Chassis Developments	C16F	1985	Ex Johnson, Newingreen, 1994
D814BVT	Ford Transit	Ford	14	1986	Ex untraced owner, 1991
D152VRP	Mercedes-Benz L608D	Alexander AM	B20F	1986	Ex Crosville Wales, 1995
D501MJA	Iveco Daily 49.10	Robin Hood City Nippy	B19F	1987	Ex Greater Manchester, 1992
F725MNB	Ford Transit	Mellor	B14F	1989	Ex Darlington, 1995
H733LOL	Mercedes-Benz 811D	Carlyle	B33F	1990	Ex Lunt, Olney, 1995
H389SYG	Mercedes-Benz 811D	Optare StarRider	B26F	1990	Ex demonstrator, 1991
H668ATN	Toyota Coaster HB31R	Caetano Optimo II	C21F	1990	Ex Buffalo, Flitwick, 1993
K540OGA	Mercedes-Benz 811D	Dormobile	B29F	1992	
M62MOG	Iveco Daily 59.12	Mellor	B27F	1994	
M848MOL	Iveco Daily 59.12	Mellor	B27F	1994	
N802GRV	Mercedes-Benz 709D	UVG Citi Star	B29F	1996	
N803GRV	Mercedes-Benz 709D	UVG Citi Star	B29F	1996	
N219HBK	Dennis Dart 9.8SDL3054	UVG Urban Star	B40F	1996	
N784JBM	Mercedes-Benz 711D	UVG Citi Star	B29F	1996	

Previous registrations
Q956UOE NFP735P

REG'S OF HERTFORD

Reg's Coaches Ltd, Spencer Street, Mead Lane, Hertford, SG13 7AH

Reg's Coaches of Hertford has been established in local coaching work for a considerable time. Bus operations have increased gradually since deregulation and now include routes from Hertford to the outlying communities. Fleet livery is white with dark green and black relief.

PHG186T	Leyland Leopard PSU5C/4R	Plaxton	C57F	1979	Ex Robinson, Great Harwood, 1985
YYL771T	Leyland Leopard PSU5C/4R	Duple	C50F	1979	Ex Cowie, London N16, 1985
CYH770V	Leyland Leopard PSU3E/4R	Duple	C53F	1979	Ex Cowie, London N16, 1988
NMJ289V	Bedford YMT	Duple	C53F	1980	
LVS418V	Leyland Leopard PSU5C/4R	Duple	C57F	1980	Ex Ribblesdale, Great Harwood, 1986
HHG193W	Leyland Leopard PSU5C/4R	Duple	C57F	1981	Ex Robinson, Great Harwood, 1988
LBZ7235	Bedford YNV	Duple	C57F	1987	Ex Casbon, Yaxley, 1996
LBZ2943	Leyland Tiger TRCTL11/3RZ	Plaxton	C53F	1987	Ex Shearings, Wigan, 1993
LBZ2944	Leyland Tiger TRCTL11/3RZ	Plaxton	C53F	1987	Ex Shearings, Wigan, 1993
LBZ2940	Hestair Duple 425	Duple	C51FT	1988	Ex Davies, New Broughton, 1994
LBZ2941	Dennis Javelin 12SDA1908	Plaxton	C49FT	1988	Ex Whittle, Kidderminster, 1989
LBZ2942	Dennis Javelin 12SDA1908	Plaxton	C57F	1988	Ex Whittle, Kidderminster, 1989
LBZ7234	Leyland Tiger TRCTL11/3ARZ	Duple	C53F	1989	Ex Bennett, Chieveley, 1996
G541JBV	Dennis Dart 9SDL3002	Duple	B39F	1989	Ex demonstrator, 1990
N990FNK	Mercedes-Benz 709D	Marshall C19	B27F	1995	
N991FNK	Mercedes-Benz 709D	Marshall C19	B27F	1995	
N617UEW	Dennis Dart 9.8SDL	Marshall	B40F	1996	

Named vehicles
PHG186T *Reg's European Cruiser*, NMJ 289V *Reg's Inter-Continental*, YYL771T *Reg's Caribbean Cruiser*, CYH770V *Reg's Sovereign Cruiser*, LVS418V *Reg's Panoramic Cruiser*, HHG193W *Reg's Pathfinder*, LBZ2943 *Reg's Highwayman*, LBZ2944 *Reg's Highlander*, LBZ2940 *Reg's Enterprise*, LBZ2941 *Reg's Starrider*, LBZ2942 *Reg's Starliner*, LBZ7234 *Reg's Viewfinder*, LBZ7235 *Reg's Nightingale*

Previous registrations

LBZ2940	E512AEY	LBZ2944	D594MVR
LBZ2941	E544JWP	LBZ7234	F783GNA
LBZ2942	E502JWP	LBZ7235	D35ONY
LBZ2943	D593MVR		

SAFEGUARD

Safeguard Coaches Ltd, Ridgemount Garage, Guildford Park Road, Guildford, Surrey, GU2 5CH

The fleet originated in a charabanc operation started in 1924 by Arthur Newman, a local coal merchant and haulier. A stage service in Guildford commenced in 1927.

For many years Safeguard pursued a vehicle policy based on the locally-produced Dennis chassis, though the current fleet is epitomised by Leylands and Volvos, together with two Dennis Darts. Farnham Coaches was acquired in 1988 together with a fleet of Setras, and other vehicles have since been repainted into Farnham Coaches white and purple livery, gaining private index marks. In addition to local services, the company operates a local bus service between Aldershot and Camberley during the week and school services in the surrounding areas.

The bus livery is dark red and cream, while coaches are painted cream, red and grey. The garage is at the licensed address. Farnham Coaches vehicles are kept at Odiham Road, Ewshot, Farnham.

SAFEGUARD

KUS244Y	Leyland Tiger TRCTL11/2R	Duple Dominant	B51F	1982	Ex Hutchison, Overtown, 1986
531FCG	Kässbohrer Setra S215HD	Kässbohrer Tornado	C49FT	1983	Ex Farnham Coaches, 1988
A60GPL	Mercedes-Benz L608D	Reeve Burgess	C19F	1984	
A62HPG	Leyland Tiger TRCTL11/3R	Plaxton Paramount 3200	C53F	1984	
277FCG	Kässbohrer Setra S215HR	Kässbohrer Rational	C53F	1984	Ex Farnham Coaches, 1988
C164SPB	Leyland Tiger TRBTL11/2R	Duple Dominant	B53F	1985	
538FCG	Kässbohrer Setra S215HR	Kässbohrer Rational	C49FT	1986	Ex Tourswift, Birtley, 1990
C105AFX	Volvo B10M-61	Plaxton Paramount 3200 2	C53F	1986	Ex Excelsior, Bournemouth, 1987
WPF926	Auwaerter N722/3	Plaxton Paramount 4000 3	CH53/18DT	1986	Ex Davies, Slough, 1996
D159HML	Mercedes-Benz 609D	Reeve Burgess	B20F	1987	
D633XVV	Volkswagen LT55	Optare CityPacer	B25F	1986	Ex Leicester, 1991
159FCG	Kässbohrer Setra S215HD	Kässbohrer Tornado	C47FT	1987	Ex Farnham Coaches, 1988
E297OMG	Leyland Lynx LX112L10ZR1R	Leyland	B49F	1988	
E298OMG	Leyland Lynx LX112L10ZR1R	Leyland	B49F	1988	
E169OMU	Volvo B10M-61	Duple 340	C49FT	1988	Ex P Kavanagh, Urlingford, 1996
F296RMH	Volvo B10M-46	Plaxton Paramount 3200 3	C39F	1988	
F623FNA	Mercedes-Benz 609D	Made-to-Measure	B24F	1988	Ex Berry, Stockton, 1994
515FCG	Kässbohrer Setra S215HD	Kässbohrer Tornado	C49F	1989	Ex Ebdon, Sidcup, 1994
F474WFX	Volvo B10M-60	Plaxton Paramount 3200 3	C53F	1989	Ex Excelsior, Bournemouth, 1989
F488UPB	Volvo B10M-60	Plaxton Paramount 3200 3	C53F	1989	Ex Excelsior, Bournemouth, 1989
DSK558	Volvo B10M-60	Plaxton Paramount 3500 3	C53F	1989	Ex Wallace Arnold, 1992
G122KUB	Mercedes-Benz 811D	Optare StarRider	C29F	1989	Ex Brents, Watford, 1993
DSK559	Volvo B10M-60	Plaxton Paramount 3500 3	C53F	1990	Ex Wallace Arnold, 1993
G514EFX	Volvo B10M-60	Plaxton Paramount 3200 3	C53F	1990	Ex Excelsior, Bournemouth, 1991
G520EFX	Volvo B10M-60	Plaxton Paramount 3200 3	C53F	1990	Ex Excelsior, Bournemouth, 1991
DSK560	Volvo B10M-60	Plaxton Paramount 3500 3	C53F	1990	Ex Wallace Arnold, 1993
H672ATN	Toyota HB31R	Caetano Optimo II	C21F	1990	Ex Rose, Broadway, 1992
196FCG	Volvo B10M-60	Plaxton Première 350	C48FT	1992	Ex Wallace Arnold, 1995
247FCG	Volvo B10M-60	Plaxton Première 350	C50F	1992	Ex Wallace Arnold, 1995
K628YPL	Dennis Dart 9.8SDL3025	Plaxton Pointer	B40F	1993	
L265EPD	Dennis Dart 9.8SDL3035	Plaxton Pointer	B40F	1994	
M296THD	Mercedes-Benz	Plaxton Beaver	B25F	1995	Acquired 1995
N561UPF	Dennis Javelin	Plaxton Pointer	C49FT	1996	
N562UPF	Dennis Javelin	Plaxton Pointer	C53F	1996	

Previous registrations

DSK558	F437DUG		196FCG	J705CWT
DSK559	G540LWU		247FCG	J745CWT
DSK560	G515LWU		515FCG	F830NNF
E169OMU	E169OMU, 88KK2240		531FCG	APA672Y
F488UPB	196FCG		538FCG	C665UPJ, DSK559
WPF926	SWN159, C358KEP			

Special liveries
Farnham Coaches: B906SPR, C105AFX, 159FCG, 277FCG, 515FCG, 531FCG, F488UPB, G122KUB, 538FCG, N562UPF
Globus Gateway: 196FCG, 247FCG, N561UPF

In addition to their local bus work, Red Rose maintain a small amount of coaching. H668ATN is a Toyota Coaster of 1990 with Caetano bodywork, seen in Watford in July 1996. Capital Transport

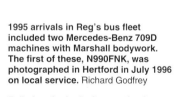

1995 arrivals in Reg's bus fleet included two Mercedes-Benz 709D machines with Marshall bodywork. The first of these, N990FNK, was photographed in Hertford in July 1996 on local service. Richard Godfrey

Full-size single-deck operation is now in the hands of Dennis Darts. N617UEW, with Marshall bodywork, was new in 1996 and photographed at Tewin in July 1996. Note how the livery is varied on the dealer white base, compared with the vehicle above. Richard Godfrey

Safeguard's L265EPD is a Dennis Dart of 1994 with Plaxton Pointer bodywork, captured at Park Barn, Southway within a few months of entering service. Richard Godfrey

Not an over-common sight, C164SPB combines a Leyland Tiger bus chassis with Duple Dominant bus bodywork. Dating from 1985, it was photographed in June 1996. Malc McDonald

SEAMARKS

Seamarks Coach and Travel Ltd, Seamarks House, 387-397 Dunstable Road, Luton, LU4 8BY

Seamarks Coach and Travel Ltd has been a major figure in the coaching scene of Bedfordshire for many years, operating a fleet of high-quality vehicles. Hertfordshire County Council contracts were gained in March 1989 for two routes, and other routes have been obtained since. An initial collection of buses hired from Hyndburn Transport has been gradually replaced by more modern vehicles, most of them bodied by Optare. Fleet livery is white with green relief.

Seamarks operate four Optare Deltas (as well as four Vectas) on their bus routes. No.219, new in 1989, was caught at Borehamwood Station in May 1995 showing the more elaborate form of livery applied to these types. Tony Smethers

The newest vehicle in the Seamarks fleet is No.232, a Mercedes-Benz 709D with Marshall bodywork, new in 1995. In February 1996 it was photographed on a Hertfordshire County Council contract service in Watford. Colin Lloyd

SEAMARKS

182	EPP819Y	Bova Europa EL26/581	Bova	C53F	1982	
183	2267MK	Kässbohrer Setra S215HD	Kässbohrer	C49FT	1982	
192	HRO982V	Bedford YMT	Duple	C53F	1979	Ex Kirby, High Wycombe, 1983
197	2917MK	Kässbohrer Setra S215H	Kässbohrer	C53F	1984	
198	Q684LPP	Kässbohrer Setra S215HU	Kässbohrer	C49FT	1984	
199	9569KM	Kässbohrer Setra S215H	Kässbohrer	C53F	1984	
200	MJI7855	Kässbohrer Setra S215H	Kässbohrer	C53F	1984	
201	MJI7856	Kässbohrer Setra S215H	Kässbohrer	C53F	1984	
202	MJI7857	Kässbohrer Setra S215H	Kässbohrer	C53F	1984	
205	B817BPP	Volvo B10M-61	Plaxton	C57F	1985	
206	MJI8660	Volvo B10M-61	Plaxton	C57F	1985	
207	MJI8661	Volvo B10M-61	Plaxton	C57F	1985	
208	MJI8662	Volvo B10M-61	Plaxton	C53F	1985	
209	MJI8663	Volvo B10M-61	Plaxton	C53F	1985	
210	25CTM	Volvo C10M-70	Ramseier & Jenzer	C49FT	1985	
211	MJI7854	Volvo B10M-61	Caetano	C53F	1985	
214	F791DWT	DAF SB220LC550	Optare Delta	B47F	1989	
215	F370BUA	DAF SB220LC550	Optare Delta	B51F	1988	Ex demonstrator, 1989
219	G971TTM	DAF SB220LC550	Optare Delta	B47F	1989	
220	G278WKX	DAF SB220LC550	Optare Delta	B47F	1989	
225	J208RVS	Optare MetroRider	Optare	DP31F	1992	
226	H846UUA	MAN 11-190	Optare Vecta	B41F	1991	Ex demonstrator, 1992
228	D81NWW	Volkswagen LT55	Optare City Pacer	B25F	1987	Ex Lancaster, 1992
229	J367BNW	MAN 11-190	Optare Vecta	B41F	1992	Ex demonstrator, 1993
230	L834MWT	MAN 11-190	Optare Vecta	B40F	1993	Ex demonstrator, 1994
231	M702RVS	MAN 11-190	Optare Vecta	B40F	1994	
232	M231SGS	Mercedes-Benz 709D	Marshall	B27F	1995	
	6101MV	Volvo C10M-70	Ramseier & Jenzer	C49F	1986	Ex Park, Hamilton, 1991
	9683ML	Volvo C10M-70	Ramseier & Jenzer	C49F	1986	Ex Park, Hamilton, 1991

Previous registrations

B817BPP	B541BMH, 9683ML		MJI8661	B543BMH	
HRO982V	GTM141T		MJI8662	B544BMH	
MJI7854	B455AUR		MJI8663	B545BMH	
MJI7855	B265XNK		9569KM	A531STM	
MJI7856	B266XNK		2917MK	A608RNM	
MJI7857	B267XNK		9683ML	C345GSD	
MJI8660	B542BMH		6101MV	C651KDS	

THE SHIRES

LDT Ltd, Castle Street, Luton, LU1 3AJ

Trading as Luton & Dunstable, Aylesbury & The Vale, Hitchin & District, The Stevenage Line, Chiltern Rover, Network Watford, Gade Valley, Elstree & Borehamwood, and with Green Line and Jetlink operations, The Shires emanates from the former Luton & District and London Country North West fleets. The latter was taken over by the former in October 1990, and has acquired a number of other local operators subsequently, including Stuart Palmer of Dunstable in October 1994, Buffalo Bus of Flitwick in May 1995 and Motts (Yellow Bus) of Aylesbury in July 1995. Vehicles acquired from these operators have added an eclectic element to a varied fleet, including Leyland Swifts, more Iveco minibuses and Bristol VRTs, and a quantity of Volvo coaches.

Luton & District had been taken over by British Bus in July 1994, and passed (with other members of the group) to the ownership of the Cowie Group in June 1996. The present local marketing names were introduced in April 1995, coupled with the adoption of the present registered name and a new livery of blue and yellow with a grey skirt. This livery has rapidly replaced the former Brunswick green and cargo grey of the LCNW-inherited fleet and the red and cream of the L&D area. A dual fleet numbering system remains in place, however, with letter prefixes in use for vehicles based at former LCNW sites.

The fleet now operates from depots at Aylesbury, Dunstable, Hemel Hempstead, High Wycombe, Hitchin, Luton, Stevenage and Watford, with outstations at Amersham and Leighton Buzzard.

Four Leyland Olympians bodied by Northern Counties on 11-metre chassis in 1989 for Ensign's found their way into the fleet by various means within two years. The extra length of LRL32 is apparent in this unusual appearance on Green Line work in Buckingham Palace Road in June 1995, when the livery was still very new. Colin Lloyd

THE SHIRES

AN165 XPG165T	Leyland Atlantean AN68A/1R	Park Royal		H43/30F	1978	Ex London Country North West, 1990

AN233-243 Leyland Atlantean AN68B/1R Roe   H43/39F 1980   Ex London Country North West, 1990

AN233 JPE233V		**AN236** JPE236V		**AN241** KPJ241W	**AN242** KPJ242W	**AN243** KPJ243W

AN245 TRN477V	Leyland Atlantean AN68A/1R	Eastern Coach Works	H43/31F	1980	Ex Ribble, 1994
BTL47 C147SPE	Leyland Tiger TRCTL11/3RH	Berkhof Everest 370	C53F	1986	Ex London Country North West, 1986
BTL48 C148SPE	Leyland Tiger TRCTL11/3RH	Berkhof Everest 370	C53F	1986	Ex London Country North West, 1986
BTL49 C149SPE	Leyland Tiger TRCTL11/3RH	Berkhof Everest 370	C53F	1986	Ex London Country North West, 1986

DC1-8 Dennis Dart 9.8SDL3004   Carlyle   B40F* 1991 * DC8 is DP39F

DC1 H922LOX	**DC3** H925LOX	**DC5** H242MUK	**DC7** H244MUK
DC2 H923LOX	**DC4** H926LOX	**DC6** H243MUK	**DC8** H245MUK

DC14 K447XPA	Dennis Dart 9.8SDL3017	Plaxton Pointer	B40F	1992	Ex Buffalo, Flitwick, 1995
DC15 K448XPA	Dennis Dart 9.8SDL3017	Plaxton Pointer	B40F	1992	Ex Buffalo, Flitwick, 1995
DE171 P671OPP	Dennis Dart SLF	East Lancs Spryte	B41F	1996	
DE172 P672OPP	Dennis Dart SLF	East Lancs Spryte	B41F	1996	
DE173 P673OPP	Dennis Dart SLF	East Lancs Spryte	B41F	1996	
DE174 P674OPP	Dennis Dart SLF	East Lancs Spryte	B41F	1996	
DT358 RDS83W	Volvo B58-56	Duple	B53F	1980	Ex Buffalo, Flitwick, 1995
DT359 RDS84W	Volvo B58-56	Duple	B53F	1980	Ex Buffalo, Flitwick, 1995

DW9-13 Dennis Dart 9.8SDL3054   Wright Handybus   B40F 1994

DW9 M247SPP	**DW10** M248SPP	**DW11** M249SPP	**DW12** M250SPP	**DW13** M251SPP

LN491 GNV658N	Leyland National 11351/1R		B49F	1974	Ex United Counties, 1986
LNB493 GNV660N	Leyland National 11351/1R		B49F	1974	Ex United Counties, 1986
LNB498 GVV889N	Leyland National 11351/1R		B49F	1974	Ex United Counties, 1986
LNG532 IAZ4037	Leyland National 11351A/1R	DAF engine, Volvo badge	B49F	1977	Ex United Counties, 1986
LR33 A698EAU	Leyland Olympian ONTL11/1R	Northern Counties	H47/33D	1984	Ex Buffalo, Flitwick, 1995
LR34 A699EAU	Leyland Olympian ONTL11/1R	Northern Counties	H47/33D	1984	Ex Buffalo, Flitwick, 1995
LR35 F506OYW	Leyland Olympian ONTL11/1RH	Northern Counties	H47/30F	1988	Ex Mott, Stoke Mandeville, 1995

LR49-55 Leyland Olympian ONTL11/1R Roe   H43/29F 1984   Ex London Country North West, 1990

LR49 A149FPG	**LR52** A152FPG	**LR54** A154FPG	
LR51 A151FPG	**LR53** A153FPG	**LR55** A155FPG	

LR70 B270LPH	Leyland Olympian ONTL11/1R	Eastern Coach Works	H43/29F	1985	Ex London Country North West, 1990
LR71 B271LPH	Leyland Olympian ONTL11/1R	Eastern Coach Works	H43/29F	1985	Ex London Country North West, 1990
LR72 B272LPH	Leyland Olympian ONTL11/1R	Eastern Coach Works	H43/29F	1985	Ex London Country North West, 1990
LR73 B273LPH	Leyland Olympian ONTL11/1R	Eastern Coach Works	H43/29F	1985	Ex London Country North West, 1990

LR81-95 Leyland Olympian ONCL10/1RZ Leyland   H47/31F 1989/90 Ex London Country North West, 1990

LR81 G281UMJ	**LR84** G284UMJ	**LR87** G287UMJ	**LR90** G290UMJ	**LR93** G293UMJ
LR82 G282UMJ	**LR85** G285UMJ	**LR88** G288UMJ	**LR91** G291UMJ	**LR94** G294UMJ
LR83 G283UMJ	**LR86** G286UMJ	**LR89** G289UMJ	**LR92** G292UMJ	**LR95** G295UMJ

LR96-102 Leyland Olympian ON2R50C13Z4 Leyland   H47/29F 1991

LR96 H196GRO	**LR98** H198GRO	**LR100** H201GRO	**LR102** H203GRO
LR97 H197GRO	**LR99** H199GRO	**LR101** H202GRO	

LR103 F747XCS	Leyland Olympian ONCL10/1RZ	Alexander RL	H47/32F	1989	Ex McMenemy, Ardrossan, 1995
LR104 IAZ2314	Leyland Olympian ONLXB/1R	Eastern Coach Works	H45/32F	1982	Ex Rhondda, 1995
LR634 F634LMJ	Leyland Olympian ONCL10/1RZ	Alexander RL	H47/32F	1988	
LR642 F642LMJ	Leyland Olympian ONCL10/1RZ	Alexander RL	H47/32F	1988	
LRL29 G129YEV	Leyland Olympian ONCL10/1RZ	Northern Counties	H49/34F	1989	Ex London Country North West, 1990
LRL30 G130YEV	Leyland Olympian ONCL10/1RZ	Northern Counties	H49/34F	1989	Ex London Country North West, 1990
LRL31 G131YWC	Leyland Olympian ONCL10/1RZ	Northern Counties	H49/34F	1989	Ex Ensign, Purfleet, 1991
LRL32 G132YWC	Leyland Olympian ONCL10/1RZ	Northern Counties	H49/34F	1989	Ex London Country North West, 1990
MBI63 D23RPP	Iveco Daily 49.10	Robin Hood	B21F	1987	Ex London Country North West, 1990

The newest double-deckers in the fleet are ten Volvo Olympians with Northern Counties bodies delivered during the early summer of 1996. ONO37, with Luton & Dunstable fleetnames, poses for the camera in July 1996.
Capital Transport

Right **Other Olympians derive from the former Luton & District fleet, including No.643, new in 1988 with Alexander bodywork. This shot was taken in Watford in July 1996.**
Capital Transport

Most of the earlier Leyland Olympians which were passed from the former London Country North West fleet are based at Watford. LR52, new in 1984, has Roe bodywork, and shows the Network Watford branding now applied locally.
Capital Transport

With the acquisition of the Buffalo, Flitwick bus fleet in 1995 came a motley collection of vehicles, including LR34, a Leyland Olympian of 1984 with Northern Counties dual-door bodywork, showing the local identity of Aylesbury & the Vale in July 1996. Colin Brown

MCW1-30 MCW Metrorider MF150/81* Metro-Cammell-Weymann B23F 1988 Ex London Country North West, 1990
* MCW19-30 are MF150/83

MCW1 E971DNK	**MCW7** E977DNK	**MCW15** E985DNK	**MCW21** E991DNK	**MCW27** E997DNK
MCW2 E972DNK	**MCW8** E978DNK	**MCW16** E986DNK	**MCW22** E992DNK	**MCW28** E998DNK
MCW3 E973DNK	**MCW9** E979DNK	**MCW17** E987DNK	**MCW23** E993DNK	**MCW29** E999DNK
MCW4 E974DNK	**MCW10** E980DNK	**MCW18** E988DNK	**MCW24** E994DNK	**MCW30** E731DNM
MCW5 E975DNK	**MCW11** E981DNK	**MCW19** E989DNK	**MCW25** E995DNK	
MCW6 E976DNK	**MCW14** E984DNK	**MCW20** E990DNK	**MCW26** E996DNK	

MCW31 E478CNM	MCW Metrorider MF150/74	Metro-Cammell-Weymann	B23F	1988	Ex Sovereign, 1990
MCW32 E479CNM	MCW Metrorider MF150/72	Metro-Cammell-Weymann	B23F	1988	Ex Sovereign, 1990
MCW33 E486CNM	MCW Metrorider MF150/74	Metro-Cammell-Weymann	B23F	1988	Ex Sovereign, 1990
MCW34 E484CNM	MCW Metrorider MF150/72	Metro-Cammell-Weymann	B23F	1988	Ex Sovereign, 1990
ML18 L326AUT	Mercedes-Benz 709D	Leicester Carriage Builders	B25F	1994	Ex Midland Fox, 1994
ML19 L327AUT	Mercedes-Benz 709D	Leicester Carriage Builders	B25F	1994	Ex Midland Fox, 1994
ML20 L328AUT	Mercedes-Benz 709D	Leicester Carriage Builders	B25F	1994	Ex Midland Fox, 1994

MP38-59 Mercedes-Benz 709D Plaxton B27F 1996

MP38 N368JGS	**MP42** N372JGS	**MP51** N381JGS	**MP55** N385JGS	**MP59** N367JGS
MP39 N369JGS	**MP43** N373JGS	**MP52** N382JGS	**MP56** N386JGS	
MP40 N370JGS	**MP44** N374JGS	**MP53** N383JGS	**MP57** N387JGS	
MP41 N371JGS	**MP50** N380JGS	**MP54** N384JGS	**MP58** N366JGS	

MP257-270 Mercedes-Benz 709D Plaxton B27F* 1995 * MP269 is DP27F

MP257 N907ETM	**MP260** N910ETM	**MP263** N913ETM	**MP266** N916ETM	**MP269** N919ETM
MP258 N908ETM	**MP261** N911ETM	**MP264** N914ETM	**MP267** N917ETM	**MP270** N920ETM
MP259 N909ETM	**MP262** N912ETM	**MP265** N915ETM	**MP268** N918ETM	

MP271 J65UNA Mercedes-Benz 709D Plaxton B23F 1992 Ex South Lancashire, St Helens, 1996

ONO36-45 Volvo Olympian YN2RV18Z4 NC Countybus Palatine I H47/30F 1996

ONO36 N36JPP	**ONO38** N38JPP	**ONO40** N46JPP	**ONO42** N42JPP	**ONO44** N35JPP
ONO37 N37JPP	**ONO39** N39JPP	**ONO41** N41JPP	**ONO43** N43JPP	**ONO45** N45JPP

SE701-720 Scania L113CRL East Lancs Cityzen DP49F* 1995 * SE717-20 are B51F

SE701 N701EUR	**SE705** N705EUR	**SE709** N709EUR	**SE717** N28KGS
SE702 N702EUR	**SE706** N706EUR	**SE710** N710EUR	**SE718** N29KGS
SE703 N703EUR	**SE707** N707EUR	**SE711** N711EUR	**SE719** N31KGS
SE704 N704EUR	**SE708** N708EUR	**SE712** N712EUR	**SE720** N32KGS

SNB328 UPB328S Leyland National 10351A/1R B41F 1977 Ex London Country North West, 1990

SNB405-523 Leyland National 10351B/1R B41F 1978/9 Ex London Country North West, 1990

SNB405 YPL405T	**SNB436** YPL436T	**SNB465** BPL465T	**SNB523** EPD523V
SNB418 YPL418T	**SNB449** YPL449T	**SNB521** EPD521V	

SNG524 IIL4821	Leyland National 10351/1R/SC	East Lancs (1993)	B41F	1974	Ex Crosville Wales, 1995
SNG525 IIL4822	Leyland National 10351/1R/SC	East Lancs (1993)	B41F	1976	Ex Crosville Wales, 1995
SNG526 IIL4823	Leyland National 10351/1R	East Lancs (1993)	B41F	1978	Ex Crosville Wales, 1995
SNG527 IIL4824	Leyland National 10351/1R	East Lancs (1993)	B41F	1975	Ex Crosville Wales, 1995
SNG528 BAZ6869	Leyland National 10351B/1R	East Lancs (1994)	B41F	1979	Ex Crosville Wales, 1995
SNG529 RJI6861	Leyland National 10351B/1R	East Lancs (1994)	B41F	1979	Ex Crosville Wales, 1995
SNG534 TIB4886	Leyland National 10351/1R/SC	East Lancs (1993)	B41F	1975	Ex Crosville Wales, 1995
SNG535 RJI6862	Leyland National 10351B/1R	East Lancs (1994)	B41F	1979	Ex Crosville Wales, 1995
SNG536 TIB4873	Leyland National 10351B/1R	East Lancs (1993)	B41F	1979	Ex Crosville Wales, 1995
SNG540 BTX152T	Leyland National 10351A/2R	East Lancs (1994)	B44F	1979	Ex Parfitt, Rhymney, 1995
SNG543 CAZ6852	Leyland National 10351B/1R	East Lancs (1994)	B41F	1978	Ex Crosville Wales, 1995
SNG544 TIB7835	Leyland National 10351B/1R	East Lancs (1994)	B41F	1979	Ex Crosville Wales, 1995
STL201 SIB8529	Leyland Tiger TRCL10/3ARZA	Plaxton	C51FT	1988	Ex London Country North West, 1990
STL202 SIB7480	Leyland Tiger TRCL10/3ARZA	Plaxton	C51FT	1988	Ex London Country North West, 1990
STL203 SIB7481	Leyland Tiger TRCL10/3ARZA	Plaxton	C51FT	1988	Ex London Country North West, 1990
TP13 A113EPA	Leyland Tiger TRCTL11/2RH	Plaxton	C53F	1983	Ex London Country North West, 1990

TPL50-57 Leyland Tiger TRCTL11/3R Plaxton Paramount 3200Exp C53F* 1984 Ex London Country North West, 1990
* TPL50 is C51F; TPL52/7 are C57F

TPL50 A150EPA	**TPL52** A152EPA	**TPL55** A155EPA	
TPL51 A151EPA	**TPL53** A153EPA	**TPL57** A157EPA	

TPL92	B292KPF	Leyland Tiger TRCTL11/3RH	Plaxton Paramount 3200 2	C51F	1985	Ex London Country North West, 1990		
TPL93	B293KPF	Leyland Tiger TRCTL11/3RH	Plaxton Paramount 3200 2	C51F	1985	Ex London Country North West, 1990		
TPL98	E323OMG	Leyland Tiger TRCTL11/3ARZA	Plaxton Paramount 3200 3	C53F	1988	Ex London Country North West, 1990		
VC198	H198AOD	Volvo B10M-60	Plaxton Expressliner	C50FT	1991	Ex Trathens, Plymouth, 1996		
VC199	H199AOD	Volvo B10M-60	Plaxton Expressliner	C50FT	1991	Ex Trathens, Plymouth, 1996		

VN310-327 Volvo B6-50   NC Countybus Paladin B40F 1994

VN310	L310HPP	**VN314**	L314HPP	**VN318**	M718OMJ	**VN322**	M722OMJ	**VN326** M726OMJ
VN311	L311HPP	**VN315**	L315HPP	**VN319**	M719OMJ	**VN323**	M723OMJ	**VN327** M727OMJ
VN312	L312HPP	**VN316**	L316HPP	**VN320**	M720OMJ	**VN324**	M724OMJ	
VN313	L313HPP	**VN317**	M717OMJ	**VN321**	M721OMJ	**VN325**	M725OMJ	

VN338	L922LJO	Volvo B6-50	NC Countybus Paladin	B40F	1994	Ex Mott, Stoke Mandeville, 1995
VN339	L923LJO	Volvo B6-50	NC Countybus Paladin	B40F	1994	Ex Mott, Stoke Mandeville, 1995
VR917	IAZ3977	Bristol VRT/SL3/501	Eastern Coach Works	H43/31F	1977	Ex South Wales, 1987
01	K8BUS	Mercedes-Benz 811D	Wright	B33F	1992	Ex Patterson, Birmingham, 1995
02	K580YOJ	Mercedes-Benz 811D	Wright	B33F	1992	Ex Patterson, Birmingham, 1995
03	H35DGD	Mercedes-Benz 811D	Dormobile	B33F	1991	Ex Pathfinder, Newark, 1995
04	G896TGG	Mercedes-Benz 811D	Reeve Burgess	B33F	1989	Ex Stevensons, Uttoxeter, 1995

6-11 Mercedes-Benz 709D   Reeve Burgess   B25F   1988   Ex Kentish Bus (6, 7, 9) or Metrobus, Orpington (8, 10/1), 1991

6	F121TRU	**8**	F123TRU	**10**	F125TRU	
7	F122TRU	**9**	F124TRU	**11**	F128TRU	

12	J917HGD	Mercedes-Benz 709D	Dormobile	B29F	1991	Ex Clydeside 2000, 1992
13	H848AUS	Mercedes-Benz 709D	Dormobile	B29F	1991	Ex Clydeside 2000, 1992
14	F598CET	Mercedes-Benz 609D	Reeve Burgess	C25F	1988	Ex Clydeside 2000, 1992

15-21 Mercedes-Benz 609D   Made-to-Measure   B24F   1992   Ex Birmingham Omnibus, Tividale, 1995

15	K25WND	**17**	K27WND	**19**	K29WND	**21**	K32WND	
16	K26WND	**18**	K28WND	**20**	K31WND			

23	H408BVR	Mercedes-Benz 709D	Reeve Burgess	B25F	1990	Ex Arrowline, Knutsford, 1995
24	H409BVR	Mercedes-Benz 709D	Reeve Burgess	B25F	1990	Ex Arrowline, Knutsford, 1995
25	K579YOJ	Mercedes-Benz 709D	Dormobile	B29F	1993	Ex Patterson, Birmingham, 1995
26	K543OGA	Mercedes-Benz 709D	Dormobile	B29F	1992	Ex Midland Fox, 1995
27	H641UWE	Mercedes-Benz 811D	Whittaker	B31F	1991	Ex Buffalo, Flitwick, 1995
28	H614CGG	Mercedes-Benz 709D	Dormobile	B33F	1991	Ex Pathfinder, Newark, 1995
29	K578YOJ	Mercedes-Benz 709D	Dormobile	B29F	1993	Ex Patterson, Birmingham, 1995
30	K202FEH	Mercedes-Benz 709D	Dormobile	B27F	1993	Ex Stevensons, Uttoxeter, 1995
31	K203FEH	Mercedes-Benz 709D	Dormobile	B27F	1993	Ex Stevensons, Uttoxeter, 1995
32	H642UWE	Mercedes-Benz 811D	Whittaker	B31F	1991	Ex Buffalo, Flitwick, 1995
33	G58BEL	Mercedes-Benz 811D	Wadham Stringer	DP31F	1989	Ex Buffalo, Flitwick, 1995
34	H231KBH	Mercedes-Benz 709D	Carlyle	B27F	1991	Ex Buffalo, Flitwick, 1995
36	H523SWE	Mercedes-Benz 709D	Whittaker	B29F	1990	Ex Rhondda, 1995

45-49 Mercedes-Benz 709D   Plaxton   B27F   1996

45	N375JGS	**46**	N376JGS	**47**	N377JGS	**48**	N378JGS	**49** N379JGS

69-76 Iveco Daily 49.10   Dormobile   B25F   1988

69	E335DRO	**70**	E341DRO	**73**	E344DRO	**75**	E346DRO	**76** E347DRO

106	E64BVS	Iveco Daily 49.10	Robin Hood	B25F	1988	Ex East Midland, 1994
107	E66BVS	Iveco Daily 49.10	Robin Hood	B25F	1988	Ex United Counties, 1994

109-113 Leyland Tiger TRCTL11/3ARZ Plaxton   C53F   1988

109	E881YKY	**110**	E882YKY	**111**	E661AWJ	**112**	E662AWJ	**113** E663AWJ

143	A143EPA	Leyland Tiger TRCTL11/3R	Plaxton Paramount 3200	C51F	1984	Ex London Country North West, 1990

150-160 Iveco Daily 59.12   Marshall   B27F   1994

150	M150RBH	**152**	M152RBH	**154**	M154RBH	**157**	M157RBH	**159** M159RBH
151	M151RBH	**153**	M153RBH	**156**	M156RBH	**158**	M158RBH	**160** M160RBH

A total of twenty-seven Scania L113 low-floor buses with East Lancs bodywork have so far joined the fleet. No.716 arrives in Watford on the trunk route from Aylesbury. Capital Transport

No fewer than 32 Volvo B6s with Northern Counties Countybus Paladin bodywork joined the fleet in 1994 to replace older Leyland Nationals. No.306 forms part of the contingent now based in the Hitchin & District fleet, and was caught at Stevenage in June 1996. Tony Wilson

The Shires have acquired all of Crosville Wales's fleet of Leyland Nationals rebuilt to Greenway specification by East Lancs. SNG529, lacking its class prefix on the vehicle, was seen in High Wycombe in July 1995 freshly-repainted into Chiltern Rover livery. Colin Lloyd

Eight Dennis Darts were bodied by Carlyle in 1991 for contract routes in the Watford and Hemel Hempstead areas. DC3, recently repainted into the new livery, comes into Watford in July 1996. Capital Transport

Leyland Lynxes entered the fleet in 1989 with a batch of five new vehicles, represented by No.404 at Stevenage in May 1996. Note how the local fleetname is more stylised than in the versions used elsewhere. Colin Lloyd

The 1995 minibus replacement programme was centred around Mercedes-Benz 709D units with Plaxton bodywork. MP261, in Elstree & Borehamwood livery, was working on Sunday route W4 in Watford during the summer of 1996. Capital Transport

164	F634UEF	Iveco Daily 49.10	Carlyle	B23F	1989	Ex OK, Bishop Auckland, 1994
169	L863BEA	Iveco Daily 59.12	Marshall C29	B23F	1993	Ex Buffalo, Flitwick, 1995
170	L864BEA	Iveco Daily 59.12	Marshall C29	B23F	1993	Ex Buffalo, Flitwick, 1995
171	F985GKJ	Iveco Daily 49.10	Robin Hood	B25F	1990	Ex Buffalo, Flitwick, 1995
172	MBZ6455	Iveco Daily 49.10	Carlyle	B25F	1988	Ex Buffalo, Flitwick, 1995
173	F969GKJ	Iveco Daily 49.10	Robin Hood	B21F	1990	Ex Buffalo, Flitwick, 1995
174	F287FLG	Iveco Daily 49.10	Carlyle	B23F	1988	Ex Buffalo, Flitwick, 1995
175	K184GDU	Mercedes-Benz 811D	Wright	B31F	1993	Ex Mott, Stoke Mandeville, 1995
176	J171GGG	Mercedes-Benz 709D	Dormobile	B29F	1991	Ex Mott, Stoke Mandeville, 1995
177	G360FOP	Mercedes-Benz 709D	Carlyle	B25F	1989	Ex Mott, Stoke Mandeville, 1995
178	M38WUR	Mercedes-Benz 811D	Plaxton	B31F	1995	
179	M39WUR	Mercedes-Benz 811D	Plaxton	B31F	1995	
180	M41WUR	Mercedes-Benz 811D	Plaxton	B31F	1995	
181	M42WUR	Mercedes-Benz 811D	Plaxton	B31F	1995	

182-190
Mercedes-Benz 709D · Plaxton · B27F · 1995

182	M43WUR	184	M46WUR	186	N186EMJ	188	N188EMJ	190	N190EMJ
183	M45WUR	185	M47WUR	187	N187EMJ	189	N189EMJ		

192	GIL6523	Volvo B10M-61	Plaxton	C50F	1987	Ex Moor-Dale, Newcastle, 1994
193	GIL6949	Volvo B10M-61	Plaxton	C50F	1987	Ex Moor-Dale, Newcastle, 1994
194	HIL7594	Volvo B10M-61	Plaxton	C53F	1988	Ex Moor-Dale, Newcastle, 1994
195	HIL7595	Volvo B10M-61	Plaxton	C53F	1988	Ex Moor-Dale, Newcastle, 1994
196	HIL7597	Volvo B10M-61	Plaxton	C53F	1988	Ex Moor-Dale, Newcastle, 1994
204	SIB4846	Leyland Tiger TRCTL11/3ARZA	Plaxton	C53F	1988	Ex London Country North West, 1990

251-256
Mercedes-Benz 709D · Plaxton · B27F · 1995

251	N191EMJ	253	N193EMJ	255	N195EMJ
252	N192EMJ	254	N194EMJ	256	N196EMJ

257	H407FGS	Mercedes-Benz 811D	Reeve Burgess	B31F	1991	Ex Sovereign, 1996
258	H408FGS	Mercedes-Benz 811D	Reeve Burgess	B31F	1991	Ex Sovereign, 1996
259	H406FGS	Mercedes-Benz 811D	Reeve Burgess	B31F	1990	Ex Sovereign, 1996
300	F300MNK	Leyland Swift LBM6T/2RAO	Wadham Stringer	B35F	1989	
301	F301MNK	Leyland Swift LBM6T/2RAO	Wadham Stringer	B35F	1989	
302	F302MNK	Leyland Swift LBM6T/2RAO	Wadham Stringer	B35F	1989	
303	F303MNK	Leyland Swift LBM6T/2RAO	Wadham Stringer	B35F	1989	
304	G97VMM	Leyland Swift LBM6T/2RS	Wadham Stringer	B39F	1989	Ex London Country North West, 1990

305-336
Volvo B6-50 · NC Countybus Paladin · B40F · 1994

305	L305HPP	308	L308HPP	329	M729OMJ	332	M712OMJ	335	M715OMJ
306	L306HPP	309	L309HPP	330	M710OMJ	333	M713OMJ	336	M716OMJ
307	L307HPP	328	M728OMJ	331	M711OMJ	334	M714OMJ		

337	L43MEH	Volvo B6-50	Plaxton Pointer	B40F	1994	Ex Stevensons, Uttoxeter, 1994
350	L133HVS	Volvo B10B-58	Alexander AF	B50F	1993	Ex Buffalo, Flitwick, 1995
351	F314RMH	Volvo B10M-56	Plaxton	B54F	1988	Ex Buffalo, Flitwick, 1995
352	F151KGS	Volvo B10M-56	Plaxton	B54F	1988	Ex Buffalo, Flitwick, 1995
353	F152KGS	Volvo B10M-56	Plaxton	B54F	1988	Ex Buffalo, Flitwick, 1995
354	F153KGS	Volvo B10M-56	Plaxton	B54F	1988	Ex Buffalo, Flitwick, 1995
355	NIB8459	Volvo B10M-61	East Lancs (1991)	B55F	1988	Ex Buffalo, Flitwick, 1995
356	MBZ6454	Volvo B10M-61	East Lancs (1991)	B55F	1985	Ex Buffalo, Flitwick, 1995
357	HIL7467	Volvo B10M-61	East Lancs (1991)	B55F	1983	Ex Buffalo, Flitwick, 1995
360	GHB574V	Volvo B58-56	East Lancs	B53F	1980	Ex Parfitt, Rhymney, 1995

400-404
Leyland Lynx LX112L10ZR1R · Leyland · B51F · 1989

400	F400PUR	401	F401PUR	402	F402PUR	403	F403PUR	404	F404PUR

405	D603ACW	Leyland Lynx LX112L10ZR1	Leyland	B51F	1987	Ex Sovereign, 1990
406	E970NMK	Leyland Lynx LX112TL11ZR1	Leyland	B49F	1987	Ex Sovereign, 1990
407	H407ERO	Leyland Lynx LX2R11C15Z4R	Leyland	DP45F	1990	
408	H408ERO	Leyland Lynx LX2R11C15Z4R	Leyland	DP45F	1990	
409	H409ERO	Leyland Lynx LX2R11C15Z4R	Leyland	DP45F	1990	
410	H410ERO	Leyland Lynx LX2R11C15Z4R	Leyland	DP45F	1990	
417	E969PME	Leyland Lynx LX112L10ZR1	Leyland	B49F	1988	Ex Atlas, London NW10, 1994
418	E970PME	Leyland Lynx LX112L10ZR1	Leyland	B49F	1988	Ex Atlas, London NW10, 1994
419	F154KGS	Leyland Swift LBM6T/2RA	Wadham Stringer	B39F	1988	Ex Buffalo, Flitwick, 1995
420	F155KGS	Leyland Swift LBM6T/2RA	Wadham Stringer	B39F	1988	Ex Buffalo, Flitwick, 1995
422	E966PME	Leyland Lynx LX112TL11ZR1	Leyland	B49F	1988	Ex Mott, Stoke Mandeville, 1995

423	E965PME	Leyland Lynx LX112TL11ZR1	Leyland		B49F	1988	Ex Mott, Stoke Mandeville, 1995
424	E420EBH	Leyland Lynx LX112TL11ZR1R	Leyland		B51F	1988	Ex Sovereign, 1996
437	UPB337S	Leyland National 10351A/1R			B41F	1977	Ex Sovereign, 1990
513	KNV513P	Leyland National 11351/1R			B49F	1976	Ex United Counties, 1986

518-579 Leyland National 11351A/1R B49F* 1976-9 Ex United Counties, 1986*
531/72/3 ex Milton Keynes Citybus, 1987; 548 is B47FL

518	OVV518R	538	XVV538S	547	BVV547T	569	MNH569V	577	MNH577V
524	SBD524R	539	XVV539S	548	IAZ3457	572	MNH572V	579	MNH579V
531	VRP531S	542	BVV542T	550	ERP550T	573	MNH573V		
537	XVV537S	545	BVV545T	560	KRP560V	574	MNH574V		

581	NRP581V	Leyland National 2 NL116L11/1R	B49F	1980	Ex United Counties, 1986
588	SVV588W	Leyland National 2 NL116L11/1R	B49F	1980	Ex United Counties, 1986

589-597 Leyland National 2 NL106AL11/2R B44F 1981 Ex Parfitt, Rhymney, 1995

589	GUW447W	591	GUW461W	593	GUW475W	595	GUW465W	597	GUW457W
590	GUW441W	592	GUW462W	594	GUW494W	596	GUW456W		

600	MUH284X	Leyland Olympian ONLXB/1R	Eastern Coach Works	H45/32F	1982	Ex Rhondda, 1995
601	MUH287X	Leyland Olympian ONLXB/1R	Eastern Coach Works	H45/32F	1982	Ex Rhondda, 1995

612-620 Leyland Olympian ONLXB/1R Eastern Coach Works H45/32F 1981/2 Ex United Counties, 1986

612	ARP612X	614	ARP614X	616	ARP616X	618	ARP618X	620	ARP620X
613	ARP613X	615	ARP615X	617	ARP617X	619	ARP619X		

633-644 Leyland Olympian ONCL10/1RZ Alexander RL H47/32F* 1988 * 636/41 are CH47/29F

633	F633LMJ	636	F636LMJ	638	F638LMJ	640	F640LMJ	643	F643LMJ
635	F635LMJ	637	F637LMJ	639	F639LMJ	641	F641LMJ	644	F644LMJ

645-657 Leyland Olympian ON2R50C13Z4 Alexander RL H47/32F* 1989/90
* 649-53 are H47/34F; 654 is CH47/29F

645	G645UPP	648	G648UPP	651	G651UPP	654	G654UPP	657	G657UPP
646	G646UPP	649	G649UPP	652	G652UPP	655	G655UPP		
647	G647UPP	650	G650UPP	653	G653UPP	656	G656UPP		

661	A141DPE	Leyland Olympian ONTL11/1R	Roe	H43/29F	1983	Ex Sovereign, 1990
663	A143DPE	Leyland Olympian ONTL11/2R	Roe	H43/29F	1983	Ex Sovereign, 1990
664	B262LPH	Leyland Olympian ONTL11/2R	Eastern Coach Works	H43/29F	1985	Ex Sovereign, 1990
665	BPF135Y	Leyland Olympian ONTL11/2R	Roe	H43/29F	1983	Ex Sovereign, 1990
666	BPF136Y	Leyland Olympian ONTL11/2R	Roe	H43/29F	1983	Ex Sovereign, 1990
667	MUH290X	Leyland Olympian ONLXB/1R	Eastern Coach Works	H45/32F	1982	Ex Rhondda, 1995

693-716 Scania L113CRL East Lancs Cityzen B51F* 1995 * 713-6 are DP49F

693	N693EUR	696	N696EUR	699	N699EUR	715	N715EUR
694	N694EUR	697	N697EUR	713	N713EUR	716	N716EUR
695	N695EUR	698	N698EUR	714	N714EUR		

779	CBD779K	Bristol VRT/SL2/6LX	Eastern Coach Works	H39/31F	1972	Ex United Counties, 1986
802	PRP802M	Bristol VRT/SL2/6LX	Eastern Coach Works	H43/31F	1974	Ex United Counties, 1986
825	GNV334N	Bristol VRT/SL2/6LX	Eastern Coach Works	H43/31F	1974	Ex United Counties, 1986
837	LDB837P	Bristol VRT/SL3/6LX	Eastern Coach Works	H43/31F	1975	Ex United Counties, 1986

851-904 Bristol VRT/SL3/6LXB Eastern Coach Works H43/31F 1976-8 Ex United Counties, 1986

851	OVV851R	855	OVV855R	877	WBD877S	895	YVV895S	899	CBD899T
852	OVV852R	865	TNH865R	893	YVV893S	897	CBD897T	900	CBD900T
853	OVV853R	874	WBD874S	894	YVV894S	898	CBD898T	904	CBD904T

916	OCY916R	Bristol VRT/SL3/501	Eastern Coach Works	H43/31F	1977	Ex South Wales, 1987

918-960 Bristol VRT/SL3/6LXB Eastern Coach Works H43/31F* 1979-81 Ex United Counties, 1986
* 918/55 are CH40/31F

918	HBD918T	929	ONH929V	934	SNV934W	947	URP947W	956	VVV956W
925	ONH925V	932	SNV932W	938	SNV938W	951	VVV951W	957	VVV957W
928	ONH928V	933	SNV933W	946	URP946W	955	VVV955W	960	VVV960W

977	RMA431V	Bristol VRT/SL3/501	Eastern Coach Works	H43/31F	1980	Ex Crosville Wales, 1995
978	UDM448V	Bristol VRT/SL3/6LXB	Eastern Coach Works	H43/31F	1980	Ex Crosville Wales, 1995

Acquired from United Counties in 1986, LNG532 was fitted with a DAF engine (and Volvo badge) in 1995 and experimentally refurbished. In this summer 1996 view it is seen at Woodside. Capital Transport

Four low-floor Dennis Darts with East Lancs Spryte bodywork joined The Shires fleet at Hemel Hempstead during the late summer of 1996. DE171 was captured in September 1996 shortly after route prefix letters were removed in a restructuring of the local network. Capital Transport

SE710, one of the low-floor Scanias bodied by East Lancs in 1995, has received this special livery primarily for use on route 607, which runs from Tring to Watford for college students. When not so required, it appears on other routes.
Capital Transport

Transferred from Midland Fox in 1994 when still only a few months old, ML19, a Mercedes-Benz 709D with Leicester Carriage Builders body, has now received its third livery in less than two years. It was caught in the old town area of Hemel Hempstead a few yards from the river Gade from which the local brand name is taken.
Capital Transport

MP262 is generally used on the local Park & Ride service at Hemel Hempstead, but on Sundays is regularly found on HCC-contracted town services. This view shows it in such use at the north end of Marlowes. In September 1996, The Shires abolished the use of letter prefixes for most local services in the former London Country area. Capital Transport

Something of a stopgap were ten Iveco Daily minibuses with Marshall bodywork received in 1994. IV151, at Hemel Hempstead in July but subsequently transferred away and renumbered 151, shows the final form of the old livery, albeit lacking any local identity. Colin Lloyd

Previous registrations

BAZ6869	JTU577T	H23KBH	CMN414C	MBZ6455	E295VOM, 7178KP
BTX752T	AYR329T, NIW4810	IAZ2314	MUH288X	NIB8459	E637NEL
CAZ6852	HMA561T	IAZ3457	BVV548T	RJI6861	HMA569T
GIL6523	D209LWX	IAZ3977	RHT917S	RJI6862	MCA677T
GIL6949	D210LWX	IAZ4037	VRP532S	SIB4846	E321OMG
GIL8487	E32SBO	IIL4579	E33SBO	SIB7480	E325OMG
GIL8488	E38SBO	IIL4580	E37SBO	SIB7481	E326OMG
HIL7467	FVA387Y, 3408WY,	IIL4821	XPD299N	SIB8529	E324OMG
	NRV859Y	IIL4822	LPB180P	TIB4873	MCA671T
HIL7594	E662UNE	IIL4823	GMB659T	TIB4886	HPF322N
HIL7595	E663UNE	IIL4824	HNB20N	TIB7835	JTU594T
HIL7596	E31SBO	J65UNA	J59MHF, J6SLT	429UFM	E614AEY
HIL7597	E660UNE	MBZ6454	B572AVW, URY598	430UFM	E615AEY

Special liveries
Airport Link: VN326
Buffalo: DT358
Dacorum Park & Ride: MP262
Green Line: BTL47/9, STL201/2, TPL50-3/5/7, TPL84, TPL92/3/8, VC198, 109-13/92-6, 204
Jetlink: BTL48, STL203
Overall advertisements: DC5, DW11, LR49, LR51/3, LR104, LRL29, MCW6/8/10/20/6, ML18, SE70210, SNB405/49/65,
       SNB523, SNG524/6/7/34/6/40/3, VN313/7/9/20, VR917, 26, 31, 46, 69, 176, 334, 400/2,
       509/18/24/31/8/50/60/3/9/72/9, 616/37/9/50/3/7/65/7, 956
Palmers: 121, 961-3
Sapphire: Route X31 637/55-7
School Bus: 802/3
White: DC5, VC199, 31

SOVEREIGN

Sovereign Bus & Coach Co Ltd, Babbage Road, Stevenage, Hertfordshire, SG1 2EQ

Sovereign was established on 9th January 1989 (at Hatfield), taking over the western part of the former London Country North East. The Stevenage area operations of Jubilee Travel were purchased on 25th January 1989, and services in the area were soon rationalised. Welwyn Hatfield Line, which had been operating since August 1987 as a result of LCNE withdrawals in the Welwyn and Hatfield area, was bought out on 10th January 1990, continuing as a subsidiary until early in 1995. Most operations in the Stevenage area were transferred to Luton & District (now part of The Shires) on 20th May 1990. Operations have subsequently spread to the Harrow area, and BTS of Borehamwood has come under the Sovereign wing; these operations are covered in the London Bus Handbook.

The Hertfordshire fleet is based at North Mymms, Stevenage and St Albans. The initial livery of cream with light blue skirt and stripes is now being augmented by a modest black stripe on at least some vehicles.

Sovereign have received ten low-floor Scanias with Wright bodywork during the past year. No.108 is branded for route 734, which was revised in March 1996 as part of a rationalisation of routes with The Shires to become a through service between Hitchin and Hemel Hempstead. The black stripe is a recent addition to standard Sovereign livery. Here it is seen at the eastern end of the route in Hitchin. Richard Godfrey

Most other full-size single-deckers in the fleet are Leyland Lynxes. No.215, seen in Welwyn Garden City in April 1996, came from Keighley & District, and is the only such vehicle to have received Welwyn Hatfield Line livery, perpetuating the name of the subsidiary operation which was absorbed in January 1996. Colin Lloyd

Sovereign's minibuses have interchanged regularly between the Hertfordshire and Harrow fleets. No.403, a Mercedes-Benz 811D with Reeve Burgess bodywork, was caught in St Albans in April 1996 after moving north from work in Greater London. Tony Smethers

SOVEREIGN

31	BPF131Y	Leyland Olympian ONTL11/1R	Roe		H43/29F	1983	Ex Keighley & District, 1996
32	BPF132Y	Leyland Olympian ONTL11/1R	Roe		H43/29F	1983	Ex London Country North East, 1989
33	BPF133Y	Leyland Olympian ONTL11/1R	Roe		H43/29F	1983	Ex London Country North East, 1989
34	BPF134Y	Leyland Olympian ONTL11/1R	Roe		H43/29F	1983	Ex Keighley & District, 1995
37	BPF137Y	Leyland Olympian ONTL11/1R	Roe		H43/29F	1983	Ex London Country North East, 1989
38	A138DPE	Leyland Olympian ONTL11/1R	Roe		H43/29F	1983	Ex London Country North East, 1989
39	A139DPE	Leyland Olympian ONTL11/1R	Roe		H43/29F	1983	Ex Keighley & District, 1993
40	A140DPE	Leyland Olympian ONTL11/1R	Roe		H43/29F	1983	Ex Keighley & District, 1994

101-105		Volvo B10B-58		Wright Endurance		DP49F	1995	
101	M101UKX	**102**	M102UKX	**103**	M103UKX	**104**	M104UKX	**105**	M105UKX

106	N106GVS	Volvo B10B-58	Wright Endurance	B51F	1996	
107	N107GVS	Volvo B10B-58	Wright Endurance	B51F	1996	
108	N108GVS	Volvo B10B-58	Wright Endurance	B51F	1996	
109	N109GVS	Volvo B10B-58	Wright Endurance	B51F	1996	
110	M310KHP	Volvo B10B-58	Wright Endurance	B51F	1995	Ex demonstrator, 1996

201-207		Leyland Lynx LX2R11C15Z4S	Leyland		B49F	1989	
201	G201URO	**203**	G203URO	**205**	G205URO	**207**	G207URO
202	G202URO	**204**	G204URO	**206**	G206URO		

213-218		Leyland Lynx LX112TL11ZR1R	Leyland		B49F*	1989	Ex Keighley & District, 1992/3*
							* 215 is B47F; 218 ex Harrogate & District, 1993
213	F203MBT	**215**	F205MBT	**217**	F207MBT		
214	F204MBT	**216**	F206MBT	**218**	F208MBT		

240	E840EUT	Leyland Lynx LX112TL11ZR1R	Leyland		B51F	1987	Ex County, 1990
258	F358JVS	Leyland Lynx LX112TL11ZR1	Leyland		B49F	1988	Ex Jubilee, Stevenage, 1989
259	F359JVS	Leyland Lynx LX112TL11ZR1	Leyland		B49F	1988	Ex County, 1990
271	E371YRO	Leyland Lynx LX112TL11ZR1	Leyland		B51F	1987	Ex County, 1990
284	G384MWX	Leyland Lynx LX112L10ZR1R	Leyland		DP47F	1990	Ex Harrogate & District, 1995
321	F421DUG	Volvo B10M-60	Plaxton Paramount 3200 3		C50F	1989	Ex Cambridge Coach Services, 1996
324	F424DUG	Volvo B10M-60	Plaxton Paramount 3200 3		C50F	1989	Ex Cambridge Coach Services, 1996
325	F425DUG	Volvo B10M-60	Plaxton Paramount 3200 3		C50F	1989	Ex Cambridge Coach Services, 1996
326	E362NEG	Volvo B10M-61	Plaxton Paramount 3200 3		C53F	1988	Ex Cambridge Coach Services, 1996
327	H827UWR	Volvo B10M-60	Plaxton		C50F	1991	Ex Wallace Arnold, Leeds, 1993
328	H828UWR	Volvo B10M-60	Plaxton		C50F	1991	Ex Wallace Arnold, Leeds, 1993
349	J749CWT	Volvo B10M-60	Plaxton		C50F	1992	Acquired 1996
358	E358NEG	Volvo B10M-61	Plaxton Paramount 3200 3		C53F	1988	Ex Sovereign (Harrow), 1996
403	H403FGS	Mercedes-Benz 811D	Reeve Burgess		B31F	1991	Ex Sovereign (Harrow), 1995
404	H404FGS	Mercedes-Benz 811D	Reeve Burgess		B31F	1990	Ex Sovereign (Harrow), 1995
409	H409FGS	Mercedes-Benz 811D	Reeve Burgess		B31F	1990	Ex Sovereign (Harrow), 1995
433	K3SBC	Mercedes-Benz 811D	Plaxton		B31F	1993	Ex Welwyn & Hatfield, 1996
434	K4SBC	Mercedes-Benz 811D	Plaxton		B31F	1993	Ex Welwyn & Hatfield, 1996

442-453

Mercedes-Benz 811D — Plaxton — B31F — 1993/4

442	L2SBC	445	L945MTM	448	L948MTM	451	L951MBH
443	L3SBC	446	L946MTM	449	L949MBH	452	L952MBH
444	L944MTM	447	L947MTM	450	L950MBH	453	L953MBH

521	FUG321T	Leyland National 10351B/1R		B44F	1979	Ex Keighley & District, 1994
525	FUG325T	Leyland National 10351B/1R		B44F	1979	Ex Keighley & District, 1995
543	DNW843T	Leyland National 10351B/1R		B44F	1979	Ex Keighley & District, 1994
699	AYJ99T	Leyland National 11351A/1R		B49F	1979	Ex Harrogate & District, 1994
803	C303CRH	Ford Transit	Carlyle	B16F	1985	Ex Associated, Bromsgrove, 1994
804	C304CRH	Ford Transit	Carlyle	B18F	1985	Ex Keighley & District, 1996
808	C308CRH	Ford Transit	Carlyle	B18F	1985	Ex Rover, Bromsgrove, 1993
811	C311DRH	Ford Transit	Carlyle	B18F	1985	Ex Welwyn & Hatfield, 1993
864	B264KPF	Leyland Tiger TRCTL11/2RH	Plaxton Paramount 3200 2	C49F	1985	Ex Keighley & District, 1995

901-917

Mercedes-Benz 709D — Reeve Burgess — B23F — 1989 — 901/2/4-8 ex Welwyn & Hatfield, 1996; 909 ex Sovereign (Harrow), 1996; 915 ex County, 1991

901	G901UPP	904	G904UPP	907	G907UPP	915	G915UPP
902	G902UPP	905	G905UPP	908	G908UPP	916	G916UPP
903	G903UPP	906	G906UPP	909	G909UPP	917	G917UPP

990	K390SLB	Mercedes-Benz 709D	Plaxton	B23F	1993	
991	K391SLB	Mercedes-Benz 709D	Plaxton	B23F	1993	
992	K392SLB	Mercedes-Benz 709D	Plaxton	B23F	1993	Ex Welwyn & Hatfield, 1996
993	K393SLB	Mercedes-Benz 709D	Plaxton	B23F	1993	Ex Welwyn & Hatfield, 1996

Special liveries
BTS: 33
Green Line: 321/4-6/49/58
Jetlink: 747 327/8
Overall advertisements: 37, 258, 914/6
Welwyn-Hatfield Line: 215, 433/4, 901/2/4-8/92/3

SOLENT BLUE LINE

Musterphantom Ltd, 160-170 High Street, Southampton, Hampshire, SO1 0BY

In May 1987, Southern Vectis and Badgerline combined to set up 'Badger Vectis' to compete with Wilts & Dorset on the Bournemouth to Poole corridor. Though this operation ceased in March 1988, Solent Blue Line has expanded in east Hampshire and west Sussex. Initially treated as one combined unit with the Southern Vectis fleet, greater independence has been evident in recent times, and some fleet numbers are now duplicated between the fleets.

In 1988 Solent Blue Line contracted out two routes to Marchwood Motorways. These were to be the first franchised bus operations in the United Kingdom. Vehicles used in this way are identified in the fleet list on pages 118 and 119.

Vehicles operate in a diagonally-structured livery of yellow and two blues. The Solent Blue Line fleet is based at depots in Southampton, Eastleigh and Hythe; those owned by Marchwood Motorways are based at that company's depot in Totton.

Amongst a batch of Bristol VRTs acquired mid-life from Cumberland in 1987, No.163, in basic fleet livery with overall advertising, waits to negotiate a junction in Southampton in April 1995.
Richard Godfrey

New in 1995 were two Volvo Olympians with East Lancs coach-seated bodywork. No.735 makes a graceful sight in Southampton in April 1996.
Malc McDonald

Recent updating of the minibus fleet has led to the arrival of many Iveco Daily models, of which four new in 1994 carry European Coach Conversions bodywork. No.244 presents a rather more rounded image than might be expected. Phillip Stephenson

The most recent Iveco Daily arrivals have Mellor bodywork, and were new in 1995. No.256 awaits departure from Southampton on the service to Fareham. Malcolm King

New in 1994 were four Volvo B10s with Alexander Strider bodywork. No.527 was photographed at Eastleigh in April 1995, and shows the style in which names are applied to some of the fleet.
Richard Godfrey

SOLENT BLUE LINE

84	NDL654R	Bristol VRT/SL3/6LXB	Eastern Coach Works	H43/31F	1977	Ex Southern Vectis, 1990
96	BFX576T	Bristol VRT/SL3/6LXB	Eastern Coach Works	H43/31F	1979	Ex Hampshire Bus, 1987
97	BFX577T	Bristol VRT/SL3/6LXB	Eastern Coach Works	H43/31F	1979	Ex Hampshire Bus, 1987
98	PTT98R	Bristol VRT/SL3/6LXB	Eastern Coach Works	H43/31F	1977	Ex Southern Vectis, 1992

101-109   Bristol VRT/SL3/6LXB   Eastern Coach Works   H43/31F 1977/78

101	ODL661R	103	ODL663R	105	ODL665R	107	ODL667R	109	UDL669S
102	ODL662R	104	ODL664R	106	ODL666R	108	UDL668S		

123	DBV23W	Bristol VRT/SL3/6LXB	Eastern Coach Works	H43/31F	1980	Ex G&G, Leamington Spa, 1995

149-165   Bristol VRT/SL3/501   Eastern Coach Works   H43/31F 1978-79   Ex Cumberland, 1987
       Modified to Gardner 6LXB engines

149	LHG449T	154	LHG454T	158	LHG458T	162	TRN462V
150	LHG450T	155	LHG455T	159	LHG459T	163	TRN463V
151	LHG451T	156	LHG456T	160	TRN460V	164	TRN464V
152	LHG452T	157	LHG457T	161	TRN461V	165	TRN465V

167	FDL678V	Bristol VRT/SL3/6LXB	Eastern Coach Works	H43/31F	1980	Ex Southern Vectis, 1996
168	FDL680V	Bristol VRT/SL3/6LXB	Eastern Coach Works	H43/31F	1980	Ex Southern Vectis, 1996
213†	H711LOL	Dennis Dart 9SDL3002	Carlyle Dartline	B36F	1990	
214†	H712LOL	Dennis Dart 9.8SDL3004	Carlyle Dartline	B40F	1991	

231-235   Iveco Daily 49.10   Car Chairs   B23F 1992

231	J231KDL	232	J232KDL	233	J233KDL	234	J234KDL	235	J235KDL

241	M241XPO	Iveco Daily 59.12	European Coach Conversions	B29F	1994
242	M242XPO	Iveco Daily 59.12	European Coach Conversions	B29F	1994
243	M243XPO	Iveco Daily 59.12	European Coach Conversions	B29F	1994
244	M244XPO	Iveco Daily 59.12	European Coach Conversions	B29F	1994

245-262

Iveco Daily 59.12 Mellor   B29F   1995

245	M245BPO	249	M249BPO	253	N253ECR	257	N257ECR	261	N261FOR
246	M246BPO	250	M250BPO	254	N254ECR	258	N258ECR	262	N262FOR
247	M247BPO	251	M251BPO	255	N255ECR	259	N259FOR		
248	M248BPO	252	M252BPO	256	N256ECR	260	N260FOR		

263†	N301FOR	Iveco Daily 59.12	Mellor	B29F	1995
264†	N302FOR	Iveco Daily 59.12	Mellor	B29F	1995
265†	N303FOR	Iveco Daily 59.12	Mellor	B29F	1995
266†	N304FOR	Iveco Daily 59.12	Mellor	B29F	1995
267†	N305FOR	Iveco Daily 59.12	Mellor	B29F	1995

277-282

Iveco Daily 49.10   Robin Hood City Nippy   B23F   1987/88

277	E277HDL	278	E278HDL	280	E280HDL	281	F281ODL	282	F282ODL

287	F287CEY	Iveco Daily 49.10	Robin Hood City Nippy	B25F	1988	Ex Crosville Wales, 1995
288	F288CEY	Iveco Daily 49.10	Robin Hood City Nippy	B25F	1988	Ex Crosville Wales, 1995
289	F289CEY	Iveco Daily 49.10	Robin Hood City Nippy	B25F	1988	Ex Crosville Wales, 1995
291†	F731OOT	Iveco Daily 49.10	Robin Hood City Nippy	B23F	1988	
292†	H975EOR	Iveco Daily 49.10	Phoenix	B23F	1991	
293†	G364FOP	Iveco Daily 49.10	Carlyle Dailybus II	B25F	1990	Ex Strathclyde, 1991
502†	F246RJX	DAF SB220LC550	Optare Delta	B47F	1989	
503†	J45GCX	DAF SB220LC550	Optare Delta	B49F	1992	
504†	L509EHD	DAF SB220LC550	Ikarus Citibus	B48F	1993	
505†	L510EHD	DAF SB220LC550	Ikarus Citibus	B48F	1993	
526	L526YDL	Volvo B10B-58	Alexander Strider	B51F	1994	
527	L527YDL	Volvo B10B-58	Alexander Strider	B51F	1994	
528	L528YDL	Volvo B10B-58	Alexander Strider	B51F	1994	
529	L227THP	Volvo B10B-58	Alexander Strider	B51F	1994	Ex Volvo Bus, Warwick, 1994
694	WDL694Y	Leyland Olympian ONLXB/1R	Eastern Coach Works	H45/30F	1983	Ex Southern Vectis, 1989
695	A295FDL	Leyland Olympian ONLXB/1R	Eastern Coach Works	DPH41/32F	1984	Ex Southern Vectis, 1992
697	A697DDL	Leyland Olympian ONLXB/1R	Eastern Coach Works	DPH41/32F	1984	Ex Southern Vectis, 1992
699	A699DDL	Leyland Olympian ONLXB/1R	Eastern Coach Works	DPH41/32F	1984	Ex Southern Vectis, 1992
700	A700DDL	Leyland Olympian ONLXB/1R	Eastern Coach Works	DPH41/32F	1984	Ex Southern Vectis, 1992

701-705

Leyland Olympian ONLXB/1R   Eastern Coach Works   H45/30F   1984   Ex Hampshire Bus, 1987

701	A201MEL	702	A202MEL	703	A203MEL	704	A204MEL	705	A205MEL

706	F706SDL	Leyland Olympian ONCL10/1RZ	Leyland	DPH39/29F	1989	
707	F707SDL	Leyland Olympian ONCL10/1RZ	Leyland	DPH39/29F	1989	
708	F708SDL	Leyland Olympian ONCL10/1RZ	Leyland	DPH39/29F	1989	
709	F709SDL	Leyland Olympian ONCL10/1RZ	Leyland	DPH39/29F	1989	
721	G721WDL	Leyland Olympian ON2R50C13Z5	Leyland	DPH39/29F	1989	
722	G722WDL	Leyland Olympian ON2R50C13Z5	Leyland	DPH39/29F	1989	

728-734

Leyland Olympian ON2R50C13Z5   Leyland   H47/31F   1991

728	H728DDL	731	H731DDL	733	H733DDL		
729	H729DDL	732	H732DDL	734	H734DDL		

735	M735BBP	Volvo Olympian YN2RV18Z4	East Lancs	DPH41/29F	1995	
736	M736BBP	Volvo Olympian YN2RV18Z4	East Lancs	DPH41/29F	1995	
817	F817URN	Leyland Olympian ONCL10/1RZ	Leyland	H47/31F	1988	Ex demonstrator, 1990

Previous registrations
A295FDL A702DDL, WDL142
F817URN BMN88G

Special liveries
Overall advertisements: 157/63, 728

Named vehicles
149 Southampton Mencap, 150 Wendy Knight, 154 T S Astrid, 155 Josie Nicholls, 160 Eileen Howlett, 161 British Diabetic Assn, Southampton, 162 RSPCA Action for Animals, 163 Romsey Lions, 164 Mary Hill, 505 County of Hampshire, 526 City of Southampton, 527 Borough of Eastleigh, 528 City of Winchester, 529 Leukaemia Busters, 707 Venturers Search & Rescue, 709 Wessex Cancer Trust, 721 Southampton-le Havre Twinning Society, 722 Training Corps, 735 Solent Dolphin

† vehicles owned by Marchwood Motorways and operated in Solent Blue Line livery.

SOUTHAMPTON CITYBUS

Southampton City Transport (1993) Ltd, 226 Portswood Road, Southampton, SO9 4XS

This company was established on 21st December 1993 in succession to Southampton Citybus Ltd, itself formed to take over the former municipal operations in October 1986. The traditional operating area is bounded by the M27 to the north, Totton in the west and Hedge End in the east, though the operation of Hampshire County Council services and several commercial services results in vehicles appearing some way outside this boundary. Competition has also been experienced from Solent Blue Line on services within Southampton and a fleet of crew-operated Routemasters was for a while operated to counteract this. Services were introduced in Portsmouth under the Red Admiral name, though this network subsequently passed to Transit Holdings. In June 1996, some of the former Hants & Sussex network was taken over when that firm ceased operations.

Fleet livery is red with a black skirt; most coaches are in overall red under the 'Red Ensign' name. Almost all buses are named.

Unique in the Southampton fleet is No.114, a Volvo B10 with Northern Counties Countybus Paladin bodywork, found on layover in April 1995. Richard Godfrey

Dennis Darts have taken over most of the single-deck role in the fleet. No.307, seen in August 1995, is however the only one to carry Wadham Stringer bodywork, having been purchased in 1990 after use as a demonstrator. Ivor Norman

Top **A particularly interesting experiment currently under way is the operation of ten Dennis Darts powered by gas. Carrying Plaxton Pointer bodies, they entered service in the spring of 1996.** Malc McDonald

Above **An unusual move in 1991 was the rebodying of five elderly Leyland Atlanteans with single-deck East Lancs bodies. Most recently, these have been transferred to cover the former Hants & Sussex operations, as evidenced by the fleetnames on No.354 in July 1996.** D. Heath

Left **Coaching operations are carried out under the Red Ensign banner, for which a revised livery has been introduced recently. No.288 is a Leyland Olympian with coach-seated East Lancs bodywork.** Malc McDonald

A few of Southampton's Leyland Atlanteans with East Lancs bodywork carry Schoolbus names, but still sometimes turn up on regular service, as shown by No.203 in May 1996.
Gerald Mead

SOUTHAMPTON CITYBUS

002	C433BHY	Ford Transit	Dormobile	B16F	1986	Ex White Horse Ferries, Hythe, 1995	
003	C443BHY	Ford Transit	Dormobile	B16F	1986	Ex White Horse Ferries, Hythe, 1995	
004	C429AHT	Ford Transit	Carlyle	B16F	1985	Ex White Horse Ferries, Hythe, 1995	
102	F102RTR	Leyland Lynx LX112L10ZR1S	Leyland	B47F	1989		

104-111   Leyland Lynx LX2R11C15ZR4   Leyland   B47F   1990

104	G104WRV	106	G106WRV	109	G109XOW	111	G111XOW
105	G105WRV	108	G108WRV	110	G110XOW		

112	G112XOW	Leyland Lynx LX112L10ZR1R	Leyland	DP47F	1990
113	G113XOW	Leyland Lynx LX112L10ZR1R	Leyland	DP47F	1990
114	K114DRV	Volvo B10B-58	Northern Counties Countybus Paladin	B51F	1993
115	M967GDU	Volvo B10B-58	Plaxton Verde	B51F	1994	Ex demonstrator, 1995

119-128   Leyland Atlantean AN68A/1R   Roe   H43/32F 1978/79   Ex Plymouth, 1992

119	OCO119S	121	STK121T	126	STK126T	127	STK127T	128	STK128T

178-197   Leyland Atlantean AN68/1R   East Lancs   H45/31F 1972-75

178	PCR301M	188	HTR558P	191	HTR561P		
182	PCR305M	190	HTR560P	197	HTR566P		

202-261   Leyland Atlantean AN68A/1R   East Lancs   H45/31F 1977-80

202	MCR202R	214	MCR214R	226	PBP226S	238	UPO238T	250	YRV250V
203	MCR203R	215	MCR215R	227	PBP227S	239	UPO239T	251	YRV251V
204	MCR204R	216	MCR216R	228	PBP228S	240	UPO240T	252	YRV252V
205	MCR205R	217	ORV90S	229	PBP229S	241	UPO241T	253	YRV253V
206	MCR206R	218	MCR218R	230	PBP230S	242	UPO242T	254	YRV254V
207	MCR207R	219	ORV89S	231	PBP231S	243	UPO243T	255	YRV255V
208	MCR208R	220	PBP220S	232	UPO232T	244	UPO244T	256	YRV256V
209	MCR209R	221	PBP221S	233	UPO233T	245	UPO245T	257	YRV257V
210	MCR210R	222	PBP222S	234	UPO234T	246	UPO246T	258	YRV258V
211	MCR211R	223	PBP223S	235	UPO235T	247	YRV247V	259	YRV259V
212	MCR212R	224	PBP224S	236	UPO236T	248	YRV248V	260	YRV260V
213	MCR213R	225	PBP225S	237	UPO237T	249	YRV249V	261	YRV261V

262-266   Leyland Atlantean AN68B/1R   East Lancs   H45/31F*   1981   * 265/6 are H40/31F

262	DBK262W	263	DBK263W	264	DBK264W	265	DBK265W	266	DBK266W

267-276   Leyland Atlantean AN68C/1R   East Lancs   H40/31F 1982

267	FTR267X	269	FTR269X	271	FTR271X	273	KOW273Y	275	KOW275Y
268	FTR268X	270	FTR270X	272	KOW272Y	274	KOW274Y	276	KOW276Y

277	A277ROW	Dennis Dominator DDA171	East Lancs		H46/30F	1984	
287	SIB3272	Leyland Olympian ONLXCT/2R	East Lancs		CH47/21F	1986	
288	SIB3273	Leyland Olympian ONLXCT/2R	East Lancs		CH47/29F	1986	
289	E289HRV	Leyland Olympian ONLXB/1RH	Eastern Coach Works		DPH43/27F	1987	
290	E290HRV	Leyland Olympian ONLXB/1RH	Eastern Coach Works		DPH43/27F	1987	

291-296   Volvo Olympian YN2RV18Z4 Northern Counties   H47/30F   1996

291	P291KPX	293	P293KPX	295	P295KPX
292	P292KPX	294	P294KPX	296	P296KPX

301-306   Dennis Dart 9SDL3002   Duple Dartline   B36F*   1990   * 306 is B35F

301	G301XCR	303	G303XCR	305	G305XCR
302	G302XCR	304	G304XCR	306	H306DRV

307	G895XPX	Dennis Dart 8.5SDL3003	Wadham Stringer Portsdown	B33F	1990	Ex demonstrator, 1990
308	H308ERV	Dennis Dart 9SDL3002	Reeve Burgess Pointer	B35F	1991	

309-313   Dennis Dart 9SDL3011   Plaxton Pointer   B35F   1993

309	L309RTP	310	L310RTP	311	L311RTP	312	L312RTP	313	L313RTP

314-323   Dennis Dart 9SDL3031   Plaxton Pointer   B35F   1994

314	M314YOT	316	M316YOT	318	M318YOT	320	M320YOT	322	M322YOT
315	M315YOT	317	M317YOT	319	M319YOT	321	M321YOT	323	M323YOT

324-329   Dennis Dart 9SDL3051   Plaxton Pointer   B35F   1995

324	N324ECR	326	N326ECR	328	N328ECR
325	N325ECR	327	N327ECR	329	N329ECR

330-339   Dennis Dart 9SDL   Plaxton Pointer   B35F   1996   CNG-powered

330	N159GOT	332	N161GOT	334	N163GOT	336	N165GOT	338	N167GOT
331	N160GOT	333	N162GOT	335	N164GOT	337	N166GOT	339	N168GOT

350-354   Leyland Atlantean AN68/1R   East Lancs Sprint (1991)   B35F*   1974   * 353 is B29F

350	OJI1870	351	OJI1871	352	OJI1879	353	OJI1873	354	OJI1874

401	N465ETR	Dennis Dart 9.8SDL3054	Plaxton Pointer	B40F	1995	
402	N466ETR	Dennis Dart 9.8SDL3054	Plaxton Pointer	B40F	1995	
403	N467ETR	Dennis Dart 9.8SDL3054	Plaxton Pointer	B40F	1995	
404	P404KOW	Dennis Dart SLF	Plaxton	B37F	1996	
405	P405KOW	Dennis Dart SLF	Plaxton	B37F	1996	
406	P406KOW	Dennis Dart SLF	Plaxton	B37F	1996	
407	P407KOW	Dennis Dart SLF	Plaxton	B37F	1996	
500	115CLT	Kässbohrer Setra S228DT	Kässbohrer Imperial	CH54/20CT	1984	Ex Harris, Catshill, 1991
501	MJI4605	Kässbohrer Setra S228DT	Kässbohrer Imperial	CH55/20CT	1984	Ex Smith, Bold Heath, 1992
502	DSU405	Kässbohrer Setra S228DT	Kässbohrer Imperial	CH54/20CT	1984	Ex Ron, Ashington, 1993
503	709LAU	Scania K112TRS	Berkhof Emperor 395	CH57/19CT	1985	Ex Thamesdown, 1993
504	WLT649	Leyland Olympian ONTL11/2Rsp	East Lancs	CH49/23F	1986	Ex London Coaches, 1990
505	SIB3275	Leyland Olympian ONTL11/2Rsp	East Lancs	CH49/20FT	1986	Ex London Coaches, 1990
	PJI4982	Leyland Leopard PSU5A/4R	Plaxton	C50F	1976	Ex Hants & Sussex, 1996
	WRO434S	Leyland Leopard PSU3E/4R	Duple	C53F	1978	Ex Hants & Sussex, 1996
	135MHT	Leyland Leopard PSU3E/4R	Plaxton	C53F	1978	Ex Hants & Sussex, 1996
	CTM406T	Leyland Leopard PSU3E/4R	Duple	C53F	1979	Ex Hants & Sussex, 1996
	CTM407T	Leyland Leopard PSU3E/4R	Duple	C53F	1979	Ex Hants & Sussex, 1996

Previous registrations

DSU405	A414GPY	OJI1874	HTR568P	SIB3275	C202DYE
MJI4605	A574GEF	OJI1879	EOW398L	WLT649	C201DYE
OJI1870	PCR299M	PJI4982	NUR82P	115CLT	B149NPE, SWH67
OJI1871	HTR567P	SIB3272	C287BBP	709LAU	C276GVX
OJI1873	HTR570P	SIB3273	C288BBP	135MHT	WOC729T

Special liveries
Overall advertisements: 265/7/70/1, 303/53
School bus livery: 184, 202-5
Hants & Sussex fleetnames:102/4,350-4
Red Ensign: 288, 500-5

Named vehicles
Almost all vehicles in the fleet carry names

SOUTHERN VECTIS

Southern Vectis Omnibus Company Ltd, Nelson Road, Newport, Isle of Wight, PO30 1RD

Southern Vectis was formed in 1929 when the Southern Railway Company took over the business of Dodson Brothers Ltd, trading as 'Vectis'. The name therefore reflects the original ownership rather than geographical confinement to the south of the island. Services expanded and many smaller stage and tour operators were acquired over the years until a near-monopoly of services was achieved. The company was nationalised in 1948 and passed to the National Bus Company in 1969. In October 1986 it became one of the first NBC subsidiaries to be sold when it was purchased by a management team. Further expansion took place in 1987 when the West Wight fleet, comprising four coaches, was acquired.

A notable feature is the development of a fleet of veteran vehicles operating on the Isle of Wight in Tilling-based liveries. The current livery is emerald green and greensand for buses, with magnolia and dark green relieved with red and white for coaches. Minibuses are in red or blue. Vehicles are based at Newport, Ryde, Freshwater, Sandown, Ventnor and East Cowes.

Below In May 1996 Southern Vectis recast many of their services, introducing colour-coding for the main routes. Dennis Dart No.813, new that spring with UVG bodywork, stands at West Cowes in May 1996 showing how the first track of the number blind is used to convey the route code. Richard Godfrey

Right The last Olympian to be delivered to Southern Vectis under the Leyland marque, No.743 carries Northern Counties coach-seated Countybus Palatine bodywork. This view shows it passing through the picturesque scenery of Totland. Richard Godfrey

Below right The newest double-deckers on the Isle of Wight are seven Volvo Olympians delivered in 1995 with Northern Counties bodywork, as represented by No.751 at Newport in April 1996. Keith Grimes

Two Bristol LHS vehicles with Eastern Coach Works bodies carry dual-purpose seating. No.203 stands at Newport in May 1996. A.W.Mead

SOUTHERN VECTIS

202	KDL202W	Bristol LHS6L	Eastern Coach Works	DP31F	1980
203	KDL203W	Bristol LHS6L	Eastern Coach Works	DP31F	1980
236	J236KDL	Iveco Daily 49.10	Car Chairs	B23F	1992
237	J237KDL	Iveco Daily 49.10	Car Chairs	B23F	1992
238	J238KDL	Iveco Daily 49.10	Car Chairs	B23F	1992
240	N240PDL	Iveco Daily 59.12	Marshall C31	DP23	1996
241	N241PDL	Iveco Daily 59.12	Marshall C31	DP23	1996
242	N242PDL	Iveco Daily 59.12	Marshall C31	DP23	1996
243	N243PDL	Iveco Daily 59.12	Marshall C31	DP23	1996
267	C267SDL	Ford Transit 190D	Carlyle	B16F	1985

271-287		Iveco Daily 49.10	Robin Hood City Nippy	B23F	1987-89

271	E271HDL	274	E274HDL	279	E279HDL	285	F285SDL
272	E272HDL	275	E275HDL	283	F283SDL	286	F286SDL
273	E273HDL	276	E276HDL	284	F284SDL	287	F287SDL

288	G565YTR	Iveco Daily 49.10	Phoenix	B23F	1990	Ex demonstrator, 1990
289	H289DDL	Iveco Daily 49.10	Phoenix	B23F	1990	
301	KDL885F	Bristol RESH6G	Duple Commander	C45F	1968	
302	CXI5971	Leyland Leopard PSU3E/4R	Plaxton Supreme IV Exp	C52F	1979	Ex Berks Bucks, 1989
307	LXI4409	Leyland Leopard PSU3E/4R	Plaxton Supreme IV	C53F	1981	
310	TJI8780	Leyland Tiger TRCTL11/2R	Plaxton Paramount 3200	C51F	1983	
311	TJI8781	Leyland Tiger TRCTL11/2R	Plaxton Paramount 3200	C51F	1983	
312	TJI8782	Leyland Tiger TRCTL11/2R	Plaxton Paramount 3200	C51F	1984	
313	TJI8783	Leyland Tiger TRCTL11/2R	Plaxton Paramount 3200	C51F	1984	
314	TJI8784	Leyland Tiger TRCTL11/3R	Plaxton Paramount 3500 2	C49F	1986	
315	473CDL	Leyland Tiger TRCTL11/3R	Plaxton Paramount 3500 2	C49F	1986	
316	390CDL	Leyland Tiger TRCTL11/3R	Plaxton Paramount 3500 2	C49F	1986	
317	VDL263	Leyland Tiger TRCTL11/3R	Plaxton Paramount 3500 2	C51F	1986	
320	TJI7520	Leyland Tiger TRCTL11/3ARZ	Plaxton Paramount 3500 3	C53F	1988	
321	WXI6291	Leyland Tiger TRCTL11/3ARZ	Plaxton Paramount 3500 3	C53F	1988	
326	934BDL	Leyland Tiger TRCTL11/3R	Plaxton Paramount 3200	C53F	1984	Ex Hill, Tredegar, 1989
500	MDL955	Bristol LD6G	Eastern Coach Works	O33/27R	1956	Ex preservation, 1993
501	MDL952	Bristol LD6G	Eastern Coach Works	O33/27R	1956	
502	CDL899	Bristol K5G	Eastern Coach Works	O30/26R	1939	
503	VDL613S	Bristol VRT/SL3/6LXB	Eastern Coach Works	CO43/31F	1977	Ex Hants & Dorset, 1979

504	UFX856S	Bristol VRT/SL3/6LXB	Eastern Coach Works	CO43/31F	1977	Ex Hants & Dorset, 1979
505	UFX857S	Bristol VRT/SL3/6LXB	Eastern Coach Works	CO43/31F	1977	Ex Hants & Dorset, 1979
506	UFX858S	Bristol VRT/SL3/6LXB	Eastern Coach Works	CO43/31F	1977	Ex Hants & Dorset, 1979
507	MDL953	Bristol LD6G	Eastern Coach Works	O33/27R	1956	Ex preservation, 1994
563u	SDL268	Bristol LD6G	Eastern Coach Works	H33/27R	1959	On extended loan from preservation
565	TDL998	Bristol FS6G	Eastern Coach Works	H33/27RD	1960	
573u	YDL318	Bristol FS6G	Eastern Coach Works	H33/27RD	1962	
611	CDL479C	Bristol FLF6G	Eastern Coach Works	H38/32F	1965	Ex Shamrock & Rambler, 1986
628	SDL638J	Bristol VRT/SL6G	Eastern Coach Works	H39/31F	1971	On extended loan to Westbrook Travel

676-685   Bristol VRT/SL3/6LXB   Eastern Coach Works   H43/31F   1979-81

676	YDL676T	679	FDL679V	682	FDL682V	684	DPX684W
677	FDL677V	681	FDL681V	683	DPX683W	685	DPX685W

686-698   Leyland Olympian ONLXB/1R   Eastern Coach Works   H40/30F   1982-84

686	RDL686X	689	RDL689X	692	WDL692Y	696	WDL696Y
687	RDL687X	690	RDL690X	693	WDL693Y	698	A698DDL
688	RDL688X	691	RDL691X	695	WDL695Y		

710	F710SDL	Leyland Olympian ONCL10/1RZ	Leyland		DPH41/29F	1989
711	F711SDL	Leyland Olympian ONCL10/1RZ	Leyland		DPH41/29F	1989
712	F712SDL	Leyland Olympian ONCL10/1RZ	Leyland		DPH41/29F	1989

713-727   Leyland Olympian ON2R50C13Z5   Leyland   DPH41/29F   1989-90

713	G713WDL	716	G716WDL	719	G719WDL	724	G724XDL	727	G727XDL
714	G714WDL	717	G717WDL	720	G720WDL	725	G725XDL		
715	G715WDL	718	G718WDL	723	G723XDL	726	G726XDL		

735-743   Leyland Olympian ON2R50C13Z4   Northern Counties
Countybus Palatine   DPH41/29F   1993

735	K735ODL	737	K737ODL	739	K739ODL	741	K741ODL	743	K743ODL
736	K736ODL	738	K738ODL	740	K740ODL	742	K742ODL		

744-751   Volvo Olympian YN2RC16Z5   Northern Counties   DPH41/29F   1995

744	M744HDL	746	M746HDL	749	M749HDL	751	M751HDL
745	M745HDL	748	M748HDL	750	M750HDL		

806u	FDL927D	Bristol MW6G	Eastern Coach Works	B43F	1966	Ex preservation, 1989

810-815   Dennis Dart 8.5SDL3052   UVG Urban Star   DP33F   1996

810	N810PDL	812	N812PDL	814	N814PDL
811	N811PDL	813	N813PDL	815	N815PDL

863	TDL563K	Bristol RELL6G	Eastern Coach Works	B53F	1971	
864	TDL564K	Bristol RELL6G	Eastern Coach Works	OB53F	1971	
865	F86TDL	Leyland Tiger TRCTL11/2R	Marshall	DP53F	1983	Ex Ministry of Defence, 1995
901	WDL142	Kässbohrer Setra S215HD	Kässbohrer Tornado	C49F	1991	
902	WDL748	Kässbohrer Setra S215HD	Kässbohrer Tornado	C47F	1992	

Previous registrations

CXI5971	WJM811T	TJI8784	C314TDL, WDL748
F86TDL	20 KB 78, A550DPA	VDL263	C317TDL, LDZ3474
LXI4409	RDL307X	VDL613S	UFX855S, 473CDL
TDL998	TDL998, ABK832A	WDL142	H901EDL
TJI7520	E320JDL	WDL748	J902LDL
TJI8780	WDL310Y, WDL142	WXI6291	E321JDL
TJI8781	WDL311Y	934BDL	A780WHB
TJI8782	A312BDL	390CDL	C316TDL
TJI8783	A313BDL	473CDL	C315TDL

Special liveries
Overall advertisements: 679/93/5, 724
Tilling: 301, 500-2/7/63/5/73, 611/28, 806/63
Shanklin's Pony: 864
Big Dipper: 503/5/6

Three Iveco Daily minibuses added to the fleet in 1992 carry rare Car Chairs bodywork. No.237 manouvres at Newport in April 1996, with a Bristol RE in evidence in the background.
Keith Grimes

Showing the immaculate turn-out of vehicles in this fleet, No.690 is a Leyland Olympian of 1982 with Eastern Coach Works body, attracting good custom at the Tesco store in Ryde during May 1996. A.W.Mead

New in 1977, No.505, a Bristol VRT with Eastern Coach Works convertible open-top bodywork, moved across the Solent from Hants & Dorset as early as 1979. In July 1995 it was caught in Ryde sporting this eye-catching livery.
Laurie Rufus

Southern Vectis has a deserved reputation for its operation of vintage vehicles. No.507 is a Bristol LD6G of 1956 with Eastern Coach Works body subsequently converted to open-top, and currently sports a Tilling-based livery. Richard Godfrey

Not only is No.863 one of the declining number of Bristol REs which can still be found with its original owner, complete with standard Eastern Coach Works body, but it has been repainted back into Tilling-group colours. This picture was taken at Ryde.
Richard Godfrey

The coaching fleet is quite a rare sight on the mainland. In June 1996 No.320, a Leyland Tiger with Plaxton coachwork, visited the Air Show Day at Biggin Hill.
Eric Baldock

STAGECOACH SOUTH

Stagecoach South Ltd, 112 Malling Street, Lewes, East Sussex, BN7 2RB

The Stagecoach South group now covers much of the southern coast, and was restructured from 29th March 1992 into three divisions to cover operations at that time: Stagecoach South Ltd, Sussex Coastline Buses Ltd and South Coast Buses Ltd. These covered the former operations of the Southdown empire, Hampshire Bus and the former Hastings operations of Maidstone & District. To these was added Stagecoach Hants & Surrey when Alder Valley was purchased in October 1992, and Stagecoach East Kent upon the absorption of the East Kent Travel group in September 1993. Most recently, Sussex Bus was acquired on 19th October 1996.

Stagecoach livery is now dominant across the operating area, apart from a handful of vehicles retaining the liveries of the constituent companies for historical reasons, and the small East Kent coaching fleet in burgundy and cream. Substantial tranches of new vehicles have arrived in the past three years to replace older non-standard types.

Stagecoach South Ltd trades as Hampshire Bus with depots at Andover, Basingstoke and Winchester and outstations at Alton, Bishops Waltham, Marlborough, Petersfield and Stockbridge, and as Hants & Surrey at Aldershot with outstations at Alton, Guildford, Haslemere, Lindford and Petersfield. South Coast Buses Ltd has depots at Eastbourne and Hastings with outstations at Lewes, Rye, Seaford and Uckfield. Sussex Coastline has depots at Chichester, Langstone Point and Worthing, with outstations at Henfield, Leigh Park and Littlehampton. Stagecoach East Kent operates at Ashford, Dover, Folkestone, Herne Bay and Thanet (Ramsgate) with outstations at Canterbury, Deal and New Romney.

In the fleet list, previous operators are shown only where they relate to the operators as constituted before absorption into the Stagecoach South group.

The past year has seen an influx of 59 new Volvo Olympians into the fleet, all bodied by Alexander. Amongst the last of these is No.355, allocated to East Kent and found in Bexhill on the lengthy coastal route to Brighton in May 1996. Three weeks later, this particular form of the route, via Lewes, was withdrawn. Terry Blackman

STAGECOACH SOUTH

1u	H101EKR	Iveco Daily 49-10	Phoenix	B23F	1991
3	H103EKR	Iveco Daily 49.10	Phoenix	B23F	1991
4u	H104EKR	Iveco Daily 49.10	Phoenix	B23F	1991
11u	J121LKO	Iveco Daily 49.10	Dormobile Routemaker	B23F	1991
12u	J112LKO	Iveco Daily 49.10	Carlyle	B23F	1991

15-20
Iveco Daily 49.10   Dormobile Routemaker   B23F   1991

15	J115LKO	17	J117LKO	19u	J119LKO
16u	J116LKO	18	J118LKO	20u	J115LKO

97	G97SKR	Iveco Daily 49.10	Phoenix	B23F	1990

100	AYJ100T	Leyland National 11351A/1R		B52F	1979
101	AYJ101T	Leyland National 11351A/1R		B52F	1979
102	AYJ102T	Leyland National 11351A/1R		B52F	1979
103	AYJ103T	Leyland National 11351A/1R		B52F	1979

107-118
Leyland National 11351A/1R   B52F   1979

107	AYJ107T	111	ENJ911V	114	ENJ914V	117	ENJ917V
109	ENJ909V	112	ENJ912V	115	ENJ915V	118	ENJ918V
110	ENJ910V	113	ENJ913V	116	ENJ916V		

119-126
Leyland National 2 NL116L11/1R   B52F   1980

119	GYG919V	121	GYG921V	123	HFG923V	125	OUF262W
120	GYG920V	122	GYG922V	124	JNJ194V	126	SYC852

127	FDV830V	Leyland National 2 NL116L11/1R	B52F	1980	Ex Devon General, 1989
128	FDV831V	Leyland National 2 NL116L11/1R	B52F	1980	Ex Devon General, 1989

129-138
Leyland National 2 NL116AL11/1R   B49F   1981

129	HUF603X	131	HUF625X	133	HUF639X	135	HUF604X	137	HUF592X
130	HUF579X	132	PMT199X	134	HUF451X	136	HUF593X	138	HUF626X

139	FDV829V	Leyland National 2 NL116L11/1R	B48F	1980	Ex Devon General, 1989
140	CPO98W	Leyland National 2 NL106L11/1R	B41F	1980	Ex Portsmouth, 1990
142	CPO100W	Leyland National 2 NL106L11/1R	DP40F	1980	Ex Portsmouth, 1990
143	ERV115W	Leyland National 2 NL106AL11/1R	B41F	1981	Ex Portsmouth, 1990
144	ERV116W	Leyland National 2 NL106AL11/1R	B41F	1981	Ex Portsmouth, 1990
145	ERV117W	Leyland National 2 NL106AL11/1R	B41F	1981	Ex Portsmouth, 1990
146	ERV118W	Leyland National 2 NL106AL11/1R	B41F	1981	Ex Portsmouth, 1990
147	BCW827V	Leyland National 2 NL106L11/1R	B44F	1980	Ex Ribble, 1994
148	UFG48S	Leyland National 11351A/2R	B52F	1977	
149	JCK849W	Leyland National 2 NL106L11/1R	B44F	1981	Ex Ribble, 1994
152	WPR152S	Leyland National 11351A/1R	B49F	1977	
154	VOD604S	Leyland National 11351A/1R	B52F	1978	Ex Devon General, 1987
155	VOD605S	Leyland National 11351A/1R	B52F	1978	Ex Devon General, 1987
157	UHG757R	Leyland National 11351A/1R	B52F	1977	Ex Ribble, 1993
159	YRN816V	Leyland National 2 NL106L11/1R	B44F	1980	Ex Ribble, 1994
160	YRN821V	Leyland National 2 NL106L11/1R	B44F	1980	Ex Ribble, 1994
162	FPR62V	Leyland National 11351A/1R	B49F	1979	
163	PCD73R	Leyland National 11351A/1R	B49F	1976	
164	VFX984S	Leyland National 11351A/1R	B49F	1978	
167	MLJ917P	Leyland National 11351/1R	B49F	1976	
169	WYJ169S	Leyland National 11351A/2R	B48F	1978	
173	YCD73T	Leyland National 11351A/2R	B52F	1978	
174	YCD74T	Leyland National 11351A/2R	B48F	1978	
176	YCD76T	Leyland National 11351A/2R	B48F	1978	
177	YCD77T	Leyland National 11351A/2R	B48F	1978	
179	PCD79R	Leyland National 11351A/1R	B49F	1977	
180	PCD80R	Leyland National 11351A/1R	B49F	1977	
182	YCD82T	Leyland National 11351A/2R	B48F	1978	
186	CBV776S	Leyland National 11351A/1R	B49F	1978	Ex Ribble, 1986
189	AYJ89T	Leyland National 11351A/1R	B52F	1979	
190	TEL490R	Leyland National 11351A/1R	DP48F	1977	

Other additions to the fleet have comprised 31 Leyland Titans surplus to the requirements of Selkent. These have been divided between Hastings and Langstone Point. No.7237, an earlier Titan with Park Royal body, was photographed in Hastings in May 1996; note how the destination display has been modified. Terry Blackman

Unusual in a Stagecoach fleet are the 22 Metrobuses which East Kent received in the late 1980s. No.7750 was found at Cliftonville; all are now concentrated at Thanet depot. Martin Smith

Shortly before Southdown was bought out by Stagecoach, an order was fulfilled in 1988 for twelve Volvos with Northern Counties bodywork. Nine survive, represented by No.7304 at Old Steine, Brighton in June 1996. Malc McDonald

Substantial inroads have been made into the Bristol VRT fleet, though there are still significant pockets of the type within the fleet. No.782, tracked down at Guildford in June 1996, was new in 1979 and was transferred from East Midland in 1993. Malc McDonald

191	AYJ91T	Leyland National 11351A/1R			B52F	1979
192	AYJ92T	Leyland National 11351A/1R			B52F	1979
195	AYJ95T	Leyland National 11351A/1R			B52F	1979
196	RJT146R	Leyland National 11351A/1R			B49F	1977
197	AYJ97T	Leyland National 11351A/1R			B52F	1979

201-206
Leyland Olympian ON2R56G13Z4 Alexander RL   H51/36F 1988

| 201 | F601MSL | 203 | F603MSL | 205 | F605MSL |
| 202 | F602MSL | 204 | F604MSL | 206 | F606MSL |

207-214
Leyland Olympian ON2R56G13Z4 Alexander RL   DPH51/31F   1989

| 207 | G807RTS | 209 | G809RTS | 211 | G211SSL | 213 | G213SSL |
| 208 | G808RTS | 210 | G210SSL | 212 | G212SSL | 214 | G214SSL |

215-219
Leyland Olympian ON2R56G13Z4 Alexander RL   H51/34F 1990

| 215 | H815CBP | 216 | H816CBP | 217 | H817CBP | 218 | H818CBP | 219 | H819CBP |

220	J720GAP	Leyland Olympian ON2R56G13Z4 Alexander RL	DPH47/27F	1991
221	J721GAP	Leyland Olympian ON2R56G13Z4 Alexander RL	DPH47/27F	1991
222	J722GAP	Leyland Olympian ON2R56G13Z4 Alexander RL	DPH47/27F	1991
223	J623GCR	Leyland Olympian ON2R56G13Z4 Alexander RL	H47/30F	1991
224	J624GCR	Leyland Olympian ON2R56G13Z4 Alexander RL	H47/30F	1991

225-234
Leyland Olympian ON2R56G13Z4 Alexander RL   H51/34F   1990

| 225 | G705TCD | 227 | G707TCD | 229 | G709TCD | 231 | G701TCD | 233 | G703TCD |
| 226 | G706TCD | 228 | G708TCD | 230 | G710TCD | 232 | G702TCD | 234 | G704TCD |

235-240
Leyland Olympian ON2R50G13Z4 Alexander RL   DPH43/27F   1992

| 235 | K235NHC | 237 | K237NHC | 239 | K239NHC |
| 236 | K236NHC | 238 | K238NHC | 240 | K240NHC |

241-250
Volvo Olympian YN2RV18Z4   Northern Counties Countybus Palatine   DPH43/25F   1993

| 241 | L241SDY | 243 | L243SDY | 245 | L245SDY | 247 | L247SDY | 249 | L249SDY |
| 242 | L242SDY | 244 | L244SDY | 246 | L246SDY | 248 | L248SDY | 250 | L250SDY |

254	K714ASC	Leyland Olympian ON2R50G13Z4 Alexander RL	H47/32F	1992	Ex Fife Scottish, 1994
255	K715ASC	Leyland Olympian ON2R50G13Z4 Alexander RL	H47/32F	1992	Ex Fife Scottish, 1994
256	K716ASC	Leyland Olympian ON2R50G13Z4 Alexander RL	H47/32F	1992	Ex Fife Scottish, 1994
257	K717ASC	Leyland Olympian ON2R50G13Z4 Alexander RL	H47/32F	1992	Ex Fife Scottish, 1994

341-399
Volvo Olympian YN2RC16V3   Alexander   CH47/28F   1995/6   * H47/32F

341	N341MPN	353	N353MPN	365*	N365LPN	377*	N377LPN	389	N389LPN
342	N342MPN	354	N354MPN	366*	N366LPN	378*	N378LPN	390	N390LPN
343	N343MPN	355	N355MPN	367*	N367LPN	379*	N379LPN	391	N391LPN
344	N344MPN	356	N356MPN	368*	N368LPN	380*	N380LPN	392	N392LPN
345	N345MPN	357	N357MPN	369*	N369LPN	381	N381LPN	393	N393LPN
346	N346MPN	358	N358MPN	370*	N370LPN	382	N382LPN	394	N394LPN
347	N347MPN	359	N359MPN	371*	N371LPN	383	N383LPN	395	N395LPN
348	N348MPN	360*	N360LPN	372*	N372LPN	384	N384LPN	396	N396LPN
349	N349MPN	361*	N361LPN	373*	N373LPN	385	N385LPN	397	N397LPN
350	N350MPN	362*	N362LPN	374*	N374LPN	386	N386LPN	398	N398LPN
351	N351MPN	363*	N363LPN	375*	N375LPN	387	N387LPN	399	N399LPN
352	N352MPN	364*	N364LPN	376*	N376LPN	388	N388LPN		

400	400DCD	Volvo B6-50	Alexander Dash	DP35F	1994
401	401DCD	Volvo B6-50	Alexander Dash	DP35F	1994
402	402DCD	Volvo B6-50	Alexander Dash	DP35F	1994
403	403DCD	Volvo B6-50	Alexander Dash	DP35F	1994

422-450
Bristol VRT/SL3/6LXB   Eastern Coach Works   H43/31F 1979-80   422/35/46-50 ex Devon General, 1988-89

| 422 | FDV818V | 438 | KRU838W | 446 | LFJ874W | 448 | LFJ870W | 450 | LFJ880W |
| 435 | FDV839V | 444 | KRU844W | 447 | LFJ881W | 449 | LFJ875W | | |

451-467
Dennis Dart 9.8SDL   Alexander Dash   DP40F   1996

451	N451PAP	455	N455PAP	459	N459PAP	463	N463PAP	467	N467PAP
452	N452PAP	456	N456PAP	460	N460PAP	464	N464PAP		
453	N453PAP	457	N457PAP	461	N461PAP	465	N465PAP		
454	N454PAP	458	N458PAP	462	N462PAP	466	N466PAP		

501-580 Dennis Dart 9.8SDL3017 Alexander Dash B40F* 1992 * 501-34 are B41F

501	J501GCD	517	J517GCD	533	J533GCD	549	J549GCD	565	K565NHC
502	J502GCD	518	J518GCD	534	J534GCD	550	J550GCD	566	K566NHC
503	J503GCD	519	J519GCD	535	J535GCD	551	J551GCD	567	K567NHC
504	J504GCD	520	J520GCD	536	J536GCD	552	J552GCD	568	K568NHC
505	J505GCD	521	J521GCD	537	J537GCD	553	K553NHC	569	K569NHC
506	J506GCD	522	J522GCD	538	J538GCD	554	K554NHC	570	K570NHC
507	J507GCD	523	J523GCD	539	J539GCD	555	K655NHC	571	K571NHC
508	J508GCD	524	J524GCD	540	J540GCD	556	K556NHC	572	K572NHC
509	J509GCD	525	J525GCD	541	J541GCD	557	K557NHC	573	K573NHC
510	J510GCD	526	J526GCD	542	J542GCD	558	K558NHC	574	K574NHC
511	J511GCD	527	J527GCD	543	J543GCD	559	K559NHC	575	K575NHC
512	J512GCD	528	J528GCD	544	J544GCD	560	K660NHC	576	K576NHC
513	J513GCD	529	J529GCD	545	J545GCD	561	K561NHC	577	K577NHC
514	J514GCD	530	J530GCD	546	J546GCD	562	K562NHC	578	K578NHC
515	J515GCD	531	J531GCD	547	J547GCD	563	K563NHC	579	K579NHC
516	J516GCD	532	J532GCD	548	J548GCD	564	K564NHC	580	K580NHC

581	J701YRM	Dennis Dart 9.8SDL3017	Alexander Dash	B40F	1991	Ex Cumberland, 1992
582	J702YRM	Dennis Dart 9.8SDL3017	Alexander Dash	B41F	1991	Ex Cumberland, 1992
583	J703YRM	Dennis Dart 9.8SDL3017	Alexander Dash	B41F	1992	Ex Cumberland, 1992

584-588 Dennis Dart 9.8SDL3017 Alexander Dash B40F* 1992 * 584 is B41F

584	K584ODY	585	K585ODY	586	K586ODY	587	K587ODY	588	K588ODY

601-605 Volvo B10M-55 Northern Counties DP49F 1994

601	L601VCD	602	L602VCD	603	L603VCD	604	404DCD	605	405DCD

606-661 Volvo B10M-55 Alexander PS DP48F 1993-5

655-658 ex Ribble, 1994; 659-661 ex Cumberland, 1994

606	406DCD	616	L616TDY	626	L626TDY	636	M636BCD	650	M650BCD
607	407DCD	617	L617TDY	627	L627TDY	637	M637BCD	651	M651BCD
608	408DCD	618	L618TDY	628	L628TDY	638	M638BCD	652	M652BCD
609	L609TDY	619	419DCD	629	L629TDY	639	M639BCD	655	415DCD
610	410DCD	620	420DCD	630	L630TDY	640	N640LPN	656	416DCD
611	411DCD	621	421DCD	631	L631TDY	641	N641LPN	657	417DCD
612	412DCD	622	422DCD	632	L632TDY	642	N642LPN	658	418DCD
613	413DCD	623	423DCD	633	L633TDY	643	N643LPN	659	K789DAO
614	414DCD	624	L624TDY	634	L634TDY	644	N644LPN	660	K790DAO
615	M615APN	625	L625TDY	635	L635TDY	645	N645LPN	661	K791DAO

662-670 Volvo B10M-55 Northern Counties DP47F 1995

662	M662ECD	664	M664ECD	667	M667ECD	669	M669ECD
663	M663ECD	665	M665ECD	668	M668ECD	670	M670ECD

671	M311YSC	Volvo B10M-55	Alexander PS	DP48F	1995
672	M312YSC	Volvo B10M-55	Alexander PS	DP48F	1995
673	M313YSC	Volvo B10M-55	Alexander PS	DP48F	1995

678-692 Bristol VRT/SL3/6LXB Eastern Coach Works H43/31F 1979-80

678	EAP978V	685	EAP985V	687	EAP987V	690	EAP990V	692	EAP992V
684	EAP984V	686	EAP986V	688	EAP988V	691	EAP991V		

749	BKE849T	Bristol VRT/SL3/6LXB	Eastern Coach Works	H43/31F 1979	Ex Maidstone & District, 1983
750	BKE850T	Bristol VRT/SL3/6LXB	Eastern Coach Works	H43/31F 1979	Ex Maidstone & District, 1983
759	BKE859T	Bristol VRT/SL3/6LXB	Eastern Coach Works	H43/31F 1979	Ex Maidstone & District, 1983
768	AAP668T	Bristol VRT/SL3/6LXB	Eastern Coach Works	H43/28F 1979	
780	BAU180T	Bristol VRT/SL3/6LXB	Eastern Coach Works	H43/31F 1978	Ex East Midland, 1993
782	AET182T	Bristol VRT/SL3/6LXB	Eastern Coach Works	H43/31F 1979	Ex East Midland, 1993
787	AET187T	Bristol VRT/SL3/6LXB	Eastern Coach Works	H43/31F 1979	Ex East Midland, 1993

841-850 Mercedes-Benz 709D Alexander AM B23F* 1990 * 841-3 are B25F

841	G71APO	843	G73APO	845	G975ARV	847	G977ARV	849	H679BTP
842	G72APO	844	G974ARV	846	G976ARV	848	G978ARV	850	H680BTP

Above **The fleet includes a large number of Volvo B10 single-deckers with Alexander dual-purpose bodywork, some from other Stagecoach companies. No.657 came from Ribble in 1994 and subsequently gained a Southdown cherished registration. It was caught at Guildford in June 1996.** Malc McDonald

Left **New in 1995, No. 665 is a Volvo B10 with Northern Counties dual-purpose bodywork which spent the first few weeks of its life on loan to East London as a driver-trainer. It was caught at Eastrop Round-about in this view.** Calvin Churchill

1996 deliveries have included eighteen Dennis Darts with dual-purpose Alexander bodywork. No.457 was freshly into service at Basingstoke when photographed in June 1996. Malc McDonald

Above **In 1994, four Volvo B6s with Alexander Dash bodies were purchased for Park-and-Ride service at Winchester. All have received cherished Southdown registrations, and three carry dedicated livery, as shown by No.402 and another in April 1995.** Richard Godfrey

Left **Canterbury is another location to support Park-and-Ride services. No.1402 is an Optare Delta painted in special livery for this service, which was extended across the city to a second site in 1994.** Malc McDonald

Four vehicles have been taken on extended loan from East London for rail-link services connecting into South West Trains, for which Stagecoach took up the franchise in February 1996. No.5004 is a Dennis Dart with Alexander bodywork, originating from Busways and given a private registration formerly on an East Kent coach. Calvin Churchill

853-904 Mercedes-Benz 709D Alexander(Belfast) B25F* 1993/5 * 894-904 are B23F

853	K853ODY	864	K864ODY	875	K875ODY	886	L886SDY	897	N197LPN
854	K854ODY	865	K865ODY	876	K876ODY	887	L887SDY	898	N198LPN
855	K855ODY	866	K866ODY	877	K877ODY	888	L188SDY	899	N199LPN
856	K856ODY	867	K867ODY	878	K878ODY	889	M889ECD	901	N201LPN
857	K857ODY	868	K868ODY	879	K879ODY	890	M890ECD	902	N202LPN
858	K858ODY	869	K869ODY	880	K880ODY	891	N191LPN	903	N203LPN
859	K859ODY	870	K870ODY	881	L881SDY	892	N192LPN	904	N204LPN
860	K860ODY	871	K871ODY	882	L882SDY	893	N193LPN		
861	K861ODY	872	K872ODY	883	L883SDY	894	N194LPN		
862	K862ODY	873	K873ODY	884	L884SDY	895	N195LPN		
863	K863ODY	874	K874ODY	885	L885SDY	896	N196LPN		

905-977 Mercedes-Benz 709D Alexander B23F* 1996 * 905-923 are B25F

905	N905NAP	920	N920NAP	935	N935NAP	950	N950NAP	965	N965NAP
906	N906NAP	921	N921NAP	936	N936NAP	951	N951NAP	966	N966NAP
907	N907NAP	922	N922NAP	937	N937NAP	952	N952NAP	967	N967NAP
908	N908NAP	923	N923NAP	938	N938NAP	953	N953NAP	968	N968NAP
909	N909NAP	924	N924NAP	939	N939NAP	954	N954NAP	969	N969NAP
910	N910NAP	925	N925NAP	940	N940NAP	955	N955NAP	970	N970NAP
911	N911NAP	926	N926NAP	941	N941NAP	956	N956NAP	971	N971NAP
912	N912NAP	927	N927NAP	942	N942NAP	957	N957NAP	972	N972NAP
913	N913NAP	928	N928NAP	943	N943NAP	958	N958NAP	973	N973NAP
914	N914NAP	929	N929NAP	944	N944NAP	959	N959NAP	974	N974NAP
915	N915NAP	930	N930NAP	945	N945NAP	960	N960NAP	975	N975NAP
916	N916NAP	931	N931NAP	946	N946NAP	961	N961NAP	976	N976NAP
917	N917NAP	932	N932NAP	947	N947NAP	962	N962NAP	977	N977NAP
918	N918NAP	933	N933NAP	948	N948NAP	963	N963NAP		
919	N919NAP	934	N934NAP	949	N949NAP	964	N964NAP		

1064	VSV564	Leyland Tiger TRCTL11/3R	Plaxton Paramount 3200Exp	C49F	1983	Ex Maidstone & District, 1985
1072	USV672	Leyland Tiger TRCTL11/3R	Plaxton Paramount 3200Exp	C49F	1983	Ex Maidstone & District, 1985
1094	GPJ894N	Leyland National 11351/1R		B49F	1975	Ex The Bee Line, 1992
1105	M105CCD	Dennis Javelin 11SDL2133	Plaxton Interurban	DP47F	1995	
1106	M106CCD	Dennis Javelin 11SDL2133	Plaxton Interurban	DP47F	1995	
1108	M108CCD	Dennis Javelin 11SDL2133	Plaxton Interurban	DP47F	1995	
1115	MFN115R	Leyland National 11351A/1R		B49F	1976	
1176	NPJ476R	Leyland National 11351A/1R		B49F	1976	Ex Thames Valley & Aldershot, 1986
1180	UMO180N	Leyland National 11351/1R		B49F	1974	
1181	NFN81R	Leyland National 11351A/1R		DP48F	1977	
1188	NFN88R	Leyland National 11351A/1R		DP48F	1977	
1201	HPK503N	Leyland National 11351/1R		B49F	1975	Ex Thames Valley & Aldershot, 1986
1203	HPK505N	Leyland National 11351/1R		B49F	1975	Ex Thames Valley & Aldershot, 1986
1215	KPA366P	Leyland National 11351/1R		B49F	1975	Ex Thames Valley & Aldershot, 1986
1218	KPA369P	Leyland National 11351/1R		B49F	1975	Ex Thames Valley & Aldershot, 1986
1223	KPA374P	Leyland National 11351/1R		B49F	1975	Ex Thames Valley & Aldershot, 1986
1228	KPA379P	Leyland National 11351/1R		B49F	1975	Ex Thames Valley & Aldershot, 1986
1232u	KPA383P	Leyland National 11351/1R		B49F	1975	Ex Thames Valley & Aldershot, 1986
1236	KPA387P	Leyland National 11351A/1R		B49F	1976	Ex Thames Valley & Aldershot, 1986
1237	KPA388P	Leyland National 11351A/1R		B49F	1976	Ex Thames Valley & Aldershot, 1986
1238	KPA389P	Leyland National 11351A/1R		B49F	1976	Ex Thames Valley & Aldershot, 1986
1247	LPF605P	Leyland National 11351/1R/SC		B49F	1976	Ex Thames Valley & Aldershot, 1986
1256	NPJ477R	Leyland National 11351A/1R		B49F	1976	Ex Thames Valley & Aldershot, 1986
1259	NPJ480R	Leyland National 11351A/1R		B49F	1976	Ex Thames Valley & Aldershot, 1986
1261	NPJ482R	Leyland National 11351A/1R		B49F	1976	Ex Thames Valley & Aldershot, 1986
1271	TPE148S	Leyland National 11351A/1R		B49F	1977	Ex Thames Valley & Aldershot, 1986
1272	TPE149S	Leyland National 11351A/1R		B49F	1977	Ex Thames Valley & Aldershot, 1986
1344	PJJ344S	Leyland National 10351A/1R		B41F	1977	
1401	J401LKO	DAF SB220LC550	Optare Delta	B49F	1991	
1402	J402LKO	DAF SB220LC550	Optare Delta	B49F	1991	
1403	J403LKO	DAF SB220LC550	Optare Delta	B49F	1991	

1404-1408 Dennis Lance SLF 11SDA3201 Berkhof 2000 B40F 1994

1404	M404OKM	1405	M405OKM	1406	M406OKM	1407	M407OKM	1408	M408OKM

1546	GFN546N	Leyland National 10351/1R		B40F	1975	
1890	JJG890P	Leyland National 11351A/1R		B49F	1976	
1898	JJG898P	Leyland National 11351A/1R		B49F	1976	
2136	N136MPN	OCC Omni	OCC	B21F	1995	Ex Sussex Bus, Pagham, 1996

2402	H402KPY	CVE Omni	CVE	B23F	1990	Ex Sussex Bus, Pagham, 1996
2586	XIA586	Leyland National 11351A/1R	(urban bus)	B62F	1976	Ex Sussex Bus, Pagham, 1996
2612	XSU612	Leyland Leopard PSU3F/4R	Willowbrook Warrior(1990)	B48F	1981	Ex Sussex Bus, Pagham, 1996
2646	G646DBG	CVE Omni	CVE	B23F	1989	Ex Sussex Bus, Pagham, 1996
2651	F651RBP	Iveco Daily 49.10	Robin Hood City Nippy	B25F	1989	Ex Sussex Bus, Pagham, 1996
2682	XSU682	Leyland Leopard PSU3B/4R	Willowbrook Warrior(1990)	B49F	1973	Ex Sussex Bus, Pagham, 1996
2705	E705LYU	MCW Metrorider MF158/2	Metro-Cammell-Weymann	DP33F	1988	Ex Sussex Bus, Pagham, 1996
2857	XIA857	Leyland National 11351A/1R	(urban bus)	B62F	1977	Ex Sussex Bus, Pagham, 1996
2978	CSU978	Leyland Leopard PSU3B/4R	Willowbrook Warrior(1988)	B53F	1975	Ex Sussex Bus, Pagham, 1996
2992	CSU992	Leyland Leopard PSU3E/4R	Willowbrook Warrior(1990)	DP60F	1979	Ex Sussex Bus, Pagham, 1996
5001	472YMF	DAF SB220LC550	Optare Delta	B40D	1992	Ex East London, 1996
5002	YLJ332	DAF SB220LC550	Optare Delta	B40D	1992	Ex East London, 1996
5003	NFX667	Dennis Dart 9.8SDL3017	Alexander Dash	DP32F	1992	Ex Busways, 1996
5004	XYK976	Dennis Dart 9.8SDL3017	Alexander Dash	DP32F	1992	Ex Busways, 1996
7201	KYV511X	Leyland Titan TNLXB2RR	Leyland	H44/24F	1982	Ex Selkent, 1995
7203	A823SUL	Leyland Titan TNLXB2RR	Leyland	H44/26F	1983	Ex Selkent, 1995
7205	KYV305X	Leyland Titan TNLXB2RR	Leyland	H44/24F	1981	Ex Selkent, 1995
7211	NUW611Y	Leyland Titan TNLXB2RR	Leyland	H44/24F	1982	Ex Selkent, 1995
7215	CUL215V	Leyland Titan TNLXB2RRSp	Park Royal	H44/26F	1980	Ex Selkent, 1995
7220	KYV420X	Leyland Titan TNLXB2RR	Leyland	H44/24F	1982	Ex Selkent, 1995
7223	KYV523X	Leyland Titan TNLXB2RR	Leyland	H44/26F	1982	Ex Selkent, 1995
7225	CUL225V	Leyland Titan TNLXB2RRSp	Park Royal	H44/24F	1980	Ex Selkent, 1995
7229	EYE229V	Leyland Titan TNLXB2RRSp	Park Royal	H44/26F	1980	Ex Selkent, 1995
7233	EYE233V	Leyland Titan TNLXB2RRSp	Park Royal	H44/26F	1980	Ex Selkent, 1995
7237	EYE237V	Leyland Titan TNLXB2RRSp	Park Royal	H44/26F	1980	Ex Selkent, 1995
7240	EYE240V	Leyland Titan TNLXB2RRSp	Park Royal	H44/26F	1980	Ex Selkent, 1995
7242	KYV442X	Leyland Titan TNLXB2RR	Leyland	H44/24F	1982	Ex Selkent, 1995
7244	EYE244V	Leyland Titan TNLXB2RRSp	Park Royal	H44/26F	1980	Ex Selkent, 1995
7245	KYV345X	Leyland Titan TNLXB2RR	Leyland	H44/26F	1981	Ex Selkent, 1995
7248	KYV348X	Leyland Titan TNLXB2RR	Leyland	H44/24F	1981	Ex Selkent, 1995
7250	EYE250V	Leyland Titan TNLXB2RRSp	Park Royal	H44/26F	1980	Ex Selkent, 1995
7251	KYV451X	Leyland Titan TNLXB2RR	Leyland	H44/24F	1982	Ex Selkent, 1995
7261	KYV361X	Leyland Titan TNLXB2RR	Leyland	H44/24F	1981	Ex Selkent, 1996
7268	CUL168V	Leyland Titan TNLXB2RRSp	Park Royal	H44/24F	1980	Ex Selkent, 1995
7269	CUL169V	Leyland Titan TNLXB2RRSp	Park Royal	H44/26F	1980	Ex Selkent, 1995
7274	KYV474X	Leyland Titan TNLXB2RR	Leyland	H44/24F	1982	Ex Selkent, 1995
7279	CUL79V	Leyland Titan TNLXB2RRSp	Park Royal	H44/26F	1979	Ex Selkent, 1995
7280	CUL180V	Leyland Titan TNLXB2RRSp	Park Royal	H44/24F	1980	Ex Selkent, 1995
7287	KYV487X	Leyland Titan TNLXB2RR	Leyland	H44/24F	1982	Ex Selkent, 1995
7288	KYN288X	Leyland Titan TNLXB2RR	Leyland	H44/24F	1981	Ex Selkent, 1995
7290	CUL190V	Leyland Titan TNLXB2RRSp	Park Royal	H44/24F	1980	Ex Selkent, 1995
7294	NUW594Y	Leyland Titan TNLXB2RR	Leyland	H44/24F	1982	Ex Selkent, 1995
7296	NUW596Y	Leyland Titan TNLXB2RR	Leyland	H44/24F	1982	Ex Selkent, 1995
7297	KYV397X	Leyland Titan TNLXB2RR	Leyland	H44/24F	1982	Ex Selkent, 1995
7298	CUL198V	Leyland Titan TNLXB2RRSp	Park Royal	H44/26F	1980	Ex Selkent, 1995

7301-7309   Volvo Citybus D10M-50   Northern Counties   DPH43/33F 1989

7301	F301MYJ	7303	F303MYJ	7305	F305MYJ	7307	F307MYJ	7309 F309MYJ
7302	F302MYJ	7304	F304MYJ	7306	F306MYJ	7308	F308MYJ	

7322	VTV172S	Bristol VRT/SL3/6LXB	Eastern Coach Works	H43/31F	1978	Ex East Midland, 1993
7347	AAP647T	Bristol VRT/SL3/6LXB	Eastern Coach Works	H43/31F	1978	
7352	JWV252W	Bristol VRT/SL3/6LXB	Eastern Coach Works	H43/31F	1980	
7353	JWV253W	Bristol VRT/SL3/6LXB	Eastern Coach Works	H43/31F	1980	
7355	SWV255W	Bristol VRT/SL3/6LXB	Eastern Coach Works	H43/31F	1980	
7356	JWV256W	Bristol VRT/SL3/6LXB	Eastern Coach Works	H43/31F	1980	
7358	JWV258W	Bristol VRT/SL3/6LXB	Eastern Coach Works	H43/31F	1980	
7359	DBV29W	Bristol VRT/SL3/6LXB	Eastern Coach Works	DPH43/31F	1980	Ex Ribble, 1986
7360	AAP660T	Bristol VRT/SL3/6LXB	Eastern Coach Works	H43/28F	1978	
7362	AAP662T	Bristol VRT/SL3/6LXB	Eastern Coach Works	H43/28F	1979	
7365	DBV25W	Bristol VRT/SL3/6LXB	Eastern Coach Works	DP43/31F	1980	Ex Ribble, 1986
7366	JWV266W	Bristol VRT/SL3/680	Eastern Coach Works	H43/31F	1981	now Gardner 6LXB engine
7367	JWV267W	Bristol VRT/SL3/680	Eastern Coach Works	DPH43/27F	1981	now Gardner 6LXB engine
7368	JWV268W	Bristol VRT/SL3/680	Eastern Coach Works	H43/31F	1981	now Gardner 6LXB engine
7369	JWV269W	Bristol VRT/SL3/680	Eastern Coach Works	H43/31F	1981	now Gardner 6LXB engine
7371	AAP671T	Bristol VRT/SL3/6LXB	Eastern Coach Works	H43/28F	1979	
7373	EAP973V	Bristol VRT/SL3/6LXB	Eastern Coach Works	H43/31F	1979	
7374	JWV274W	Bristol VRT/SL3/680	Eastern Coach Works	H43/31F	1981	
7375	JWV275W	Bristol VRT/SL3/680	Eastern Coach Works	H43/31F	1981	
7376	JWV976W	Bristol VRT/SL3/680	Eastern Coach Works	H43/31F	1981	now Gardner 6LXB engine

Leyland Nationals have also been reduced in number. No.121, a Mk2 example dating from 1980, was photographed in Chichester working for Sussex Coastline in June 1996. Malc McDonald

Renewal and standardisation of the minibus fleet has been achieved through generous doses of Mercedes-Benz 709D vehicles with Alexander bodywork. The newest such vehicles, bodied at Falkirk, have virtually eliminated the large contingent of Ivecos in the East Kent fleet. No.971 leaves Folkestone Bus Station in April 1996. Laurie Rufus

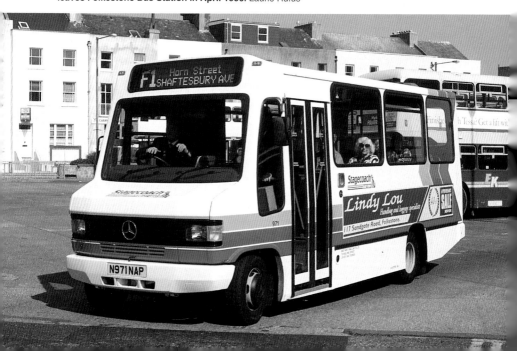

Two of the former Southdown convertible open-top Bristol VRTs survive. No.7623, allocated to Hastings, has been painted into dedicated livery to operate local tours on behalf of Guide Friday; note the legend for "1066 Country" on the nearside. Terry Blackman

Stagecoach South is the only major operator in the area with National Express work. No.8915, a Plaxton Expressliner in the East Kent fleet, was new in 1995, and was photographed at the Eastern Docks, Dover in June 1996. Eric Baldock

7377	EAP977V	Bristol VRT/SL3/6LXB	Eastern Coach Works	H43/31F	1979	
7382u	EAP982V	Bristol VRT/SL3/6LXB	Eastern Coach Works	H43/31F	1979	
7392	VPR491S	Bristol VRT/SL3/6LXB	Eastern Coach Works	H43/31F	1978	
7394	HFG193T	Bristol VRT/SL3/6LXB	Eastern Coach Works	H43/31F	1978	
7395	YEL2T	Bristol VRT/SL3/6LXB	Eastern Coach Works	H43/31F	1978	
7397	YEL4T	Bristol VRT/SL3/6LXB	Eastern Coach Works	H43/31F	1978	
7621u	UWV621S	Bristol VRT/SL3/6LXB	Eastern Coach Works	CO43/31F	1978	
7623u	UWV623S	Bristol VRT/SL3/6LXB	Eastern Coach Works	CO43/31F	1978	

7650-7685 Bristol VRT/SL3/6LB   Eastern Coach Works   H43/31F   1980-81
7655 rebodied 1983

7650 XJJ650V	**7658** XJJ658V	**7665** XJJ665V	**7672** BJG672V	**7681** SKL681X
7651 XJJ651V	**7659** XJJ659V	**7666** XJJ666V	**7673** BJG673V	**7682** SKL682X
7652 XJJ652V	**7660** XJJ660V	**7667** XJJ667V	**7674** BJG674V	**7683** SKL683X
7653 XJJ653V	**7661** XJJ661V	**7668** XJJ668V	**7675** BJG675V	**7684** SKL684X
7654 XJJ654V	**7662** XJJ662V	**7669** XJJ669V	**7677** CJJ677W	**7685** SKL685X
7655 XJJ655V	**7663** XJJ663V	**7670** XJJ670V	**7679** CJJ679W	
7657 XJJ657V	**7664** XJJ664V	**7671** BJG671V	**7680** SKL680X	

7746-7755 MCW Metrobus 2 DR132/11   Metro-Cammell-Weymann H46/31F   1988

7746 E746SKR	**7748** E748SKR	**7750** E750SKR	**7752** E752SKR	**7754** E754UKR
7747 E747SKR	**7749** E749SKR	**7751** E751SKR	**7753** E753SKR	**7755** E755UKR

7761-7767 MCW Metrobus 2 DR132/15   Metro-Cammell-Weymann DPH43/27F 1989

7761 F761EKM	**7763** F763EKM	**7765** F765EKM	**7767** F767EKM
7762 F762EKM	**7764** F764EKM	**7766** F766EKM	

7771-7775 MCW Metrobus 2 DR132/14   Metro-Cammell-Weymann H46/31F   1989

7771 F771EKM	**7772** F772EKM	**7773** F773EKM	**7774** F774EKM	**7775** F775EKM

7781	F781KKP	Scania N113DRB	Alexander RH	H47/33F	1989
7782	F782KKP	Scania N113DRB	Alexander RH	H47/33F	1989

7801-7810 Leyland Olympian ON2R56C16Z4 Northern Counties   H51/34F   1990

7801 H801BKK	**7803** H803BKK	**7805** H805BKK	**7807** H807BKK	**7809** H809BKK
7802 H802BKK	**7804** H804BKK	**7806** H806BKK	**7808** H808BKK	**7810** H810BKK

7811	J811NKK	Leyland Olympian ON2R50C13Z4	Northern Counties	
			Countybus Palatine	H47/30F	1992
7812	J812NKK	Leyland Olympian ON2R50C13Z4	Northern Counties	
			Countybus Palatine	H47/30F	1992
7813	J813NKK	Leyland Olympian ON2R50C13Z4	Northern Counties	
			Countybus Palatine	H47/30F	1992
7814	J814NKK	Leyland Olympian ON2R50C13Z4	Northern Counties	
			Countybus Palatine	H47/30F	1992

7821-7830 Leyland Olympian ON2R50C13Z4 Northern Counties
Countybus Palatine   H47/30F   1993

7821 K821TKP	**7823** K823TKP	**7825** K825TKP	**7827** L827BKK	**7829** L829BKK
7822 K822TKP	**7824** K824TKP	**7826** L826BKK	**7828** L828BKK	**7830** L830BKK

7950-7988 Bristol VRT/SL3/6LXB   Eastern Coach Works   H43/31F   1978-80 Ex Thames Valley & Aldershot, 1986

7950 TPE156S	**7962** GGM82W	**7969** WJM829T	**7980** CJH120V
7956 GGM86W	**7965** WJM825T	**7972** WJM832T	**7982** CJH142V
7960 GGM80W	**7966** WJM826T	**7977** CJH117V	**7985** CJH145V
7961 GGM81W	**7968** WJM828T	**7979** CJH119V	**7988** KKK888V

8211	D211VEV	Scania K112CRB	Berkhof Esprite 350	C41FTL	1987	
8243	SIB8243	Volvo B10M-60	Plaxton Paramount 3500 3	C49FT	1991	Ex Park, Hamilton, 1993

8404-8410 Volvo B10M-62   Plaxton Première 350   C53F*   1995   * 8410 is C49FT

8404 M404BFG	**8406** M406BFG	**8408** M408BFG	**8410** M410BFG
8405 M405BFG	**8407** M407BFG	**8409** M409BFG	

8503	IIL3503	Volvo B10M-61	Van Hool Alizée	C49FT	1988	Ex Cumberland, 1995
8505	IIL3505	Volvo B10M-61	Van Hool Alizée	C49FT	1988	Ex Cumberland, 1995
8618	WVT618	Volvo B10M-61	Plaxton Paramount 3500 3	C50F	1987	Ex Cumberland, 1995
8856	J856NKK	Scania K93CRB	Plaxton Paramount 3500 3	C49FT	1992	
8909	J909NKP	Volvo B10M-60	Plaxton Expressliner	C49FT	1992	

142

8910-8918 Volvo B10M-62*   Plaxton Expressliner 2   C49FT   1993-5   * 8910 is Volvo B10M-60

8910 K910TKP	**8912** M912WJK	**8914** M914WJK	**8916** M916WJK	**8918** M918WJK
8911 M911WJK	**8913** M913WJK	**8915** M915WJK	**8917** M917WJK	

8996 PFN873   Bova FHD12-280   Bova Futura   C49FT   1986   Ex Marinair, Canterbury, 1991

Special events vehicles

0135	CD7045	Leyland G7	Short (1926)	O27/24RO	1922	Ex preservation, 1970
0409	409DCD	Leyland Titan PD3/4	Northern Counties	FCO39/30F	1964	
0424	424DCD	Leyland Titan PD3/4	Northern Counties	FCO39/30F	1964	
0770	HKE690L	Bristol VRT/SL2/6LX	Eastern Coach Works	O43/34F	1973	Ex Maidstone & District, 1983
0813	UF4813	Leyland Titan TD1	Brush	O27/24RO	1929	
0946	MFN946F	AEC Regent V 3D3RA	Park Royal	H40/32F	1967	Ex East Kent, 1983

Previous registrations

CJV978	HWY718N, CSU934	SIB8243	H826AHS	407DCD	L607TDY
CSU992	OMA506V, TCS157	SYC852	JWV126W	408DCD	L608TDY
HFG193T	YEL1T	USV672	FKL172Y	410DCD	M610APN
HUF451X	RUF434X, XLD244	VSV564	FKL171Y	411DCD	M611APN
HUF579X	RUF430X, 400DCD	WVT618	D202LWX	412DCD	M612APN
HUF592X	RUF437X, 407DCD	XIA586	RYG773R	413DCD	M613APN
HUF593X	RUF436X, 406DCD	XIA857	PKP548R, XIA256	414DCD	M614APN
HUF603X	RUF429X, 415DCD	XSU612	PWT278W	415DCD	L345KCK
HUF604X	RUF435X, 405DCD	XSU682	OKG158M	416DCD	L346KCK
HUF625X	RUF431X, 411DCD	XYK976	K719PCN	417DCD	L347KCK
HUF626X	RUF438X, 410DCD	YLJ332	J715CYG	418DCD	L348KCK
HUF639X	RUF433X, MSV533, 420DCD	400DCD	M490BFG	419DCD	L619TDY
IIL3503	E625UNE, TXI2426, E936XSB	401DCD	M401BFG	420DCD	L620TDY
IIL3505	E623UNE, XIA257, E942XSB	402DCD	M402BFG	421DCD	L621TDY
JNJ194V	HFG924V, DSV943	403DCD	M403BFG	422DCD	L622TDY
NFX667	K716PCN	404DCD	L604VCD	423DCD	L6223TDY
OUF262W	JWV125W, LYJ145	405DCD	L605VCD	424DCD	424DCD, AOR158B
PFN873	C996FKM	406DCD	L606TDY	472YMF	J713CYG
PMT199X	RUF432X, YLJ332				

Special liveries
East Kent Coach: 8243, 8404-10, 8856, 8996
East Sussex County Rider: 2891/2
Freedom Coach for the Disabled: 8211
Guide Friday: 0770, 7623
Hastings Buses: 0946
National Express: 8909-18
Overall advertisements: 13, 97, 139, 219/35/46, 509/24/41/63/4/81/3, 877/8, 938/77, 1546, 7205, 7347, 7661/64/72/4/82/4, 7763/5, 7805/7/9
Canterbury Park & Ride: 1401-8, 7801
South West Trains: 5001-4
Sussex Bus: 2136/402/586/612/46/51/82/705/857/978/92
Traditional Southdown: 0135, 0409/24, 0813
Winchester Park & Ride: 400/2/3
White: 401, 8503

Fleet disposition
Coastline: 118-35/7-9, 209/15-24/8-35/7-40/3-5, 341-50/95-9, 464-7, 551-69/74/9/80, 610/1/21-3/6/8-30/84/6/7/91/2, 849/89-93, 917-21, 1180, 1203/72, 7201/11/20/5/9/42/5/8/51/61/9/94/6-8, 7365/7/8/75/6
East Kent: 3, 15/7/8, 97, 195/7, 225-7/54-7, 355/60-5/8-78/81/9/90, 632-4/9/40/59-61, 894-9, 901-4/22-77, 1105/6/8/15/81, 1344, 1401-8, 1546, 1890/8, 7355, 7652/3/5/7-66/8-75/7/9-85, 7746-55/61-7/71-5/81/2, 7801-14/21-30, 7977, 8211/43, 8404-10, 8503/5, 8618, 8856, 8909-18/96
Hampshire Bus: 100/2/3/13/5-7/52/4/64/7/74/80/2/6/90-2/6, 201-6/8/10-4/46-50, 366/7/91-4, 400-3/22/35/8/44/6-50/6-62, 524-40/2-50/73/81/2, 606-8/15-7/25/7/31/41-3/51/2/5/8/62-5/7-70, 749/87, 841-3/6-8/50/3, 915/6, 1072, 1176, 1247/56, 5001-3, 7322/47/52/3/6/8/60/2/6/9/73/4/7/92/4/5/7, 7651, 7950/6/61/5/6/88
Hants & Surrey: 162/89, 207/36, 351-3/79/80, 522/3/70-2/5-8/84-8, 618/24/35/56/7/85/8, 759/80/2, 854-80, 905-14, 1064/94, 1201/15/8/23/8/36-8/59/61/71, 5004, 7650/4/67, 7960/8/9/72/9/80/2/5
South Coast Buses: 101/7/10-2/4/36/40/2-9/55/9/60/3/9/73/6/7/9, 241/2, 356-9/82-8, 451-5, 501-21/41/83, 601-5/9/12-4/9/20/36-8/44/5/50/71-3, 750/68, 844/5/81-8, 7203/5/15/23/33/7/40/4/50/68/74/9/80/7/8/90, 7301-9/71
Reserve fleet: 354, 463, 680
Unallocated: 16
Repaint float: 109/57, 678, 7359
Sussex Bus: 2136, 2402, 2586, 2612/46/51/82, 2705, 2857, 2978/92
Unlicensed: 1, 4, 11/2/9, 20, 7382, 7621/3, 7962

THAMES TRANSIT

Thames Transit Ltd, Unit 4, Horspath Road, Cowley, Oxford, OX4 2RY

Thames Transit, then part of the Transit Holdings group based at Exeter, started operations in Oxford on 7th March 1987 with a half-hourly coach service between Oxford and London marketed as "Oxford Tube". This has subsequently been increased in frequency and extended in London to Victoria. A minibus service in Oxford started from the same date and the network has been further expanded since, notably through the acquisition of South Midland from City of Oxford Motor Services in December 1988. Some rationalisation took place with City of Oxford services on the London and Heathrow corridors from 28th July 1996.

The fleet was for a long while based on standard Ford Transit/Mellor machines, although updating has taken place with Mercedes-Benz vehicles. More recently Ivecos and Dennis Darts with dual-door bodywork have been introduced, of which all but one of the Ivecos have been withdrawn. The fleet includes coaches for the London services. Inter-fleet changes occurred regularly with other members of the group until its recent fragmentation. A new bus livery has been introduced of silver grey with dark blue and red relief, coupled with route branding in many cases. Oxford Tube coaches operate in a distinctive livery of red with grey relief; their fleet numbers are related to radio control numbers and are liable to change according to operational need.

The fleet is based at Cowley, Chipping Norton and Witney.

In 1990 Thames Transit turned to Carlyle for bodies on Mercedes-Benz chassis. Amongst a large intake of the type received by the group in Oxford and elsewhere was No.352, seen in Oxford. Stephen Madden

THAMES TRANSIT

| 1 | L723JUD | Volvo B10M-60 | | Jonckheere Deauville P599 | C49FT | 1994 |
| 2 | L724JUD | Volvo B10M-60 | | Jonckheere Deauville P599 | C49FT | 1994 |

| **3-7** | | Volvo B10M-60 | | Jonckheere | | C49FT | 1993 |
| 3 | L210GJO | **4** | L211GJO | **5** | L212GJO | **6** | L213GJO | **7** | L214GJO |

8	N41MJO	Volvo B10M-62	Berkhof	C51FT	1996	
9	M103XBW	Volvo B10M-62	Berkhof	C51FT	1995	
10	H639UWR	Volvo B10M-60	Plaxton	C48FT	1991	Ex Wallace Arnold, 1994
11	H640UWR	Volvo B10M-60	Plaxton	C48FT	1991	Ex Wallace Arnold, 1994
12	N42MJO	Volvo B10M-62	Berkhof	C51FT	1996	
14	N43MJO	Volvo B10M-62	Berkhof	C51FT	1996	
15	H641UWR	Volvo B10M-60	Plaxton	C48FT	1991	Ex Wallace Arnold, 1994
16	M104XBW	Volvo B10M-62	Berkhof	C51FT	1995	
17	H650UWR	Volvo B10M-60	Plaxton	C48FT	1991	Ex Wallace Arnold, 1994
18	L155LBW	Volvo B10M-62	Jonckheere Deauville	C49FT	1994	
19	N45MJO	Volvo B10M-62	Berkhof	C51FT	1996	
20	H914FTT	Volvo B10M-60	Ikarus Blue Danube	C49FT	1991	
21	L159LBW	Volvo B10M-62	Jonckheere Deauville	C49FT	1994	
22	H916FTT	Volvo B10M-60	Ikarus Blue Danube	C49FT	1991	
23	N46MJO	Volvo B10M-62	Berkhof	C51FT	1996	
24	J499MOD	Volvo B10M-60	Ikarus Blue Danube	C49FT	1992	
25	M105XBW	Volvo B10M-62	Berkhof	C51FT	1995	
26	M106XBW	Volvo B10M-62	Berkhof	C51FT	1995	
27	H916PTG	Volvo B10M-60	Ikarus Blue Danube	C49FT	1991	Ex Hills, Tredegar, 1992
28	M107XBW	Volvo B10M-62	Berkhof	C51FT	1995	
29	L156LBW	Volvo B10M-62	Jonckheere Deauville	C49FT	1994	
30	L157LBW	Volvo B10M-62	Jonckheere Deauville	C49FT	1994	
31	L158LBW	Volvo B10M-62	Jonckheere Deauville	C49FT	1994	
32	N47MJO	Volvo B10M-62	Berkhof	C51FT	1996	
33	N48MJO	Volvo B10M-62	Berkhof	C51FT	1996	
50	E829ATT	Mercedes-Benz 709D	Reeve Burgess	DP25F	1988	Ex Devon General, 1993
64	F724FDV	Mercedes-Benz 709D	Reeve Burgess	DP25F	1988	Ex Bayline, 1994
74	F734FDV	Mercedes-Benz 709D	Reeve Burgess	DP25F	1988	Ex Bayline, 1994

109-139		Ford Transit VE6		Mellor		B16F	1986-8
109	D109PTT	**122**	D122PTT	**133**	D133PTT	**137**	D137PTT	**139**	D139PTT ·
115	D115PTT	**132**	D132PTT	**136**	D136PTT	**138**	D138PTT		

| 200 | LRV992 | Leyland Titan PD2/12 | Metro-Cammell | O33/26R | 1956 | Ex Blue Admiral, 1996 |
| 287 | XTP287L | Leyland Atlantean AN68/1R | Alexander AL | H45/30D | 1973 | Ex Blue Admiral, 1996 |

300-324		Mercedes-Benz 709D		Reeve Burgess Beaver		DP25F	1988	Ex South Midland, 1988
300	E300BWL	**305**	E305BWL	**310**	F310EJO	**315**	F315EJO	**320**	F320EJO
301	E301BWL	**306**	E306BWL	**311**	F311EJO	**316**	F316EJO	**321**	F321EJO
302	E302BWL	**307**	E307BWL	**312**	F312EJO	**317**	F317EJO	**322**	F322EJO
303	E303BWL	**308**	E308BWL	**313**	F313EJO	**318**	F318EJO	**323**	F323EJO
304	E304BWL	**309**	E309BWL	**314**	F314EJO	**319**	F319EJO	**324**	F324EJO

326-346		Mercedes-Benz 709D		Reeve Burgess Beaver		B25F	1989	339 ex Bayline, 1994
326	F776FDV	**329**	F766FDV	**332**	F769FDV	**344**	F402KOD
327	F764FDV	**330**	F767FDV	**333**	F770FDV	**345**	F403KOD
328	F765FDV	**331**	F768FDV	**339**	F409KOD	**346**	F746FDV

347-354		Mercedes-Benz 709D		Carlyle		B29F	1990
347	G947TDV	**349**	G949TDV	**351**	G951TDV	**353**	G953TDV
348	G948TDV	**350**	G950TDV	**352**	G952TDV	**354**	G954TDV

355-366		Mercedes-Benz 811D		Carlyle		B29F	1990	Ex Bayline, 1992/3
355	G831UDV	**358**	G834UDV	**361**	G837UDV	**364**	G840UDV
356	G832UDV	**359**	G835UDV	**362**	G838UDV	**365**	G841UDV
357	G833UDV	**360**	G836UDV	**363**	G839UDV	**366**	G842UDV

| 901 | N901PFC | Dennis Lance 11SDA3113 | Plaxton Verde | B49F | 1996 |

Renewal of the fleet in 1995 brought thirty-two Dennis Darts with dual-door Plaxton bodywork into the fleet. This nearside view of No.3036 shows this body arrangement as well as route branding for The City Cavalier in July 1996. Capital Transport

Thames Transit took delivery of three Dennis Lances with Plaxton Verde bodywork for the Chipping Norton service in July 1996. No.902 was found in pristine condition on 15th September. Stephen Madden

Thames Transit No.11, a Volvo B10 with Plaxton coachwork which started life with Wallace Arnold, was found at Victoria in August 1996 shortly after the 390 Heathrow Tube service was upgraded from short-lived minicoach operation. A new livery for this service was introduced at the same time. Colin Lloyd

Most vehicles used on Oxford Tube services are named after Oxford colleges. No.26, a Volvo B10 with Berkhof coachwork, carries the name of Worcester College, and was captured a few days before the rationalisation of these services in July 1996. Capital Transport

902	N902PFC	Dennis Lance 11SDA3113	Plaxton Verde	B49F	1996	
903	N903PFC	Dennis Lance 11SDA3113	Plaxton Verde	B49F	1996	
2017	K718UTT	Iveco Daily 59.12	Mellor Duet	B26D	1993	

3000-3013
Dennis Dart 9.8SDL3035   Plaxton Pointer   B37D*   1994   *3007/11 are B39D

3000	L709JUD	3003	L712JUD	3006	L715JUD	3009	L718JUD	3012	L721JUD
3001	L710JUD	3004	L713JUD	3007	L716JUD	3010	L719JUD	3013	L722JUD
3002	L711JUD	3005	L714JUD	3008	L717JUD	3011	L720JUD		

3014-3050
Dennis Dart 9.8SDL3054   Plaxton Pointer   B37D   1995

3014	M59VJO	3022	M69VJO	3030	M81WBW	3038	M91WBW	3046	M101WBW
3015	M61VJO	3023	M71VJO	3031	M82WBW	3039	M92WBW	3047	M102WBW
3016	M62VJO	3024	M73VJO	3032	M83WBW	3040	M93WBW	3048	M103WBW
3017	M63VJO	3025	M74VJO	3033	M84WBW	3041	M94WBW	3049	N47EJO
3018	M64VJO	3026	M75VJO	3034	M85WBW	3042	M95WBW	3050	N48EJO
3019	M65VJO	3027	M76VJO	3035	M86WBW	3043	M96WBW		
3020	M67VJO	3028	M78VJO	3036	M87WBW	3044	M97WBW		
3021	M68VJO	3029	M79VJO	3037	M89WBW	3045	M98WBW		

3051-3062
Dennis Dart 9.8SDL3054   Plaxton Pointer   B40F   1996

3051	N51KBW	3054	N54KBW	3057	N58KBW	3060	N62KBW
3052	N52KBW	3055	N56KBW	3058	N59KBW	3061	N63KBW
3053	N53KBW	3056	N57KBW	3059	N61KBW	3062	N64KBW

Named vehicles
1 New College, 2 Nuffield, 3 Merton, 4 Queens College, 5 Magdelen, 6 Pembroke, 7 St Catherine's College, 9 Manchester College, 12 St Edmund Hall, 16 Somerville, 18 Mansfield, 21 Christ Church Oxford, 22 Lincoln College, 23 Lady Margaret Hall, 24 Hertford College, 25 Corpus Christi College, 26 Worcester College, 29 Trinity, 30 Keble, 31 St Hilda's, 3025 Lillian Board, 3026 Christopher Brasher, 3027 Dave Moorcroft, 3028 Mary Rand, 3029 Steve Ovett

Special liveries
Blackbird Flyer: 3000-8/10-3
Carousel: 3041-8
City Cavalier: 3030-4/6-40
Heathrow Tube: 10/1/5/7, 20/7
Kidlington Cavalier: 3017-24
Oxford Tube: 1-9, 12/4/6/8/9, 21-6/8-33
Rose Hill Runner: 3025-9
Weaver: 3051-62

THANET BUS

P.A. Booth & C.H. Wright, Wingham Yard, Goodnestone Road, Wingham, Kent

Thanet Bus has developed from local bus operations introduced in the Isle of Thanet during 1988. These initially led to keen competition with East Kent, although both parties withdrew to a compatible position in March 1990. Subsequently Thanet Bus gained Kent County Council contracts covering former East Kent work from Ramsgate to the westerly villages, and for a short period weekday evening and Sunday work for the main service linking Canterbury with Thanet towns. From June 1994 a more recent service from Canterbury via Sandwich, Ramsgate, Broadstairs and Margate to Westgate was reformed as a complete loop to and from Canterbury via Upstreet, though the Canterbury sections have since been withdrawn.

The original midibuses were largely supplanted by a variety of second-hand single-deckers in the 1990s. Most recently these have been replaced by Ivecos, operating in a white and red livery. The fleet is garaged at Wingham.

THANET BUS

NDU998P	Bedford YLQ	Plaxton Supreme Express	C43F	1976	Ex Bovington, Margate, 1995
D128DRV	Iveco Daily 49.10	Robin Hood City Nippy	B19F	1986	Ex Kelvin Central, 1996
D756MUR	Iveco Daily 49.10	Robin Hood City Nippy	B21F	1986	Ex LDT, 1995
D549HNW	Iveco Daily 49.10	Robin Hood City Nippy	B21F	1986	Ex McPherson, Port Glasgow, 1996
D408FRV	Iveco Daily 49.10	Robin Hood City Nippy	B19F	1987	Ex Kelvin Central, 1996
D733YBV	Iveco Daily 49.10	Robin Hood City Nippy	B19F	1987	Ex Kelvin Central, 1996
E855ENR	Volkswagen LT55	Optare City Pacer	B25F	1987	Ex Chisholm, Cliftonville, 1995
E338DRO	Iveco Daily 49.10	Dormobile Routemaker	B25F	1988	Ex LDT, 1995
K536RJX	DAF MB230LTRH615	Van Hool Alizée	C51FT	1993	Ex Bluebird, 1995
L206MAV	Mercedes-Benz 709D	Marshall C19	B27F	1993	Ex Chisholm, Cliftonville, 1995
N616DWY	Mercedes-Benz 709D	Plaxton Beaver	B27F	1995	

The entire Thanet Bus fleet has been replaced during the past year. The only vehicle now owned which has been purchased new is N616DWY, a Mercedes-Benz 709D with Plaxton bodywork, photographed at Birchington in February 1996. Brian Weeden

TILLINGBOURNE

Tillingbourne Bus Co. Ltd, Littlemead Industrial Estate, Alford Road, Cranleigh, Surrey, GU6 8ND

Tillingbourne Bus Company dates back to 1924 when Mr G. Trice, a country carrier based in Chilworth near Guildford, started motor bus operation under the name of Tillingbourne Valley Services. A Guildford town service started in 1931 and lasted for 40 years. A limited company was formed in 1935 and since 1972 has run under its own title.

Activities extended into Sussex in 1972 when North Downs Rural Transport ceased, Tillingbourne taking the Horsham and Rusper circular service. A separate company, Tillingbourne (Sussex) Ltd was formed in May 1974 to administer this operation. Tillingbourne expanded again in 1981 when services in the Orpington and East Croydon areas were taken over from Orpington & District. These were handed over to Metrobus in September 1983. The Surrey Hills and Sussex Weald services were revised in November 1982 following the takeover of Tony McCann Coaches of Forest Green. The goodwill of Dorking Coaches was acquired in 1994.

The present network consists of a variety of services in the Guildford, Cranleigh, Fleet, Camberley, Staines, Reading, Wokingham, Farnborough, Horsham, Reigate and Crawley areas. A new livery of dark yellow with dark blue relief has been introduced, replacing the former blue, white and yellow. The main garage is at Cranleigh with subsidiary sites at Horsham and Aldershot.

In 1994, Tillingbourne purchased two Volvo B6s with Northern Counties Countybus Paladin bodywork. The first of these, No.103 was caught leaving Reading in June 1996. Terry Blackman

The only Scania in the Tillingbourne fleet is No.401, new in 1989 with a Plaxton Derwent II body. This view shows it at Bramley in March 1996. Richard Godfrey

Somewhat unusual is No.364, which combines a 1988 Volvo B10M chassis with a 1992 Northern Counties body. In May 1996 it was seen going about its business in Guildford. Malc McDonald

Participating in the Surrey Sunday network during 1996 is Tillingbourne 280, a Bristol SUL4A of 1962 with dual-purpose ECW bodywork. Originating in the Western National fleet, it had been in preservation until 1995. Here it is seen in Shere in May 1996. Richard Godfrey

TILLINGBOURNE

11	H11TBC	Volvo B10M-60	Ikarus Blue Danube	C53F	1991	
101	K101XPA	Volvo B10M-55	Plaxton Derwent II	B55F	1993	
102	K102XPA	Volvo B10M-55	Plaxton Derwent II	B55F	1993	
103	L103EPA	Volvo B6-50	NC Countybus Paladin	B40F	1994	
104	L104EPA	Volvo B6-50	NC Countybus Paladin	B40F	1994	
195	C195WJT	Leyland Tiger TRBTL11/2R	Duple Dominant	B53F	1985	
206	B206EKY	Mercedes-Benz L608D	Whittaker	C23F	1985	Ex Lamb, Stockport, 1996
215	E215MFX	Bedford YMT	Plaxton Derwent II	B53F	1988	
216	E216MFX	Bedford YMT	Plaxton Derwent II	B53F	1987	
279	F279HOD	Leyland Tiger TRBTL11/2RP	Plaxton Derwent II	B54F	1988	Ex Thames Transit, 1995
280	280KTA	Bristol SUL4A	Eastern Coach Works	DP33F	1962	Ex preservation, 1995
280	F280HOD	Leyland Tiger TRBTL11/2RP	Plaxton	B54F	1988	Ex Thames Transit, 1996
281	F281HOD	Leyland Tiger TRBTL11/2RP	Plaxton	B54F	1988	Ex Thames Transit, 1996
282	F282HOD	Leyland Tiger TRBTL11/2RP	Plaxton	B54F	1988	Ex Thames Transit, 1996
285	JIL2285	Volvo B10M-61	Ikarus Blue Danube	C53F	1989	Ex Goode & Bevan, West Bromwich, 1995
286	JIL2286	Volvo B10M-60	Ikarus Blue Danube	C53F	1990	Ex Goode & Bevan, West Bromwich, 1995
293	D293XUF	Volvo B10M-46	Plaxton	B39F	1987	Ex Terminus, Crawley, 1994
359	E359VUM	Leyland Tiger TRBTL11/2RP	Plaxton Derwent II	B54F	1988	Ex Allander, Milngavie, 1996
364	E364NEG	Volvo B10M-61	NC Paladin (1992)	B51F	1988	Ex County, 1991(chassis)
401	G401DPD	Scania K93CRB	Plaxton Derwent II	B57F	1989	
403	G403DPD	Iveco Daily 49.10	Carlyle Dailybus 2	B25F	1989	
404	G404DPD	Iveco Daily 49.10	Carlyle Dailybus 2	B25F	1989	
406	G406DPD	Iveco Daily 49.10	Carlyle Dailybus 2	B25F	1989	
421	H421GPM	Mercedes-Benz 709D	Dormobile Routemaker	B27F	1990	
422	H422GPM	Mercedes-Benz 709D	Phoenix	B27F	1990	
423	H423GPM	Mercedes-Benz 709D	Phoenix	B27F	1990	
425	D425XPJ	Iveco Daily 49.10	Robin Hood City Nippy	B21F	1986	
426	H426KPA	Mercedes-Benz 811D	Dormobile Routemaker	B29F	1991	
427	H427KPA	Mercedes-Benz 811D	Dormobile Routemaker	B29F	1991	
428	H428KPD	Mercedes-Benz 811D	Whittaker-Europa	B28F	1991	
429	H429KPD	Mercedes-Benz 811D	Whittaker-Europa	B28F	1991	
430	J430PPF	Mercedes-Benz 709D	Dormobile Routemaker	B29F	1991	
432	L432APC	Mercedes-Benz 709D	Wadham Stringer Wessex	B29F	1994	

433-437 | | Mercedes-Benz 709D | Pentagon Vehicle Builders | B27F | 1994 |

| 433 | M433JPD | | 434 | M434JPD | | 435 | M435JPD | | 436 | M436JPD | | 437 | M437JPD |

438	N438RPG	Mercedes-Benz 711D	WSC Wessex	B27F	1995	
439	N439RPG	Mercedes-Benz 709D	WSC Wessex	B29F	1995	
440	N440RPG	Mercedes-Benz 709D	WSC Wessex	B29F	1995	
441	N441RPG	Mercedes-Benz 709D	WSC Wessex	B29F	1995	
561	F561HPP	MCW Metrorider MF158/9	Metro Cammell-Weymann	B33F	1988	Ex Selkent, 1996
602	LFX602	Volvo B58-61	Plaxton	C53F	1981	Ex British Aerospace, Kingston, 1993
603	D603RGJ	Bedford YMT	Plaxton Derwent II	B53F	1987	Ex Cheney, Banbury, 1994
658	TBC658	Volvo B10M-56	Plaxton Paramount 3200Exp	C53F	1984	Ex Woodstone, Kidderminster, 1988
687	MIL4687	Volvo B10M-56	Plaxton Paramount 3500	C53F	1984	Ex Ford, Gunnislake, 1990
694	D694WAU	Bedford YMT	Plaxton Derwent II	B60F	1987	Ex Felix, Stanley, 1988
810	G810DPH	Iveco Daily 49.10	Phoenix	B25F	1990	
827	FGD827X	Volvo B10M-56	Duple Dominant	B51F	1982	Ex Graham, Paisley, 1990
851	MIL1851	Volvo B10M-61	Ikarus Blue Danube	C53F	1988	Ex Bere Regis, Dorchester, 1995
852	MIL1852	Volvo B10M-61	Ikarus Blue Danube	C49FT	1988	Ex Shorthouse, Droitwich, 1994
853	MIL1853	Volvo B10M-61	Duple Dominant	C53F	1982	Ex Goodwin, Stockport, 1994
854	MIL1854	AEC Reliance 6U2R	Duple Dominant II Express	C53F	1981	Ex Metrobus, Orpington, 1991
870	F870TLJ	Leyland Tiger TRBTL11/2RP	Plaxton Derwent II	B52F	1988	
877	B877OLJ	Leyland Tiger TRCTL11/2R	Duple Dominant	B55F	1984	
914	F914TBP	Mercedes-Benz 709D	Robin Hood City Nippy	B26F	1989	Ex Tenby Bus & Coach, 1991
942	FOD942Y	Dennis Dorchester SDA802	Wadham Stringer Vanguard	B59F	1983	
943	FOD943Y	Dennis Dorchester SDA802	Wadham Stringer Vanguard	B59F	1983	

Previous registrations

JIL2285	F634FDH	MIL1854	ODV404W
JIL2286	G474UHA	MIL4687	A298XUK, 353TPF, A489GYL, TBC658,
LFX602	FTH992W		A475JPB, HFB89
MIL1851	E220GCG	TBC658	A339HNR
MIL1852	F193TNP	280KTA	280KTA, 31920 (Jersey)
MIL1853	OHE271X		

Special liveries
Dorking Coaches 285/6, 658/87, 851/2

TIMEBUS TRAVEL

D Pring, 7 Boleyn Drive, St Albans, Hertfordshire, AL1 2BP

Timebus operate local routes in Watford, generally using Routemasters, and also undertake private hire work. Vehicles are parked at Park Street, Frogmore and are in traditional London red but with flake grey relief in Green Line style. Competition from The Shires has been successfully resisted and in November 1996 the Abbots Langley routes were extended to Hemel Hempstead.

TIMEBUS TRAVEL

MXX223	AEC Regent III 0961	Weymann	L27/28R	1952	Ex preservation, 1993
MXX468	AEC Regal IV 9821LT	Metro-Cammell	B39F	1953	Ex preservation, 1995
WFO410	AEC Routemaster 5RM	Park Royal	H36/24R	1961	Ex Southend, 1996
394CLT	AEC Routemaster 5RM	Park Royal	H36/24R	1963	Ex preservation, 1996
571CLT	AEC Routemaster 5RM	Park Royal	H36/24R	1963	Ex Routemaster, Watford, 1996
ALD871B	AEC Routemaster 5RM	Park Royal	H36/24R	1964	Ex preservation, 1996
CUV156C	AEC Routemaster 5RM	Park Royal	H36/24R	1965	Ex Routemaster, Watford, 1994
CUV180C	AEC Routemaster 5RM	Park Royal	H36/24R	1965	Ex preservation, 1993
CUV198C	AEC Routemaster 5RM	Park Royal	H36/24R	1965	Ex preservation, 1995
KGJ612D	AEC Routemaster 9RM	Park Royal	H32/24F	1966	Ex Browne, Motcombe, 1886

Previous registration
WFO410   WLT378

Timebus services are normally operated by their collection of Routemasters. CUV156C, one of the later standard Routemasters to be built, was photographed in Watford on the 73 service, which has been the subject of competition from The Shires. Capital Transport

TOWN & AROUND

Town & Around (Folkestone) Ltd, 9 Burrow Road, Folkestone, Kent, CT19 6DH

In October 1986 Robert Miller started a local service in Folkestone between Holywell Avenue and Broadmead Village. The network was expanded in March 1988 with the acquisition of Kent County Council contracts for weekday routes 558 and 559 between Hythe and Canterbury through Stelling Minnis and a Sunday route from Folkestone to Maidstone, although these were lost in the 1990 round of re-tendering. Instead, Kent County Council route 593 from Dover (Western Heights) to Martin was gained from April 1990. Other local services have since been introduced in Folkestone and Hythe, though on a complementary rather than competitive basis with East Kent.

The present company was authorised in November 1989, reflecting the trading name which had been used since inception. The fleet is in a smart livery of white with blue skirt and light blue stripes.

TOWN & AROUND

KBU892P	Leyland National 10351/1R		B41F	1975	Ex Seabrook Coaches, Hythe, 1990
MGR528P	Leyland National 11351/1R		B49F	1975	Ex Amberley, Pudsey, 1989
UPB330S	Leyland National 10351A/1R		B41F	1977	Ex London Country SW, 1990
JSS202V	Ford R1014	Alexander AYS	B45F	1980	Ex Northern Scottish, 1988
JSS203V	Ford R1014	Alexander AYS	B45F	1980	Ex Northern Scottish, 1988
H264GKK	Leyland Swift LBM6T/2RA	Wadham Stringer Vanguard 2	B39F	1991	

Town & Around's fleet includes two Ford R1014s, an increasingly rare chassis type in the area, with Alexander bodywork. JSS203V came from Northern Scottish in 1988 and has now spent half its life in Kent. Here it is seen at Dover on a KCC-contracted service. Eric Baldock

TURNER'S

T.C. Turner (Turner's of Maidstone), 9 Charlton Lane, West Farleigh, Maidstone, Kent

Turner's commenced bus operations in July 1990, working on the route from Maidstone to Coxheath, on which a significant presence is still maintained. Other work includes school contracts in the Maidstone area. The fleet is based at Redwall Lane, Linton, and is operated chiefly in cream and maroon with red relief.

TURNER'S

Reg	Make	Body	Seating	Year	Notes
26YKO	Leyland Titan PD2A/30	Massey	H33/28R	1963	Ex preservation, 1995
GAE371N	Leyland National 11351/2R		B44D	1974	Ex Morgan, Biddenden, 1990
NFB596R	Leyland National 11351A/1R		B52F	1976	Ex Frontline, Lichfield, 1995
SKN901R	Leyland National 11351A/1R		DP48F	1977	Ex Harmer, Bexhill, 1996
SKN909R	Leyland National 11351A/1R		DP48F	1977	Ex Harmer, Bexhill, 1996
CBV783S	Leyland National 11351A/1R		B49F	1977	Ex Vanguard, Bedworth, 1995
SAE758S	Leyland National 11351A/1R		B52F	1978	Ex Frontline, Lichfield, 1995
BUR437T	Bedford YMT	Plaxton Supreme	C53F	1978	Ex Craker, Maidstone, 1995
YDW399T	Leyland National 10351A/1R		B44F	1979	Ex Red & White, 1993
LKE869V	Bedford YMT	Plaxton Supreme IV	C53F	1980	Ex Rowland & Goodwin, St Leonard's, 1993
HKP126	Leyland Tiger TRCTL11/3R	Plaxton Paramount 3500	C49FT	1983	Ex King Offa Travel, Westbury, 1995
TIB8559	Scania K112CRS	Jonckheere Jubilee P50	C53F	1983	Ex Lock, South Norwood, 1996
LIL2178	Bedford YNT	Plaxton Paramount 3200	C53F	1984	Ex BB Travel, Halesowen, 1994
TCT51	Leyland Tiger TRCTL11/3RZ	Plaxton Paramount 3200 3	C53F	1987	Ex Thamesway, 1995

Previous registrations

HKP126	BRN4Y	TCT51	D598MVR
LIL2178	A283STS	TIB8559	A127SNH
LKE869V	JJF880V, SDY788, 405UPJ, TCT51		

Named vehicles
TCT51 Sir Teddy Taylor

Freshly-painted following acquisition, Turner's NFB596R is an 11.3-metre Leyland National caught at Loose in September 1995 on their main route between Maidstone and Coxheath, operated in competition with Maidstone & District. Eric Baldock

UNIVERSITYBUS

Universitybus Ltd, College Lane, Hatfield, Hertfordshire, AL10 9AB

Originally set up to provide services for students and staff to and from the sites of what is now the University of Hertfordshire, an increasing number of routes have been opened for public use, and local authority contracts have been gained to supplement a wide-ranging network of commercial services. An eclectic collection of vehicles has already been assembled, including some most unusual Blue Bird vehicles of American design. The present fleet title was adopted in 1994. Vehicles are based at Comet Way, Hatfield.

Left **Unusual arrivals in the Universitybus fleet in 1994 were four Blue Bird 51-seaters. OV323 shows the rather bulbous front-end appearance of the type in this May 1995 shot at Welwyn Garden City.**
Colin Lloyd

Below **The rear aspect of the same type. M51HUT passes Hatfield House in August 1996.**
Capital Transport

Four Dennis Darts with Marshall bodywork joined the fleet in 1995. OV336 represents the type in this view at Hatfield Station in August 1996. Capital Transport

UNIVERSITYBUS

OV304	H748CBP	Mercedes-Benz 811D	Phoenix	B33F	1990	Ex Hertfordshire County Council (npsv), 1992
OV305	H749CBP	Mercedes-Benz 811D	Phoenix	B33F	1990	Ex Hertfordshire County Council (npsv), 1992
OV306	H840NOC	Dennis Dart 9.8SDL3004	Carlyle	B40F	1991	Ex Hertfordshire County Council (npsv), 1992
OV307	H849NOC	Dennis Dart 9.8SDL3004	Carlyle	B43F	1991	Ex Hertfordshire County Council (npsv), 1992
OV309	THX204S	Leyland National 10351A/2R		B39D	1978	Ex Hertfordshire County Council (npsv), 1992
OV310	THX216S	Leyland National 10351A/2R		B39D	1978	Ex Hertfordshire County Council (npsv), 1992
OV311	THX261S	Leyland National 10351A/2R	East Lancs (1993)	B41F	1978	Ex London Buses, 1992
OV314	THX243S	Leyland National 10351A/2R		B39D	1978	Ex Wright, Rainham, 1993
OV315	G472PGE	Leyland Lynx LX112L10ZR1R	Leyland	B51F	1989	Ex Whitelaw, Stonehouse, 1993
OV323	M47HUT	Blue Bird RE	Blue Bird	B51F	1994	
OV324	M48HUT	Blue Bird RE	Blue Bird	B51F	1994	
OV325	M49HUT	Blue Bird RE	Blue Bird	B51F	1994	
OV326	M51HUT	Blue Bird RE	Blue Bird	B51F	1994	
OV327	M527UGS	Mercedes-Benz OH1416	Wright	B47F	1995	
OV328	M255UKX	Mercedes-Benz OH1416	Wright	B47F	1995	
OV329	F930TBP	Mercedes-Benz 609D	Reeve Burgess	C24F	1989	Ex van, 1995
OV330	EUI4415	Volvo B10M-61	Berkhof	C49FT	1983	Ex Time, Thornton Heath, 1995
OV331	M146VVS	Dennis Dart 9.8SDL3054	Wright	B42F	1995	
OV332	M148VVS	Dennis Dart 9.8SDL3054	Wright	B42F	1995	
OV333	B761OPJ	Mercedes-Benz L608D	Reeve Burgess	C21F	1984	Ex Chivers, Elstead, 1995
OV334	N421ENM	Dennis Dart 9.8SDL3054	Marshall C37	B40F	1995	
OV335	N422ENM	Dennis Dart 9.8SDL3054	Marshall C37	B40F	1995	
OV336	N423ENM	Dennis Dart 9.8SDL3054	Marshall C37	B40F	1995	
OV337	N424ENM	Dennis Dart 9.8SDL3054	Marshall C37	B40F	1995	
	HIL6246	Leyland Tiger TRCTL11/3RH	Berkhof Everest 370	C53F	1986	Ex Speedlink, 1996
	P780PTM	Marshall Midibus	Marshall	B29F	1996	
	P664PNM	Dennis Dart SLF 10.8m	Wright Crusader	B41F	1996	
	P665PNM	Dennis Dart SLF 10.8m	Wright Crusader	B41F	1996	
	P667PNM	Dennis Dart SLF 10.8m	Wright Crusader	B41F	1996	
	P668PNM	Dennis Dart SLF 10.8m	Wright Crusader	B41F	1996	

Previous registrations
B761OPB B967MLF, KXI599   EUI4415 BDV862Y   HIL6246 C146SPB

Special liveries
Overall advertisements: OV307/14

WEALDEN-BEELINE

Wealden PSV Ltd, Whetsted Road, Five Oak Green, Tonbridge, Kent, TN12 6RT

Wealden PSV has developed an increasing presence in local bus operation in recent years, and now operates several routes in the Tonbridge and Tunbridge Wells area, some of these on a co-ordinated basis with East Surrey and Fuggles. A Kent Karrier network is also operated under local authority contract in Tonbridge. The fleet of Beeline, Southborough was acquired early in 1989 and led to the introduction of a service from Tunbridge Wells to Heathfield, part of which is operated under contract to East Sussex County Council. Commercial services now reach Gravesend and extend to Eastbourne.

The fleet has included a number of unusual vehicles loaned or transferred from the associated dealing firm, Wealden PSV Sales. The basic fleet livery is two shades of green with cream relief.

A remarkable vehicle is No.701, which combines a 1978 Leyland Leopard chassis with 1985 Wadham Stringer body built for the Ministry of Defence. To confuse matters, many of the mechanical units are of Tiger specification. Acquired in 1995, it was photographed in Tunbridge Wells.
Richard Godfrey

Wealden currently operate two Leyland Fleetlines with Northern Counties bodywork; both arrived from South Yorkshire in 1994.
Gerald Mead

Four Dennis Darts have been purchased with Wadham Stringer bodywork. No.502, new in 1995, is the only one with pure bus seating. The livery is particularly effective on these vehicles. Richard Godfrey

WEALDEN-BEELINE

101	N101CKN	Mercedes-Benz 711D	UVG Citi-Star	B25FL	1996	
102	N102CKN	Mercedes-Benz 711D	UVG Citi-Star	B25FL	1996	
103	C344VVN	Mercedes-Benz L608D	Reeve Burgess	DP19F	1985	Ex United, 1996
295	DWX395T	Leyland Fleetline FE30ALR	Northern Counties	H39/31F	1978	Ex South Yorkshire, 1994
298	KWY198V	Leyland Fleetline FE30ALR	Northern Counties	H39/31F	1979	Ex South Yorkshire, 1994
320	ULS320T	Leyland Leopard PSU3E/4R	Alexander AYS	B53F	1979	Ex Graham, Paisley, 1990
337	OSJ37X	Leyland Leopard PSU3G/4R	Duple Dominant	B53F	1982	Ex Gilchrist, East Kilbride, 1993
359	PUS159W	Leyland Leopard PSU3F/4R	Alexander AYS	B53F	1981	Ex North Devon, 1993
361	MGP151P	Leyland Leopard PSU3C/4R	Duple Dominant	B53F	1976	Ex County, 1993
366	PUB66W	Leyland Leopard PSU3E/4R	Duple Dominant (1980)	B65F	1981	Ex United, 1993
380	SSU780W	Leyland Leopard PSU3F/4R	Duple Dominant	B55F	1980	Ex Sussex Bus, 1996
411	PRA111R	Leyland Leopard PSU3C/4R	Alexander AT	DP49F	1976	Ex Park Hill School, Croydon, 1993
419	VUM919X	Leyland Tiger TRCTL11/2R	Plaxton Supreme IVExpress	C53F	1981	Ex South Yorkshire, 1994
420	YUG820X	Leyland Tiger TRCTL11/2R	Plaxton Supreme IVExpress	C53F	1982	Ex South Yorkshire, 1994
466	OUF66W	Leyland Leopard PSU3F/4R	Plaxton Supreme IVExpress	C48F	1981	Ex United Counties, 1993
493	WIB7493	Leyland Leopard PSU3G/4R	Eastern Coach Works B51·	DP49F	1982	Ex East Kent, 1995
500	L500DKT	Dennis Dart 9.8SDL3032	WSC Portsdown	DP43F	1994	
501	M501PKJ	Dennis Dart 9.8SDL3032	WSC Portsdown	DP43F	1994	
502	M502RKO	Dennis Dart 9.8SDL3032	WSC Portsdown	B43F	1995	
555	L766DPE	Dennis Dart 9SDL3034	Wadham Stringer Winchester	C37F	1993	Ex demonstrator, 1994
701	B701AKM	Leyland Leopard PSU5C/4R	Wadham Stringer Vanguard (1985)	B72F	1978	Body ex Ministry of Defence, 1995

Previous registrations
B701AKM	VVU228S
OUF66W	MAP352W, SYC852
WIB7493	BKR837Y

W&H MOTORS

A G & G M Heron, Kelvin Centre, Crawley, West Sussex, RH10 2SE

W&H Motors operate minibus routes in Horley, Crawley and Haywards Heath, together with circular route 526 between Crawley and Horley. Vehicles carry a white livery, with red and blue relief.

W&H MOTORS

LIW1937	Leyland Royal Tiger B50	Roe	C47FT	1985	Ex Lehane, Sturry, 1995
D921GRU	Bedford YNV	Duple	C57F	1987	Ex Silver Fern, Crawley, 1993
E968NMK	Leyland Swift LBM6T/2RS	Wadham Stringer	B33F	1988	Ex Gatwick Motors, Horley, 1991
G555BPJ	Leyland Swift LBM6T/2RA	Wadham Stringer	B39F	1989	
G140WOT	Iveco Daily 49.10	LHE	B25F	1990	
G111VPG	Leyland Swift LBM6T/2RS	Reeve Burgess	C37F	1990	
G112VPG	Leyland Swift ST2R44C97T5	Reeve Burgess	C37F	1990	
L3WHC	Iveco Daily 59.12	ECC	C25F	1994	
M367CUF	Iveco Daily 59.12	Marshall C31	B29F	1995	
M368CUF	Iveco Daily 59.12	Marshall C31	B29F	1995	

Previous registrations
LIW1937   B295AMG

G555BPJ is a Leyland Swift of 1989 with Wadham Stringer bodywork, seen here at Crawley in April 1996. Colin Brown